The Trusted Name

(but don't take our word for it)

"In Nolo you can trust."

THE NEW YORK TIMES

"Nolo is always there in a jam as the nation's premier publisher of do-it-yourself legal books."

NEWSWEEK

"Nolo publications…guide people simply through the how, when, where and why of the law."

THE WASHINGTON POST

"[Nolo's]…material is developed by experienced attorneys who have a knack for making complicated material accessible."

LIBRARY JOURNAL

"When it comes to self-help legal stuff, nobody does a better job than Nolo…"

USA TODAY

"The most prominent U.S. publisher of self-help legal aids."

TIME MAGAZINE

"Nolo is a pioneer in both consumer and business self-help books and software."

LOS ANGELES TIMES

12th Edition

How to Write a
Business Plan

Mike P. McKeever

TWELFTH EDITION	JANUARY 2015
Editor	DAVID GOGUEN
Cover Design	SUSAN PUTNEY
Production	COLLEEN CAIN
Proofreading	IRENE BARNARD
Index	MEDEA MINNICH
Printing	BANG PRINTING

McKeever, Mike P.
  How to write a business plan / by Mike P. McKeever. -- 12th edition.
    pages cm
  Includes index.
  ISBN 978-1-4133-2078-7 (pbk) -- ISBN 978-1-4133-2079-4 (epub ebook)
  1. Business planning. 2. New business enterprises--Planning. 3. New business enterprises--Finance. 4. Small business--Planning. 5. Small business--Finance. I. Title.
  HD30.28.M3839 2014
  658.15'224--dc23

                    2014019580

This book covers only United States law, unless it specifically states otherwise.

Please note

We believe accurate, plain-English legal information should help you solve many of your own legal problems. But this text is not a substitute for personalized advice from a knowledgeable lawyer. If you want the help of a trained professional—and we'll always point out situations in which we think that's a good idea—consult an attorney licensed to practice in your state.

Dedication

This book is dedicated to the memory of my late grandmother, Elizabeth Eudora Woodall Darby, whose influence I acknowledged only recently.

Acknowledgments

After more than two decades of working with many people at Nolo, I am amazed at the uniform spirit of goodwill and cooperation.

My first editor, Ralph "Jake" Warner, showed patience working with a first-time author. My second editor, Lisa Goldoftas, challenged the grammar while gracefully deferring to my knowledge about the subject.

Also at Nolo: Steve Elias designed many charts; Adam Stanhope educated me about computers; Mark Stuhr tuned sections on computer-related material; Stephanie Harolde worked her word-processing wonders on the manuscript; Terri Hearsh designed the book; Eddie Warner gave helpful suggestions on online information; and many more folks at Nolo improved the book greatly.

A special thanks to a number of generous individuals, each of whom knows a great deal about starting and operating a small business: Peg Moran, Terri Hearsh, Roger Pritchard, Jason Wallach, Harry Keller, Dan Peters, Sharyn Simmons, Larry Healy, and finally, Hugh Codding and Leroy Knibb of Codding Investments. For these and all my readers, clients, and students who have shared their hopes, dreams, and problems with me over the years, thank you for your help. The best parts are yours—all the mistakes are mine. Many of your stories and suggestions appear here in disguised form. I hope all the readers will profit from your wisdom and generosity.

Mike P. McKeever
Oakland, California

About the Author

Mike P. McKeever's education, work experience, business ownership, writing, and teaching careers give him a broad and unique perspective on business planning. He has a BA in Economics from Whittier College and a Master's in Economics from the London (England) School of Economics, and has done postgraduate work in financial analysis at the USC Business School. Mike has taught classes at numerous community colleges in entrepreneurship and small business management. He has published articles on entrepreneurship for Dow Jones publications, the *Sloan Publications Business Journal,* and numerous newspapers and periodicals.

Mike has successfully purchased, expanded, and sold a number of businesses, including a manufacturing company, tune-up shop, gas station, retail store, and commercial building. He has worked for a variety of companies ranging from small groceries to multimillion-dollar manufacturers. As an independent business broker, he assessed the strengths and weaknesses of hundreds of companies. As senior financial analyst for a Fortune 500 company, he wrote and analyzed nearly 500 business plans.

Currently, Mike enjoys email correspondence with a few readers relating to business plan issues. You can contact him at mckeever.mp@gmail.com.

Table of Contents

Setting the Stage..1

What Kind of Plan Do You Need?.. 2

Meet Antoinette.. 4

Getting Started... 5

And a Few More Words... 5

1 Benefits of Writing a Business Plan..................................7

What Is a Business Plan?.. 8

Why Write a Business Plan?... 8

Issues Beyond the Plan 11

2 Do You Really Want to Own a Business?........................ 13

Introduction.. 14

Self-Evaluation Exercises.. 15

How to Use the Self-Evaluation Lists................................21

Reality Check: Banker's Analysis.......................................22

3 Choosing the Right Business 25

Introduction..26

Know Your Business...26

Be Sure You Like Your Business 28

Describe Your Business 29

Taste, Trends, and Technology: How Will the Future Affect Your Business?.......37

Break-Even Analysis: Will Your Business Make Money? 42

What You Have Accomplished..60

4 Potential Sources of Money to Start or Expand Your Small Business 61

Introduction...63

Ways to Raise Money...63

Common Money Sources to Start or Expand a Business....................74

Now That You've Proven Yourself, How About Expanding?.............86

If No One Will Finance Your Business, Try Again 90

Secondary Sources of Financing for Start-Ups or Expansions 91

Conclusion...96

5 Your Résumé and Financial Statement 97

Introduction...98

Draft Your Business Accomplishment Résumé 98

Draft Your Personal Financial Statement..108

6 Your Profit and Loss Forecast 127

Introduction...128

What Is a Profit and Loss Forecast?...129

Determine Your Average Cost of Sales..130

Complete Your Profit and Loss Forecast...134

Review Your Profit and Loss Forecast...150

7 Your Cash Flow Loss Forecast and Capital Spending Plan 153

Introduction...154

Prepare Your Capital Spending Plan..157

Prepare Your Cash Flow Forecast...159

Required Investment for Your Business...172

Check for Trouble 172

8 Write Your Marketing and Personnel Plans 177
Introduction 178
Marketing Plan 178
Personnel Plan 193

9 Editing and Finalizing Your Business Plan 199
Introduction 200
Decide How to Organize Your Plan 200
Write Final Portions of Your Plan 202
Create the Appendix 209
Create Title Page and Table of Contents 211
Complete Your Final Edit 211
Consider Using a Business Consultant 213

10 Selling Your Business Plan 215
How to Ask for the Money You Need 216
How to Approach Different Backers 219
What to Do When Someone Says "Yes" 224
Plan in Advance for Legal Details 225

11 After You Open—Keeping on the Path to Success 229
Introduction 230
Watch Out for Problem Areas 230
Getting Out of Business 237

12 Good Resources for Small Businesses 241
Introduction 243
Business Consultants 243
Books 246
Pamphlets 255

Magazines—Continuing Small Business Help...255

Computers and Business...256

Online Business Resources...260

Formal Education..263

Appendixes

A **Business Plan for a Small Service Business**..................................... 265

B **Business Plan for a Manufacturing Business**.....................................281

C **Business Plan for Project Development**... 299

D **How to Use the Interactive Forms**.. 309

    Editing RTFs... 310

    Files on the Book's Companion Page 311

Index

Index.. 313

Setting the Stage

What Kind of Plan Do You Need? 2

Meet Antoinette 4

Getting Started 5

And a Few More Words 5

"Nine to five ain't takin' me where I'm bound."
     —Neil Diamond, from "Thank the Lord for the Night Time"

*"You've got to be careful if you don't know where you're going because you
might not get there."*
     —Yogi Berra

Are you concerned about whether you can put together a first-rate business plan and loan application? Don't worry.

How to Write a Business Plan contains detailed forms and step-by-step instructions designed to help you prepare a well-thought-out, well-organized plan. Coupled with your positive energy and will to succeed, you'll be able to design a business plan and loan package that you will be proud to show to the loan officer at your bank, the Small Business Administration, or your Uncle Harry.

After working with hundreds of business owners, I have observed an almost universal truth about business planning: Writing a plan is a journey through the mind of one person. Even in partnerships and corporations, usually one person has the vision and energy to take an idea and turn it into a business by writing a business plan. For that reason, I have addressed this book to the business owner as a single individual rather than a husband-and-wife team, group, committee, partnership, or corporation. And you'll find that the same financial and analytical tools necessary to convince potential lenders and investors that your business idea is sound can also help you decide whether your idea is the right business for you.

What Kind of Plan Do You Need?

You can use *How to Write a Business Plan* to write whatever type of plan best suits your needs:

- **Complete business plan.** A complete business plan is especially helpful for people who are starting a new business. This form of plan is also excellent for convincing prospective backers to support your business. You'll be more successful in raising the money you need if you answer all of your potential backers' questions. A complete plan should include the following elements: Title Page, Plan Summary, Table of Contents, Problem Statement, Business Description, Business Accomplishments, Marketing Plan, Sales Revenue Forecast, Profit and Loss Forecast, Capital Spending Plan, Cash Flow Forecast, Future Trends, Risks Facing Your Business, Personnel Plan, Business Personality, Staffing Schedule, Job Descriptions, Specific Business Goals, Personal Financial Statement, Personal Background, Appendix, and Supporting Documents.

- **Quick plan (one-day plan).** If you know your business, are familiar with and able to make financial projections, and have done the necessary research, you may be able to create a plan in one day. But understand that a quick plan is a stripped-down version of a business plan. It won't convince either you or your prospective backers that your business idea is sound. It is appropriate only if your business idea is very simple or someone has already committed to backing your venture. A stripped-down quick plan has these few components: Title Page, Plan Summary, Table of Contents, Problem Statement, Business Description, Business Accomplishments, Sales Revenue Forecast, Profit and Loss Forecast, Capital Spending Plan, Cash Flow Forecast, Appendix, and Supporting Documents.

QUICK PLAN

The "quick plan" icon appears at the beginning of every chapter that contains "quick plan" components, and you'll be guided to the sections that are relevant to you.

- **Customized plan.** You can start with a quick plan and add components from the complete business plan to suit your needs. When deciding what to include and what to exclude, ask yourself:
  - Which of my statements are the strongest?
  - Which statements do my backers want to see?

> ## Get Forms, Updates, and More on This Book's Companion Page on Nolo.com
>
> You can download all business plans and forms in this book by accessing this book's online companion page, which includes blank forms as well as business plans for a small service business, a manufacturing business, and a project development. The forms—for calculating sales forecasts, personal financial information, profit and loss forecasts, and cash flow forecasts— are provided in Microsoft *Excel* spreadsheet format and include helpful formulas for making calculations.
>
> See Appendix D for instructions on accessing the companion page, and for a list of all forms and resources available there. When there are important changes to the information in this book, we'll post those updates on the companion page too.

Meet Antoinette

In an effort to make sense out of the thousands of types of small businesses, I have roughly divided them into five main ones: retail, wholesale, service, manufacturing, and project development. All the financial tools I present can be used by all five. However, for the sake of simplicity, I follow one particular retail business—a dress shop. In so doing, I illustrate most of the planning concepts and techniques necessary to understand and raise money for any business.

As you read through the text you'll meet Antoinette Gorzak, a friend of mine. Antoinette wants to open a dress shop, and she has allowed me to use her plans and thought processes as an example of a complete and well-prepared business plan for a retail store. You'll find parts of her plan presented in different chapters as we discuss the various components of a complete business plan.

Getting Started

Before you sit down to write your plan, you'll want to gather together these essentials:

- a computer with word-processing program
- a calculator or computer spreadsheet program
- a good supply of 8½" by 11" paper
- several pencils and a good eraser, and
- a printer or access to a copy machine.

Now, here's a word about revisions and changing your plan. I firmly believe in writing your first thoughts on paper and letting them rest for a day or two. Then you can edit, expand, and revise later to get a more perfect statement. In this book, I show examples of Antoinette's writing process. (I'm grateful she's such a good sport.)

Most people discover about halfway through writing their plan that they want to change either their assumptions or some of the plan they've already written. My best advice is this: Complete the plan all the way through on your original set of assumptions. That way you can see the financial impact of your ideas, and it will be much easier to make the right changes in the second draft. If you start revising individual parts of the plan before you have the complete picture, you'll waste a lot of energy. If you're like me, you'll rewrite and edit your plan several times once you've finished the first run-through.

And a Few More Words

As I write this, the book has been in print for over 30 years and has sold more than 150,000 copies. I have heard that it has been pirated in some parts of the former Soviet Union. Since it first came out I have taught, lectured, and consulted on business plans in a wide variety of forums. I have taken that experience and reformulated the exercises in the book to make them more effective as well as easier and quicker to use.

I remain friends with many of the people I met through the book and occasionally help them over rough spots in their planning, which is the most gratifying part of the experience for me. My business is helping people write business plans that find money for their businesses. Call me at 415-816-2982 and I'll listen or help if I can. This really is my cell phone, so please remember I am on Pacific Standard Time: 9:00 a.m. in New York is 6:00 a.m. in California! You can also email me at mckeever.mp@gmail.com. Please mention "Nolo Business Plan Book" in the subject line of your email, otherwise I might delete it as a spam message. Finally, to avoid always using the pronoun "he" when referring to individuals in general, and to further avoid clumsy neologisms like "s/he" and awkward phraseologies like "he/she" and "he or she," I have compromised by the random use of "he" in some instances and "she" in others. I hope I have arrived at a fair balance. Also, keep in mind that wherever possible, this book uses plain language, not jargon. As a result, you may find that I have often substituted simple terminology for traditional business plan lingo.

Benefits of Writing a Business Plan

What Is a Business Plan?..8

Why Write a Business Plan? 8

   Helps You Get Money...8

   Helps You Decide to Proceed or Stop...9

   Lets You Improve Your Business Concept 9

   Improves Your Odds of Success 10

   Helps You Keep on Track...10

Issues Beyond the Plan...11

   Bookkeeping and Accounting..11

   Taxes..11

   Securities Laws..12

   Your Management Skill..12

   Issues Specific to Your Business...12

"Marry in haste, repent at leisure."

(proverb)

"A stitch in time saves nine."

(proverb)

What Is a Business Plan?

A business plan is a written statement that describes and analyzes your business and gives detailed projections about its future. A business plan also covers the financial aspects of starting or expanding your business— how much money you need and how you'll pay it back.

Writing a business plan is a lot of work. So why take the time to write one? The best answer is the wisdom gained by literally millions of business owners just like you. Almost without exception, each business owner with a plan is pleased she has one, and each owner without a plan wishes he had written one.

Why Write a Business Plan?

Here are some of the specific and immediate benefits you will derive from writing your business plan.

Helps You Get Money

Most lenders or investors require a written business plan before they will consider your proposal seriously. Even some landlords require a sound business plan before they will lease you space. Before making a commitment to you, they want to see that you have thought through critical issues facing you as a business owner and that you really understand your business. They also want to make sure your business has a good chance of succeeding.

In my experience, about 35% to 40% of the people currently in business do not know how money flows through their business. Writing a business plan with this book teaches you where money comes from and where it goes. Is it any wonder that your backers want to see your plan before they consider your financial request?

There are as many potential lenders and investors as there are prospective business owners. If you have a thoroughly thought-out business and financial plan that demonstrates a good likelihood of success and you are persistent, you will find the money you need. Of course, it may take longer than you expect and require more work than you expect, but you will ultimately be successful if you believe in your business.

Helps You Decide to Proceed or Stop

One major theme of the book may surprise you. It's as simple as it is important. You, as the prospective business owner, are the most important person you must convince of the soundness of your proposal. Therefore, much of the work you are asked to do here serves a dual purpose. It is designed to provide answers to all the questions that prospective lenders and investors will ask. But it will also teach you how money flows through your business, what the strengths and weaknesses in your business concept are, and what your realistic chances of success are.

The detailed planning process described in this book is not infallible—nothing is in a small business—but it should help you uncover and correct flaws in your business concept. If this analysis demonstrates that your idea won't work, you'll be able to avoid starting or expanding your business. This is extremely important. It should go without saying that a great many businesspeople owe their ultimate success to an earlier decision not to start a business with built-in problems.

Lets You Improve Your Business Concept

Writing a plan allows you to see how changing parts of the plan increases profits or accomplishes other goals. You can tinker with individual parts of your business with no cash outlay. If you're using a computer spreadsheet to make financial projections, you can try out different alternatives even more quickly. This ability to fine-tune your plans and business design increases your chances of success.

For example, let's say that your idea is to start a business importing Korean leather jackets. Everything looks great on the first pass through your plan. Then you read an article about the declining exchange ratio of U.S. dollars to Korean currency. After doing some homework about exchange rate fluctuations, you decide to increase your profit margin on the jackets to cover anticipated declines in dollar purchasing power. This change shows you that your prices are still competitive with other jackets and that your average profits will increase. And you are now covered for any likely decline in exchange rates.

Improves Your Odds of Success

One way of looking at business is that it's a gamble. You open or expand a business and gamble your and the bank's or investor's money. If you're right, you make a profit and pay back the loans and everyone's happy. But if your estimate is wrong, you and the bank or investors can lose money and experience the discomfort that comes from failure. (Of course, a bank probably is protected because it has title to the collateral you put up to get the loan. See Chapter 4 for a complete discussion.)

Writing a business plan helps beat the odds. Most new, small businesses don't last very long. And, most small businesses don't have a business plan. Is that only a coincidence, or is there a connection between these two seemingly unconnected facts? My suggestion is this: Let someone else prove the connection wrong. Why not be prudent and improve your odds by writing a plan?

Helps You Keep on Track

Many business owners spend countless hours handling emergencies, simply because they haven't learned how to plan ahead. This book helps you anticipate problems and solve them before they become disasters.

A written business plan gives you a clear course toward the future and makes your decision making easier. Some problems and opportunities may represent a change of direction worth following, while others may be distractions that referring to your business plan will enable you to avoid. The black and white of your written business plan will help you face facts if things don't work out as expected. For example, if you planned to be making a living three months after start-up, and six months later you're going into the hole at the rate of $100 per day, your business plan should help you see that changes are necessary. It's all too easy to delude yourself into keeping a business going that will never meet its goals if you approach things with a "just another month or two and I'll be there" attitude, rather than comparing your results to your goals.

Issues Beyond the Plan

I have written this book to provide you with an overview of the issues that determine success or failure in a small business. Experienced lenders, investors, and entrepreneurs want a plan that takes these issues into account. Of course, this book can't cover everything. Here are some of the key business components that are left out of this initial planning process.

Bookkeeping and Accounting

This book discusses the numbers and concepts you as the business owner need in order to open and manage your small business. You have the responsibility to create bookkeeping and accounting systems and make sure they function adequately. (Some suggestions for setting up a system are contained in Chapter 6.)

One of the items generated by your accounting system will be a balance sheet. A balance sheet is a snapshot at a particular moment in time that lists the money value of everything you own and everything you owe to someone else.

Taxes

While there are a few mentions of tax issues throughout the book, most of the planning information doesn't discuss how taxes will be calculated or paid. The book focuses its efforts on making a profit and a positive cash flow. If you make a profit, you'll pay taxes and if you don't make a profit, you'll pay fewer taxes. A CPA or tax adviser can help you with tax strategies.

Securities Laws

If you plan to raise money by selling shares in a corporation or limited partnership, you'll fall under state or federal securities regulations. You can, however, borrow money or take in a general partner without being affected by securities laws. A complete discussion of these issues is beyond the scope of this book. For now, take note that you must comply with securities regulations after you complete your plan and before you take any money into your business from selling shares or partnership interests.

Your Management Skill

This book shows you how to write a very good business plan and loan application. However, your ultimate success rests on your ability to implement your plans—on your management skills. If you have any doubts about your management ability, check out the resources in Chapter 12. Also see Chapter 11 for a thought-stimulating discussion of management.

Issues Specific to Your Business

How successfully your business relates to the market, the business environment, and the competition may be affected by patents, franchises, foreign competition, location, and the like. Of necessity, this book focuses on principles common to all businesses and does not discuss the specific items that distinguish your business from other businesses. For example, this book doesn't discuss how to price your products to meet your competition; I assume that you have enough knowledge about your chosen business to answer that question.

Do You Really Want to Own a Business?

Introduction 14

Self-Evaluation Exercises 15

    Your Strong and Weak Points 17

    General and Specific Skills Your Business Needs 18

    Your Likes and Dislikes 19

    Specific Business Goals 20

How to Use the Self-Evaluation Lists 21

Reality Check: Banker's Analysis 22

    Banker's Ideal 22

    Measuring Up to the Banker's Ideal 23

    Use the Banker's Ideal 23

Introduction

"Hope springs eternal in the human breast," said English poet and essayist Alexander Pope several centuries ago. He wasn't describing people expanding or starting a business, but he may as well have been. Everyone who goes into business for themselves hopes to meet or surpass a set of personal goals. While your particular configuration is sure to be unique, perhaps you will agree with some of the ones I have compiled over the years from talking to hundreds of budding entrepreneurs.

Independence. A search for freedom and independence is the driving force behind many businesspeople. Wasn't it Johnny Paycheck who wrote the song "Take This Job and Shove It?"

Personal Fulfillment. For many people, owning a business is a genuinely fulfilling experience, one that lifetime employees never know.

Lifestyle Change. Many people find that while they can make a good income working for other people, they are missing some of life's precious moments. With the flexibility of small business ownership, you can take time to stop and smell the roses.

Respect. Successful small business owners are respected, both by themselves and their peers.

Money. You can get rich in a small business, or at least do very well financially. Most entrepreneurs don't get wealthy, but some do. If money is your motivator, admit it.

Power. When it is your business, you can have your employees do it your way. There is a little Ghengis Khan in us all, so don't be surprised if power is one of your goals. If it is, think about how to use this goal in a constructive way.

Right Livelihood. From natural foods to solar power to many types of service businesses, a great many cause-driven small businesses have done very well by doing good.

If owning a small business can help a person accomplish these goals, it's small wonder that so many are started. Unfortunately, while the potential for great success exists, so do many risks. Running a small business may require that you sacrifice some short-term comforts for long-term benefits. It is hard, demanding work that requires a wide

variety of skills few people are born with. But even if you possess
(or more likely acquire) the skills and determination you need to
successfully run a business, your business will need one more critical
ingredient: Money.

You need money to start your business, money to keep it running,
and money to make it grow. This is not the same thing as saying you
can guarantee success in your small business if you begin with a fat
wallet. Now, let me confess to one major bias here. I believe that most
small business owners and founders are better off starting small and
borrowing, or otherwise raising, as little money as possible. Put another
way, there is no such thing as "raising plenty of capital to ensure success."
Unless you, as the prospective business founder, learn to get the most
mileage out of every dollar, you may go broke and will surely spend
more than you need to. But that doesn't mean that you should try to
save money by selling cheap merchandise or providing marginal services.
In today's competitive economy, your customers want the best you can
give them at the best price. They will remember the quality of what they
get from you long after they have forgotten how much they paid.

In practical terms, that means you must buy only the best goods
for your customers. Anything that affects the image your business has
in your customer's mind should be first-rate. It also means that you
shouldn't spend money on things that don't affect the customer. For
example, unless you're a real estate broker your customers probably won't
care if you drive an old, beat-up car to an office in a converted broom
closet, as long as you provide them an honest product or service for an
honest price. Save the nice car and fancy office, until after your business
is a success.

Self-Evaluation Exercises

Here's a question to ponder: Are you the right person for your business?
Because running a business is a very demanding endeavor that can take
most of your time and energy, your business probably will suffer if you're
unhappy. Your business can become an albatross around your neck if

you don't have the skills and temperament to run it. Simply put, I've learned that no business, whether or not it has sound financial backing, is likely to succeed unless you, as the prospective owner, make two decisions correctly:

- You must honestly evaluate yourself to decide whether you possess the skills and personality needed to succeed in a small business.
- You must choose the right business. (How to select the right business is covered extensively in Chapter 3.)

A small business is a very personal endeavor. It will honestly reflect your opinions and attitudes, whether or not you design it that way. Think of it this way: The shadow your business casts will be your shadow. If you are sloppy, rude, or naively trusting, your business will mirror these attributes. If your personal characteristics are more positive than those, your business will be more positive, too. To put this concretely, suppose you go out for the Sunday paper and are met by a store clerk who is groggy from a hangover and badmouths his girlfriend in front of you. Chances are that next Sunday will find you at a different newsstand.

I'm not saying you need to be psychologically perfect to run a small business. But to succeed, you must ask people for their money every day and convince a substantial number of them to give it to you. While providing your goods or services, you will create intimate personal relationships with a number of people. It makes no difference whether you refer to people who give you money as clients, customers, patients, members, students, or disciples. It makes a great deal of difference to your chances of ultimate success if you understand that these people are exchanging their money for the conviction that you are giving them their money's worth.

The following self-evaluation exercises will help you assess whether you have what it takes to successfully run a small business. Take out a blank sheet of paper or open a computer file.

Your Strong and Weak Points

Take a few minutes to list your personal and business strengths and weaknesses. Include everything you can think of, even if it doesn't appear to be related to your business. For instance, your strong points may include the mastery of a hobby, your positive personality traits, and your sexual charisma, as well as your specific business skills. Take your time and be generous.

To provide you with a little help, I include a sample list for Antoinette Gorzak, a personal friend who has what she hopes is a good business idea: a slightly different approach to selling women's clothing. You'll get to know her better as we go along. Her strengths, weaknesses, fantasies, and fears are surely different from yours. So, too, almost certainly, is the business she wants to start. So be sure to make your own lists—don't copy Antoinette's.

Antoinette Gorzak: My Strong and Weak Points

Strong Points (in no particular order)

1. Knowledge of all aspects of women's fashion business
2. Ability to translate abstract objectives into concrete steps
3. Good cook
4. Faithful friend and kind to animals
5. When I set a goal, I can be relentless in achieving it
6. Ability to make and keep good business friends—I have had many repeat customers at other jobs

Weak Points

1. Impatience
2. Dislike of repetitive detail
3. Romantic (is this a weak point in business?)
4. Tendency to postpone working on problems
5. Tendency to lose patience with fools (sometimes I carry this too far—especially when I'm tired)

Your list of strong and weak points will help you see any obvious conflicts between your personality and the business you're in or want to start. For example, if you don't like being around people but plan to start a life insurance agency with you as the primary salesperson, you may have a personality clash with your business. The solution might be to find another part of the insurance business that doesn't require as much people contact.

Unfortunately, many people don't realize that their personalities will have a direct bearing on their business success. An example close to the experience of folks at Nolo involves bookstores. In the years since Nolo began publishing, they have seen all sorts of people, from retired librarians to unemployed Ph.D.s, open bookstores. A large percentage of these stores have failed because the skills needed to run a successful bookstore involve more than a love of books.

General and Specific Skills Your Business Needs

Businesses need two kinds of skills to survive and prosper: skills for business in general and skills specific to the particular business. For example, every business needs someone to keep good financial records. On the other hand, the tender touch and manual dexterity needed by glassblowers are not skills needed by the average paving contractor.

Next, take a few minutes and list the skills your business needs. Don't worry about making an exhaustively complete list, just jot down the first things that come to mind. Make sure you have some general business skills as well as some of the more important skills specific to your particular business.

If you don't have all the skills your business needs, your backers will want to know how you will make up for the deficiency. For example, let's say you want to start a trucking business. You have a good background in maintenance, truck repair, and long distance driving, and you know how to sell and get work. Sounds good so far—but, let's say you don't know the first thing about bookkeeping or cash flow management and the thought of using a computer makes you nervous. Because some trucking businesses work on large dollar volumes, small profit margins, and slow-paying customers, your backers will expect you to learn cash flow management or hire someone qualified to handle that part of the business.

Antoinette Gorzak:
General and Specific Skills My Business Needs

1. How to motivate employees
2. How to keep decent records
3. How to make customers and employees think the business is special
4. How to know what the customers want—today and, more important in the clothing business, to keep half-a-step ahead
5. How to sell
6. How to manage inventory
7. How to judge people

Your Likes and Dislikes

Take a few minutes and make a list of the things you really like doing and those you don't enjoy. Write this list without thinking about the business—simply concentrate on what makes you happy or unhappy.

If you enjoy talking to new people, keeping books, or working with computers, be sure to include those. Put down all the activities you can think of that give you pleasure. Antoinette's list is shown as an example.

As a business owner, you will spend most of your waking hours in the business, and if it doesn't make you happy, you probably won't be very good at it. If this list creates doubts about whether you're pursuing the right business, I suggest you let your unconscious mind work on the problem. Most likely, you'll know the answer after one or two good nights' sleep.

Antoinette Gorzak: My Likes and Dislikes

Things I Like to Do

1. Be independent and make my own decisions

2. Keep things orderly—I am almost compulsive about this

3. Take skiing trips

4. Work with good, intelligent people

5. Cook with Jack

6. Care about my work

Things I Don't Like to Do

1. Work for a dimwit boss

2. Feel like I have a dead-end job

3. Make people unhappy

CAUTION

If your list contains several things you really don't like doing and nothing at all that you like doing, it may be a sign that you have a negative attitude at this time in your life. If so, you may wish to think carefully about your decision to enter or expand a business at this time. Chances are your negative attitude will reduce your chances of business success.

Specific Business Goals

Finally, list your specific business goals. Exactly what do you want your business to accomplish for you? Freedom from 9 to 5? Money—and if so, how much? More time with the children? Making the world or your little part of it a better place? It's your wish list, so be specific and enjoy writing it.

Antoinette Gorzak: My Specific Business Goals

1. Have my own business that gives me a decent living and financial independence
2. Work with and sell to my friends and acquaintances as well as new customers
3. Introduce clothing presently unavailable in my city and provide a real service for working women
4. Be part of the growing network of successful businesswomen
5. Be respected for my success

How to Use the Self-Evaluation Lists

After you've completed the four self-evaluation lists, spend some time reading them over. Take a moment to compare the skills needed in your business to the list of skills you have. Do you have what it takes?

Show them to your family and, if you're brave, to your friends or anyone who knows you well and can be objective. Of course, before showing the lists to anyone, you may choose to delete any private information that isn't critical to your business. If you show your lists to someone who knows the tough realities of running a successful small business, so much the better. You may want to find a former teacher, a fellow employee, or someone else whose judgment you respect.

What do they think? Do they point out any obvious inconsistencies between your personality or skills and what you want to accomplish? If so, pay attention. Treat this exercise seriously and you will know yourself better. Oh, and don't destroy your lists. Assuming you go ahead with your business and write your business plan, the lists can serve as background material or even become part of the final plan.

You have accomplished several things if you have followed these steps. You have looked inside and asked yourself some basic questions about who you are and what you are realistically qualified to do. As a result, you should now have a better idea of whether you are willing to pay the price required to be successful as a small business owner. If you are still eager to have a business, you have said, "Yes, I am willing to make short-term sacrifices to achieve long-term benefits and to do whatever is necessary—no matter the inconvenience—to reach my goals."

Reality Check: Banker's Analysis

Banks and institutions that lend money have a lot of knowledge about the success rate of small businesses. Bankers are often overly cautious in making loans to small businesses. For that very reason it makes sense to study their approach, even though it may seem discouraging at first glance.

Banker's Ideal

Bankers look for an ideal loan applicant, who typically meets these requirements:

- for an existing business, a cash flow sufficient to make the loan payments
- for a new business, an owner who has a track record of profitably owning and operating the same sort of business
- an owner with a sound, well-thought-out business plan, and
- an owner with financial reserves and personal collateral sufficient to solve the unexpected problems and fluctuations that affect all businesses.

Why does such a person need a loan, you ask? He or she probably doesn't, which, of course, is the point. People who lend money are most comfortable with people so close to their ideal loan candidate that they don't need to borrow. However, to stay in business themselves, banks and other lenders must lend out the money deposited with them. To do this, they must lend to at least some people whose creditworthiness is less than perfect.

Measuring Up to the Banker's Ideal

Who are these ordinary mortals who slip through bankers' fine screens of approval? And more to the point, how can you qualify as one of them? Your job is to show how your situation is similar to the banker's ideal.

A good bet is the person who has worked for, or preferably managed, a successful business in the same field as the proposed new business. For example, if you have profitably run a clothing store for an absentee owner for a year or two, a lender may believe you are ready to do it on your own. All you need is a good location, a sound business plan, and a little capital. Then, watch out Neiman-Marcus!

Further away from a lender's ideal is the person who has sound experience managing one type of business, but proposes to start one in a different field. Let's say you ran the most profitable hot dog stand in the Squaw Valley ski resort, and now you want to market computer software in the Silicon Valley of California. In your favor is your experience running a successful business. On the negative side is the fact that computer software marketing has no relationship to hot dog selling. In this situation, you might be able to get a loan if you hire people who make up for your lack of experience. At the very least, you would need someone with a strong software marketing background, as well as a person with experience managing retail sales and service businesses. Naturally, both of those people are most desirable if they have many years of successful experience in the software marketing business, preferably in California.

Use the Banker's Ideal

It's helpful to use the bankers' model in your decision-making process. Use a skeptical attitude as a counterweight to your optimism to get a balanced view of your prospects. What is it that makes you think you will be one of the minority of small business owners who will succeed? If you don't have some specific answers, you are in trouble. Most new businesses fail, and the large majority of survivors do not genuinely prosper.

Many people start their own business because they can't stand working for others. They don't have a choice. They must be either boss or bum. They are more than willing to trade security for the chance to call the shots. They meet a good chunk of their goals when they leave their paycheck behind. This is fine as far as it goes, but in my experience, the more successful small business owners have other goals as well.

A small distributor we know has a well-thought-out business and a sound business plan for the future. Still, he believes that his own personal commitment is the most important thing he has going for him. He puts it this way: "I break my tail to live up to the commitments I make to my customers. If a supplier doesn't perform for me, I'll still do everything I can to keep my promise to my customer, even if it costs me money." This sort of personal commitment enables this successful business owner to make short-term adjustments to meet his long-range goals. And while it would be an exaggeration to say he pays this price gladly, he does pay it.

Choosing the Right Business

Introduction..26

Know Your Business...26

Be Sure You Like Your Business..28

Describe Your Business...29

    Identify Your Type of Business 30

    Problem Statement 32

    Business Description...33

Taste, Trends, and Technology: How Will the Future Affect Your Business? 37

    Taste 38

    Trends..39

    Technology 39

    Write a Future Trends Statement..41

Break-Even Analysis: Will Your Business Make Money? 42

    Forecast Sales Revenue..44

    Forecast Fixed Costs 50

    Forecast Gross Profit for Each Sales Dollar................................52

    Forecast Your Break-Even Sales Revenue...................................54

What You Have Accomplished..60

QUICK PLAN

If you've chosen the quick plan method to prepare a business plan (see Introduction), you need to read and complete only these sections of Chapter 3:

- "Problem Statement"
- "Business Description," and
- "Forecast Sales Revenue."

Introduction

This chapter helps you determine whether you have chosen the "right" business for you—one that you know, like, and will work hard for and that makes economic sense. Most experienced businesspeople complete several steps as a rough and ready template to decide whether to complete a plan. If your business passes all these steps with flying colors, it means it's a good idea to write a full business plan (although it doesn't guarantee success). On the other hand, if your proposal doesn't pass, you'll probably want to modify or change your plans altogether.

If you're like most people, chances are your business will pass some tests easily and fail some of the others. Antoinette faces just that problem in this chapter. Pay careful attention to how she approaches that dilemma; her method of proceeding may help you in your decision.

Know Your Business

One of the most common questions people ask me is this: What business should I start? My answer is always the same—start a venture that you know intimately already. I don't believe any business exists that is so foolproof that anyone can enter and make a sure profit. On the other hand, a skilled, dedicated owner often can make a venture successful when others have failed. Remember, your potential customers will exchange their money only for the conviction that you are giving them their money's worth. And that means you'll need to know what you're doing. While this point should appear obvious, sadly—it isn't.

Many people enter businesses they know little or nothing about. I did it once myself. I opened an automobile tune-up shop at a time when, seemingly, they couldn't miss. I knew a good deal about running a small business, had a personality well suited for it, and could borrow enough money to begin. The end of what turned out to be a very sad story is that it took me two years and $30,000 to get rid of the business. Why? Because in my hurry to make a profit, I overlooked several crucial facts. The most important of these was that I knew virtually nothing about cars and I didn't really want to learn. Not only was I unable to roll up my sleeves and pitch in when it was needed, I didn't even know enough to properly hire and supervise mechanics. In short, I made a classic mistake—I started a business in a "hot" field because someone was foolish enough to lend me the money.

How can you apply my lesson to your situation? Let's say you've heard pasta shops make lots of money and you want to start one. First, if at all possible, get a job working in one, even if you work for free. Learn everything you can about every aspect of the business. After a few months, you should be an expert in every aspect of pasta making, from mixing eggs and flour, flattening the dough, and slicing it into strips. Ask yourself whether you enjoy the work and whether you are good at it. If you answer "Yes," go on to the second important question: Is the business a potential money maker? You should have a pretty good answer to this question after working in the field for a few months.

If you're unable to find employment in the pasta business, make a tour of delicatessens and shops that make their own pasta. Interview the owners. To get reliable answers, it's best to do this in a different locale from the one in which you plan to locate. Small business owners are often quite willing to share their knowledge once they are sure you will not compete with them.

I remember reading a management philosophy that said that a good manager doesn't have to know every job, only how to get other people to do them. That approach may work well in a large corporation, but for a small business, it's dangerously naive. In short, don't start your small venture until you know it from the ground up. I mean this literally. If you're opening a print shop, you should be able to run the presses and use all the popular print presentation software, as well as keep a coherent set of books. If it's your elegant little restaurant and the food isn't perfect, you're the one who either improves it in a hurry or goes broke. If you don't like getting your hands dirty, choose a clean business.

Are You Choosing a Risky Business?

When considering the businesses you know, it is helpful to know how well they typically fare. For instance, these businesses have higher than average failure rates:

- computer stores
- laundries and dry cleaners
- florists
- used car dealerships
- gas stations
- local trucking firms
- restaurants
- infant clothing stores
- bakeries
- machine shops
- car washes
- e-commerce, and
- grocery and meat stores.

If your business idea is on this list, it doesn't mean you should abandon it automatically. However, it should remind you to be extra critical and careful when preparing your plan. I've known successful businesspeople in every category listed, just as I have known people who have failed in each one.

Be Sure You Like Your Business

Does the business you want to own require skills and talents you already possess? If you have the necessary skills, do you enjoy exercising them? Think about this for a good long time. The average small business owner spends more time with his venture than with his family. This being so, it makes sense to be at least as careful about choosing your endeavor as you are about picking your mate. A few of us are sufficiently blessed that we can meet someone on a blind date, settle down a week later, and have it work out wonderfully. However, in relationships, as in business, most of us make better decisions if we approach them with a little more care.

Be sure you aren't so blinded by one part of a small business that you overlook all others. For example, suppose you love music and making musical instruments. Running your own guitar shop sounds like it would be great fun. Maybe it would be, but if you see yourself contentedly making guitars all day in a cozy little workroom, you'd better think again. Who is going to meet customers, keep the books, answer the phone, and let potential customers know you are in business? If you hate all these activities, you either have to work with someone who can handle them, or do something else.

Here's one last thing to think about when considering how much you like your business idea. In fact, it's a danger that threatens almost every potential entrepreneur. Precisely because your business idea is yours, you have an emotional attachment to it. You should. Your belief in your idea will help you wade through all the unavoidable muck and mire that lies between a good idea and a profitable business. However, your ego involvement can also entail a loss of perspective. I've seen people start hopeless endeavors and lose small fortunes because they were so enamored with their "brilliant ideas" that they never examined honestly the negative factors that doomed their ventures from the start.

Describe Your Business

What is your good idea? What business do you want to be in? It's time to look at the specifics. Let's say you want to open a restaurant. What will you serve? What will your sample menu look like? What equipment will you need? Note that including french fries means you'll have to install french-fryers, grease traps in the sewer line, hoods, and fire extinguishing systems. On the other hand, by not serving fried foods you will save a lot of money in the kitchen, but maybe you'll go broke when all the grease addicts go next door.

Or suppose you want to sell DVDs, games, or digital cameras. Do you plan to have a service department? If so, will you make house calls, or only accept repairs at your store? What sort of security system will you install to protect your inventory? What about selling component sound systems or home entertainment centers? What about competition from nearby retailers?

Answers to these types of questions will be crucial to the success of your venture and to writing your business plan. Let me tell you from hard, personal experience that you need a written document—even if you're sure you know exactly what your business will do.

With this foundation document to refer to, you are less likely to forget your good plans and resolutions in the heat of getting your business under way. Any changes you later make can be made both consciously and with consideration.

To write a complete description of your proposed business, simply follow the suggestions on the next few pages.

Identify Your Type of Business

Find the business category listed below that most closely matches your business. You'll use the description that follows as a reference when you describe your own business.

CAUTION

Each of the business categories requires different skills to run efficiently. Many small businesses involve one or two types of business in the same endeavor. But if your idea will involve you in several types of business, it may be too complicated for you to run efficiently. As a general rule, small businesses work best when their owners know exactly what they are about and strive for simplicity.

- **Retail.** Retail businesses buy merchandise from a variety of whole-salers and sell it directly to consumers. Some retailers provide service and repair facilities, while most do not. Most retailers just take in the goods and mark up the price, sometimes doubling their purchase price to arrive at a sales price.

Supermarkets, mail order catalogue merchants, online stores (e-tailers), computer stores, dress shops, department stores, and convenience marts are retailers.

- **Wholesale.** Wholesalers buy merchandise from manufacturers or brokers and resell the goods to retailers. Normally, a wholesaler maintains an inventory of a number of lines. A wholesaler normally does not sell to consumers, in order to avoid competing with his retailer customers. Wholesalers usually offer delivery service and credit to customers. This type of business is characterized by low gross profit margins (sometimes varying between 15% and 33% of the wholesaler's selling price) and high inventory investment.

  Wholesalers typically buy in large lots and sell in smaller lots. Like retailers, they seldom make any changes to the products. Most wholesalers aren't well known to the general public.

- **Service.** People with a particular skill sell it to consumers or to other businesses, depending on the skill. The end product of a service business is normally some sort of advice or the completion of a task. Occasionally, a service business sells products as an ancillary function. For example, a baby diaper cleaning service may also sell diapers and baby accessories. Service business customers normally come from repeats and referrals. It's common to have to meet state licensing requirements.

  Hairdressers, carpet cleaners, consultants, housecleaners, accountants, building contractors, and architects are examples of service businesses.

- **Manufacturing.** Manufacturers assemble components or process raw materials into products usable by consumers or other businesses. This type of business ranges from an artisan who makes craft items to Toyota. The most difficult part of the manufacturing business is to find a product, or even better, a series of products, that have acceptance in the marketplace and generate a steady sales volume.

Or, as one businessperson put it: "Production without sales is scrap."

- **Project development.** Developers create and finish a saleable commodity by assembling resources for a onetime project. Normally, the developer knows the market value of the finished product before she begins work. When the project is complete, the developer sells her interest in the project, normally directly to the user or consumer.

    To understand project developers, consider a woman building a single-family house on speculation. She buys the lot, secures permits, hires a contractor, gets a loan, builds a house, and sells it. She is then ready to go on to another project. Other examples of project developers include someone who buys, restores, and sells antique cars and someone who purchases dilapidated buildings at a bargain price, fixes them up, and sells them.

TIP

Software development note: Software development differs from software production and sales in that software developers create a product that another entity produces and markets. For example, Fred Jones creates a bookkeeping program for employment agencies on his own time. Then he sells or licenses production and marketing rights to the Acme Programs Co. for $1,000 cash and 5% of future sales. Fred is the project developer and Acme is the manufacturer. If Fred also produces copies and markets them himself, he acts as both developer and manufacturer.

Problem Statement

Successful businesses share a common attribute: They do something useful for their customers. One way to determine what is useful for your customers is to identify and describe the problem that your business will solve. For example, a window washing service solves the customer's twin problems of wanting clean windows and lacking either the time or physical ability to clean windows himself. If you accurately understand your customers' problems and needs, your business will have a better chance of success.

For example, here's a problem faced by a customer of a pizza-by-the-slice stand: "I'm hungry and I don't have much time or money, but I'm tired of hamburgers and want a change of pace. Also, I'd like to be able to specify the exact ingredients I want in my meal. And, it would be really swell to have a glass of wine or beer with the meal."

Now, think about your customers for a minute. What is the problem that you solve for them? Write out your description of the problem your business solves for its customers. This statement will become part of your completed business plan.

Problem Antoinette's Dress Shop Will Solve

Professional working women like to buy fashionable, slightly conservative clothing at moderate prices. They prefer shopping at convenient times and patronizing stores that offer a wide selection of merchandise. These women like to talk to sales clerks who understand fashion and know their store's merchandise; few clerks in the local department stores have this knowledge. At the present time, many of these women travel 45 miles to shop because no local store meets their needs or carries today's most popular labels.

Business Description

Next, describe how your business will solve your customers' problem. Take your time and do a thorough job. It's very likely that the first time you attempt this task, questions will occur to you that you didn't consider previously. If so, figure out a good answer and rewrite your description. The important thing is not how long it takes to do this, but that you end up with a realistic, well-thought-out business description. After all, it's cheaper to answer questions and solve problems on paper than it is with real money.

Your business description should explain exactly what you will provide for the customer as well as what you'll exclude. Each of the choices you make in your business description will affect the amount of money you'll need to start or expand and how much sales revenue you can expect.

Consider the following series of questions when writing your business description. If you answer both the general business questions and each question that applies to your business, you'll present your business accurately and fairly.

For an example of a well-thought-out business, refer to the accompanying sample, which contains the first draft of Antoinette's Dress Shop's business description. You will find three additional business descriptions in Appendixes A, B, and C at the back of the book.

General Business Questions

These questions apply to most small businesses. Feel free to skip any questions that don't pertain to you.

1. What problem do I solve for my customers?
2. Who is my typical (target) customer?
3. How will I communicate with my target customer?
4. What products and/or services will I provide? Are there any products or services my customers may expect me to provide that I don't plan to provide?
5. Where will my business be located?
6. Where will I buy the products I need?
7. What hours will I operate?
8. Who will work for me and how will they be paid?
9. Who will handle critical tasks like selling, ordering, bookkeeping, marketing, and shipping?
10. How will I advertise and promote my business?
11. What are the competition's strengths and weaknesses?
12. How am I different from the competition, as seen through the eyes of my customers? (Make sure that you answer this question from a customer's perspective and not from an owner's point of view.)

Specific Business Questions

Some issues your business faces can be categorized by business type. Make sure your business description addresses both the general business questions that apply to your business and the questions specific to your type of business.

 CAUTION

If you plan to conduct operations in more than one category, be sure to use the specific questions for each type of business that applies.

Retail

1. How will I keep abreast of fashion and taste in my field?
2. Does my location have enough drive-by or walk-by traffic to support my business, or must I rely on heavy advertising for sales?
3. Is it better to be in a shopping center with high rents and operating restrictions, or in a separate location with lower costs and less drive-by or walk-by traffic?
4. How much inventory will I buy in comparison to my expected sales revenues? (This is a critical question in the retail field and deserves your close attention.)

Wholesale

1. Which product lines will I carry in inventory and which will I order as required?
2. Will I carry accounts for my customers or work on cash only?
3. Are there any exclusive distributorships available to me?
4. Will I have to market all the products myself or will the manufacturers have marketing programs?

Service

1. Are my credentials and skills equal to or better than others in my field?
2. Can I sell my service as well as I can perform it?
3. Will I take work on speculation or will I insist on cash for each job?

Business Description for Antoinette's Dress Shop

Antoinette's Dress Shop will be a women's retail clothing store designed to serve the growing market of professional working women. Our store will buy clothing and accessories from the most popular labels that provide consistent quality and service. Antoinette's Dress Shop will resell them "as is" to our target market. Antoinette's will specialize in fashionable, reasonably priced clothing suitable to this city's working environment. The store will sell a limited line of sportswear or leisure wear. We will carry business suits, pantsuits, and dresses for daytime wear, together with accessories like purses and belts. We will make prompt minor alterations at no charge.

Antoinette's will regularly publish a newsletter containing clothing tips for working women, which we will send to customers on our email list. We will maintain a file on each customer that contains their size and style and color preferences. Antoinette's will schedule fashion shows for our customer base as a marketing device.

Antoinette's will offer a relaxed atmosphere with personalized attention and unlimited fitting-room time. Our store will feature a contemporary design and inviting feeling. All our employees will be knowledgeable about fashion in general and about the clothing we sell. Antoinette's will be located in approximately 2,000 square feet in the downtown mall and will maintain regular mall hours of Monday through Friday from 11:00 a.m. until 9:00 p.m. and Saturdays from 10:00 a.m. until 6:00 p.m. These hours will be a convenience to our customer base. The store will not offer delivery on a regular basis, although we will offer Federal Express shipments when requested and we will maintain a website together with an active email correspondence with customers so they can express their feelings about any concerns.

4. Do I have a client list to begin with or will I start cold?

5. Am I better off associating with others or being independent?

Manufacturing

1. Does my manufacturing process create toxic or polluting materials? If so, how will I deal with them and what regulatory agencies handle them?

2. Is there a pool of readily available, affordable skilled labor where I want to locate?

3. Will I make products for inventory or per order?

4. Will I make one product only or a line of products?

5. If I succeed on a small scale, do I plan to sell out to a larger company or try to compete nationally or internationally?

6. Is my competition from small or large firms?

Project Development

1. Am I sure of the selling price of my project?

2. Am I sure of my projected costs? What will happen if my costs are higher than estimated?

3. Am I sure of the time factors? What will happen if it takes longer than expected to complete and sell the project?

4. What portions of the work will I contract with others to perform?

5. Is there a definite buyer for my project? If not, what costs will I incur before it's sold?

Taste, Trends, and Technology: How Will the Future Affect Your Business?

Let's assume you have a good description of your proposed business, and the business is an extension of something you like and know how to do well. Perhaps you have been a chef for ten years and have always dreamed of opening your own restaurant. So far, so good—but you aren't home free yet. There is another fundamental question that needs answering: Does the world need, and is it willing to pay for, the product or service you want to sell? For example, do the people in the small town where you live really want an Indonesian restaurant? If your answer is "Yes" because times are good and people have extra money, ask yourself what is likely to happen if the economy goes into a slump ten minutes after you open your doors.

To make this point more broadly, let's use a railroad train as a metaphor for our economic society. And let's have you, as a potential new businessperson, stand by the tracks. How do you deal with the train when it arrives? You can get on and ride. You can continue to stand by the tracks and watch the train disappear in the distance. Or you can stand in the middle of the tracks and get run over.

To continue this metaphor, let's now assume the economic train has three engines: taste, trends, and technology. Together they pull the heavy steel cars that can give you a comfortable ride or flatten you. Let's take a moment to think more about each of these engines.

Taste

People's tastes drive many of the changes our society speeds through. For example, in the 1970s, many of us changed our taste in automobiles from large gas guzzlers to small, well-built cars. American manufacturers didn't recognize this change in taste until they almost went broke. The Japanese were in the right place with small, reliable cars and realized great prosperity.

Consider popular music as another example. Music styles change every few years, and some bright businesspeople succeed by selling clothing and other accessories associated with each new music style.

What does this mean to you? Look at your business idea again. How does it fit with today's tastes? Is your business idea part of a six-month fad? Are you going into something that was more popular five years ago than it is now and is declining rapidly? If so, you are likely to go broke no matter how good a manager you are and how much you love your business.

Trends

It's one thing to understand that people's tastes have changed and will undoubtedly change again and again, but it's a lot harder to accurately predict what will be popular in a few years. I wish there were a central source of information about predicting future trends in any field, but there isn't. You have the task of looking into the future and deciding where it is going and how that affects what you do today. Fortunately, a little research can do wonders. Here are some tips on how to proceed.

Read everything you can about your field of interest. Attend trade shows and talk to people in small businesses at the cutting edge of the field. Talk to people in similar businesses. Read back issues of magazines aimed at your proposed field. Your goal is to know enough about your proposed business to spot the trends that will continue into the next decade. For example, if you're interested in opening a nightclub featuring imported beer and a designated area for smokers, you should know that lounges offering artisan cocktails and local craft beer are doing very well, and many states have moved to prohibit smoking in bars and restaurants. Putting this information together with other factors, such as your anticipated location and target customers, should give you a pretty good idea of the sort of drinks and environment you should offer. You might decide on a beverage menu featuring signature cocktails alongside a few local beers on tap, and make your lounge a smoke-free establishment.

Technology

Technology is the latest tablet device, your teapot that connects to the Internet, NASA's new spacecraft, and even the proverbial better mousetrap. For example, lots and lots of people are working feverishly to come up with better video games, smart watches, TVs, and the like. Sometimes it takes years to perfect an item. That can be good news for small business owners, as there is plenty of time to prepare to profit.

Of course, there is a downside to new technology, too. It often involves high risk. There's no guarantee of success just because the product is new.

E-Business Basics

From the initial dot-com boom in the late 1990s through the subsequent "dot bomb" in 2001, through the post-2001 rebound and 2008 mortgage meltdown, the only "constant" in the online business world is "constant change."

One thing is certain: The pre-2001 approach of just exploiting a hot domain name and buying up cyber "real estate" no longer guarantees success. Today, successful online companies track the same metrics as their offline counterparts—that is, they carefully watch revenues, costs, and profit and loss analysis. For example, one savvy Internet entrepreneur eventually closed his retail sporting goods store because employees—too busy shipping orders to Internet customers—were neglecting brick-and-mortar customers.

Some trends for success have emerged: A successful online retailer commonly carries a wider assortment of goods than a traditional brick-and-mortar store. Online retailers cater to an international market that operates around the clock. Many online retailers try to keep inventory investment as low as possible by having some of their suppliers ship orders directly from the manufacturer's location to the retail customer (known as "drop shipping"). In this model, the online retailer pays the manufacturer's invoice at a wholesale cost and collects cash via the customer's credit card before an electronic purchase order is issued to the manufacturer.

And online retail business also requires intensive management and sometimes requires a bit more vigilance than a typical retail store. These businesses often work on lower than average gross profit margins. Since many online shoppers use a shopping "bot," savvy retailers make sure their products are found by the search engines. Finally, online retailers must either know—or must hire others who know—website programming as well as online banking and fulfillment operations, all of which are necessary to generate profits.

Online retail sales have been growing steadily and are forecast to continue growing. The same is true for online companies that provide services. Google, for example, earns steady profits from its online advertising program where a business pays a fee for each click through to a sponsored link. One advantage of this program is that a merchant can track the cost effectiveness of the program on a daily basis (and stop or start it at any time).

In fact, something like 80% of the new products introduced into the marketplace die a quick death. Look at the Wikipedia list of more than 100 products that have been discontinued by Apple; it will open your mind. Remember HD-DVD players, the Edsel, and eight-track tape players?

What should you do to take advantage of new technologies? First, recognize that large-scale new technology ventures require vast amounts of money and will be beyond your reach unless you plan to have your small business grow in a hurry. Many companies expect to lose money for years during product development and approval before developing a big hit. However, there are often ways creative small business owners can find to participate in new technological trends. For example, many computer software companies started with little more than a good idea and a computer. Or to think even smaller—but not necessarily less profitably—lots of carpenters have done well making ergonomically correct furniture for computer workstations.

Pay attention to new developments in your chosen field and think about how you can take advantage of them. The explosion in mobile devices has popularized applications (or "apps") that enable users to accomplish many functions previously associated with deskbound computers. Can your business benefit from creating such an app? Can you modify your software or website development business to accommodate the massive app market?

In short, new technology is a mighty engine that can pull the economy in new directions at terrific speed. Be sure you are riding on the train and not picking daisies on the tracks in front of it.

Write a Future Trends Statement

With this discussion of taste, trends, and technology, I have attempted to focus your attention on the broad movements in the economy that can affect your business idea. Also, remember that there are similar trends in your local community. It's at least as important that you pay attention to these. For example, perhaps you live in a farming community with no manufacturing industries and many migrant workers. It is unlikely that a high fashion clothing store would do well there, but you might do very well selling a new lighter, stronger, cheaper work boot, or chain saw, or stump puller.

Write down your first thoughts about what trends affect your business and where they will be in five years. Nobody expects a perfect forecast, but most financial backers want to know that you have thought through how your business will fit into the world in the next few years.

Future Trends Affecting Antoinette's Dress Shop

There are two conflicting trends affecting my business. First, more women are entering the workforce. However, women increasingly must work to pay for family necessities rather than to make money for extras. For my business, this means that professional working women will appreciate even more in the years ahead the extra service and convenience that we offer.

Second, as the baby boom matures, the number of women in the age group that enters the workforce is declining. This means that I cannot count on an ever-expanding population base for my business.

To accommodate these trends, I plan to pay attention to my customers' changing tastes as they grow older. I also intend to find new ways to market to the smaller number of younger women entering the workforce.

Break-Even Analysis: Will Your Business Make Money?

Some people have a bigger problem than others when opening a new business. These are folks who are positively enamored with their business concept and are desperately eager to begin. They are so smitten and eager to start, they have no patience with the economic realities involved in their business. If you recognize this tendency in yourself, it's extra important that you prepare a financial forecast carefully and pay attention to what it tells you. This step tells you whether your idea is a sure winner or a sure loser or, like most ideas, whether it needs work and polishing to make it presentable.

How can you tell if your business idea will be profitable before you implement it? The honest answer is, you can't. This essential fact makes business scary. It also makes it adventurous. After all, if it were a sure thing, everyone would go into business.

Just because you can't be sure you will make money doesn't mean you should throw up your hands and ignore the whole problem. You can and should make some educated guesses. I like to call them SWAGs ("Scientific," Wild Ass Guesses). The challenging part is to make your profit estimate SWAGs as realistic as possible and then make them come true.

The best way to make a SWAG about your business profitability is to do a break-even forecast. Although a break-even analysis or forecast can never take the place of a complete business plan, it can help you decide if your idea is worth pursuing.

Most financial backers expect you to know how to apply break-even analyses to your business. Your backer may ask what your profits will be if sales are slightly higher or lower than your forecast.

Many experienced entrepreneurs use a break-even forecast as a primary screening tool for new business ventures. They won't write a complete business plan unless their break-even forecast shows that the sales revenue they expect to obtain far exceeds what they need just to pay all the bills. Otherwise, they know their business will not last very long.

CAUTION

You can use this technique as a "quick and dirty" profit analysis, but don't use it as a substitute for the full profit and loss forecast presented in Chapter 6. A break-even forecast is a great screening tool, but you need a more complete analysis before spending any money.

TIP

Project development note: The break-even analysis described below does not apply to a project development, since only one sale occurs. This exercise is designed for a continuing business with ongoing sales revenue. Before beginning, a developer must know how much profit she will make after the project is completed. A developer prepares a break-even forecast every time she calculates the likely sale proceeds and subtracts estimated costs. Developers can skip this section, unless they need a refresher course on break-even analyses.

To complete a break-even forecast of your business, you'll make four separate estimates:

- **Sales revenue.** This consists of the total dollars from sales activity that you bring into your business each month, week, or year.
- **Fixed costs.** These are sometimes called "overhead," and you must pay them regardless of how well you do. Fixed costs don't vary much from month to month. They include rent, insurance, and other set expenses.
- **Gross profit for each sale.** This is defined as how much is left from each sales dollar after paying for the direct costs of that sale. For example, if Antoinette pays $100 for a dress that she sells for $300, her gross profit for that sale is $200.
- **Break-even sales revenue.** This will be the dollar amount your business needs each week or month to pay for both direct product costs and fixed costs. It will not include any profit.

CAUTION

Math alert: The following section requires that you make some simple mathematical calculations, which you'll use to analyze your business before writing a complete plan. If the very thought of math makes your head spin, you'll probably want to find someone to help you.

Forecast Sales Revenue

Your first task is to estimate your most likely sales revenue by month for your first two years of operation. This is both the hardest thing to do and the most important part of your business plan. Much of your hope for success rides on how accurately you estimate sales revenue.

Keep in mind that you're honestly trying to decide if your business will be profitable. This means that you must base your forecast on the volume of business you really expect—not on how much you need to make a good profit. If you estimate sales too high, your business won't have enough money to operate. But if you estimate sales too low, you won't be prepared or able to handle all the business you get.

Here are some methods that different types of businesses use to forecast sales revenues.

FORM

You'll find a copy of the Sales Revenue Forecast on this book's companion page on Nolo.com; see Appendix D for details on accessing this form and all others in this book. Note that formulas have been embedded in the spreadsheet document to automatically calculate revenue totals.

TIP

You may decide to round off your forecasts to the nearest $1,000 instead of writing out each single dollar amount. For instance, a monthly sale of $33,333 would become $33,000. After all, these are guesses, and it's hard to guess at single dollar amounts when you're in the five-figure area.

Retail Sales Revenue Forecast

The simplest way to forecast retail sales revenue is to find the annual sales revenue per square foot of a comparable store. Then multiply that dollar figure by your estimated floor space to derive an estimate of your annual sales revenue.

> **EXAMPLE:** A similar business shows $200 of sales per square foot per year. If you have 1,000 square feet of floor space, your estimated annual sales revenue will be $200,000 (1,000 × $200). Naturally, your estimate should take into account everything that makes you different from the other store.

Some chain stores, such as supermarkets and drugstores, have refined the art of estimating sales to a science. Of course, they have the advantage

Sales Revenue Forecast for Antoinette's Dress Shop

Antoinette wants to open a 2,000-square-foot dress store in a downtown shopping mall. The shopping mall manager says that revenue for women's clothing stores in the mall averages between $200 and $250 per foot per year.

After checking with other clothing retailers, reading trade magazines, visiting similar stores in other cities, and integrating her own experience in the business, Antoinette decides that she can achieve the $250-per-foot-per-year figure. This means her annual sales should be $500,000 (2,000 × $250). To be conservative, she plans for the first year's sales to be about 20% below that level to allow for her business to build. This means that first-year sales will be about $400,000, or $200 per foot.

Because Antoinette must forecast monthly sales for the first two years, she now has to decide how the sales revenue will occur each month. She could simply divide this $400,000 by 12 months and get $33,333 per month. But in the dress business, Antoinette knows, this would be inaccurate. In women's clothing, there are four sales seasons: spring, early summer, fall, and Christmas. The kind of shop Antoinette plans to open is slow in midsummer and in January and February. Antoinette also figures that sales will be a little lower than the average for the first few months until her advertising campaign catches on.

Antoinette's monthly sales add up to $401,000 for the first year, so she reduces the December figure by $1,000 to make a nice, round $400,000. For the second year, she increases revenues to $504,000 to allow for normal growth.

of learning from their experience with their other stores. Even so, they occasionally make bad estimates.

Supermarket executives first gather statistics on how much the average person living in town spends every week in grocery stores. In some states, these numbers are available by obtaining total sales volume of grocery stores from the state sales tax agency; normally that data is broken down by county. They estimate how many people live in the area for which sales volume statistics are gathered. Dividing the sales volume data by

Sales Revenue Forecast for Antoinette's Dress Shop (continued)

Sales Revenue Forecast	Year 1: March 1, 20xx to February 28, 20xx	
Month		**Revenue**
Month 1: March	20% below average due to just opening	$ 27,000
Month 2: April	10% below average due to just opening	30,000
Month 3: May	20% above average because of cumulative effects of grand opening & seasonal peak	40,000
Month 4: June	An average month	33,000
Month 5: July	10% below average due to seasonal slowdown	30,000
Month 6: August	10% below average due to summer slowdown	30,000
Month 7: September	10% above average due to back to school	37,000
Month 8: October	10% above average due to fall season	37,000
Month 9: November	20% above average due to fall season	40,000
Month 10: December	40% above average due to Christmas	47,000
Month 11: January	30% below average since everybody's broke after Christmas	23,000
Month 12: February	20% below average	27,000
	Year One Total:	$ 401,000

the number of people in the area gives them the average sales per person from grocery stores.

Then they compare the average sales per person with state averages. If it's higher, it might mean that people living in the area have a higher-than-average income. They can verify that by referring to the United States Census, which lists average income per family and per person for every census tract. If the income per person is average or below average, and sales per person are higher than average, it probably means that people come from surrounding areas to do their shopping. If the sales per person are lower than average in the area, it might mean that income is below average or that people leave the area to do their shopping. On the basis of this sort of data, together with an analysis of competition and demographics, supermarket executives can develop relatively accurate estimates of sales volume for a new store.

Service Business Sales Revenue Forecast

To estimate sales revenue for a service business, you'll need a good understanding of what steps you go through to generate a billable sale. Then make a forecast of how many times you expect to go through all those steps every week or month and how much revenue you'll derive from those steps.

Don't forget to allow time for internal matters and marketing. If you're a sole proprietor, you'll need to allow somewhere between 20% and 40% of your time for nonbillable activities. If you have employees or partners, you'll want to make similar allowances for them.

The sales revenue forecasting process for Central Personnel Agency shows the kind of logical process you'll need to go through. (Central's complete business plan is provided in Appendix A.)

Manufacturing or Wholesale Business Sales Revenue Forecast

If you plan to be in a manufacturing or wholesale business, read the sections "Retail Sales Revenue Forecast" and "Service Business Sales Revenue Forecast," just above, and combine some of the concepts to estimate your sales volume. If you know as much about your business as you should, it shouldn't be difficult to develop a reasonable estimate. If you're having great difficulty, the chances are that you need to learn more about your business.

EXAMPLE: Patty plans to import and wholesale modems for Acme computers. Acme has told her that they have sold 100,000 computers to date and projections show about 1,000 per month for the next three years. Patty realizes she doesn't know what percentage of Acme owners will want modems and decides to conduct a mail survey of Acme owners before completing her sales forecast.

Sales Revenue Forecast for Central Personnel Agency

I like to allow room for mistakes in my forecast, so this sales forecast seems like overkill; my experience shows the overage is needed.

Since it's harder to find qualified people than it is to find job openings, I'll concentrate on finding people after I build a backlog of openings. I estimate I can find about ten job openings per week. I will allow myself two weeks to find 20 job openings. After the first 20, I'll get plenty of openings by referrals and repeats. My income goal is to gross $3,000 to $4,000 per month, and I know that the average job order filled is worth $500 to $600 in gross fees, so filling only ten openings per month should give me about $5,000 to $6,000 in gross fees.

This means that to fill six to eight job orders per month and meet my gross income goal, I need 25 to 30 good people on file. Finding good people is the hard part. It takes me up to 20 interviews to find one excellent person. Some of these interviews are done in a few minutes over the phone, but just the same, I allow one hour per interview. I can average five to eight per day, and it will take me about 60 days of interviewing to build a base of qualified people. It takes an average of three good people sent out on interviews to fill one job. Of course, once I have a good person, I send that person out on every interview I can. I anticipate three months of fairly low income before I begin to reach my income goals.

Project Development Sales Revenue Forecast

Project developers are not required to complete a monthly sales revenue forecast. They need to know the likely amount they can sell the project for before they begin work; all revenue comes when the project is sold.

Forecast Fixed Costs

For most small businesses, the difference between success and failure lies with keeping costs down. Many smart people start successful businesses in a spare room in their house, the corner of a warehouse, or a storefront in a low-rent neighborhood. Unfortunately, others sink their original capital into essentially cosmetic aspects of their business, such as fancy offices, and then go broke.

Make a list of the fixed or regular monthly expenses of your business. Your objective is to develop a dollar amount of expense that you are committed to pay every month. This is your "nut," or the dollar figure you must be able to pay to keep the business viable. Include rent, utilities, salaries of employees, payroll taxes, insurance payments, postage, telephone, utilities, bookkeeping, and so forth. Some costs will be paid each month and others will be paid once or twice a year. If a cost is less than about 10% of your total fixed costs, you can divide the cost by 12 and show an amount each month. If the cost is larger than 10% of the total, record the cost in the month you expect to pay it. You can choose whether to include a draw for yourself as part of the fixed costs. If you plan to take your compensation only if the business shows a profit, do not include your draw.

Your fixed-cost list should also include some "discretionary costs"—expenses that change from time to time due to your conscious decision. For example, your promotion expenses may change occasionally as you increase or decrease advertising to take advantage of slow or busy times. Include them in the fixed-cost category even though the amount may fluctuate from time to time.

CAUTION

Certain expenses are not "fixed costs." Do not include as fixed costs:

- the costs to actually open your business (covered in Chapter 7)
- loan repayments (covered in Chapter 7), or
- the costs you pay for any goods you'll resell or use in the manufacturing or development process (covered in Chapter 6).

By completing this simple exercise, Antoinette has gained important information. She now knows that she must sell enough every month so that she has at least $16,050 left after accounting for the merchandise she sells. On an annual basis, that's $192,600 ($16,050 multiplied by 12). Antoinette must also bear in mind that she has not shown any salary or draw for herself. To prosper, she obviously must not only cover fixed costs, but also must take in enough to make a decent living.

Fixed Costs Forecast for Antoinette's Dress Shop

Antoinette estimates her fixed costs on a monthly basis:

Rent, including taxes, maintenance	$ 3,850
Wages, employees only (average including payroll taxes, etc.)	3,600
Utilities	800
Advertising	1,000
Telephone	600
Supplies	900
Insurance	1,500
Freight	700
Accounting/Legal	600
Bad debts	500
Miscellaneous	2,000
Total per month	$ 16,050

Forecast Gross Profit for Each Sales Dollar

How much of each sales dollar will be left after subtracting the costs of the goods sold? That number will pay fixed costs and determine your profit for your business. At this stage, you are trying for a broad-brush, quick and dirty forecast, so it's okay to make a rough estimate of your average gross profit.

Let's look at how Antoinette calculates her gross profit for her first year of business. Antoinette plans to sell about half her products at double the cost she pays. A dress she buys for $125 she sells for $250. That means that her gross profit per dress sale is 50%. She plans to derive her selling price for sale dresses, markdowns, and accessories by adding one-half of her cost to her selling price; for example, if a belt cost her $10, she'll sell it for $15.

The calculations are similar for different type businesses. Service businesses will have higher gross profit margins than retailers; most revenue is gross profit because little merchandise is sold. Wholesale businesses will be similar to the retail example. Manufacturing businesses will be similar in appearance even though the cost of goods will include materials from a variety of sources and any labor that is paid per piece.

Project developers have only variable costs in each project. There are usually no fixed costs since the developer's business ends with the sale of the project. However, if a project developer works on several projects at the same time, he may have some fixed costs that continue after any particular project is sold. For a project developer, the gross profit is the difference between the project's selling price and all the project costs.

TIP
The prices in the Sale Dresses & Accessories column illustrate gross profit calculations; they do not represent the selling price of sale items.

Forecast Gross Profit for a Start-Up Business

For a new business, calculate the average gross profit for your business by following these steps:

1. For each product or service that you sell, list every individual item that goes into that product, including piece-rate labor and commissions. For example, Antoinette buys dresses from outside suppliers and resells them. The cost of the dress is the major component of the total product cost. She may add the cost of the preprinted bag to derive the total cost of the sale.
2. Once you have a complete list of all the cost components for your products or services, add up the cost of each item.
3. Write the selling price of the item below the total cost of the item.
4. Subtract the total cost from the selling price to derive the gross profit from each sale of that item.
5. Divide the selling price into the gross profit to derive the gross profit percentage for each product.
6. Repeat for each product you'll sell; if you have more than four or five individual products, then it's better to group them by gross profit percentage rather than to make an estimate for each individual product.

Gross Profit Calculation for Antoinette's Dress Shop

	Regular Dresses	Sale Dresses & Accessories	Total
Average cost each	$ 125	$ 10	N/A
Bags, wrap	1	1	N/A
Average total cost	126	11	N/A
Average selling price	250	15	N/A
Gross profit (selling price less total cost)	124	4	N/A
Gross profit % (gross profit ÷ selling price)	49.6% (or 0.496)	26.7% (or 0.267)	N/A
Total Annual Sales	200,000	200,000	$ 400,000
Total Annual Gross Profit	$ 99,200	$ 53,400	$ 152,600

Average gross profit percentage = 38.2% ($152,600 ÷ $400,000 = 38.2%)

7. Write down how much total dollar sales you expect for each product or product group.
8. Multiply the gross profit percentage by the total dollar sales to derive the dollar gross profit from each product.
9. Add together the total dollar gross profit figures to derive the total dollar gross profit from the year's sales.
10. Divide the dollar gross profit by the annual sales revenue to derive the average gross profit percentage for the year's sales.

Completing this gives you an average gross profit percentage for your business.

Forecast Gross Profit for an Existing Business

If you're already operating and have a profit and loss statement for your business from prior months, your job is even easier. Simply subtract the total cost of sales from the total revenue to get the gross profit for the period. Then, convert the dollar gross profit figures to a percentage of sales revenue by dividing total dollar gross profit by total sales for the period. The percentage gross profit figure you get will be the percentage gross profit figure you use for your break-even forecast.

If you're already operating and your expansion will change the percentage of total sales revenue that each product group brings, then you will need to forecast your new average gross profit by following the procedure for a new business listed just above.

Forecast Your Break-Even Sales Revenue

Now that you have the fixed costs per month for your business and the average gross profit per sale, you can estimate how much revenue you will need to just break even. You can use any period you wish, although most people use a month or a year. As this chart shows, it's simple to calculate. Just divide the fixed costs by the average gross profits expressed as a decimal.

Break-Even Sales Revenue Forecast		
A	B	C
Fixed costs per month (or year)	Average gross profit percentage expressed as a decimal	Break-even sales revenue (A ÷ B)

EXAMPLE: Ronnie Ryann runs the Religious Sounds Round Table in Rye, New York. It's a small business, but she loves it dearly. The gross profit on the CDs and DVDs she sells is 50%. This is the same as saying that after adding up the cost of the products, packaging, and postage (all variable costs), Ronnie is able to sell at double this amount. Ronnie rents 1,000 square feet for $800 per month, pays her part-time clerk $950 per month, and budgets $650 per month for utilities, taxes, and so forth. This means her operating expenses (all fixed costs) are $2,400 per month. (Her costs seem low because some parts of New York State are behind the inflation curve.) Therefore, Ronnie has to sell $4,800 of records per month to break even. Her salary comes out of the money she takes in over the $4,800. Fortunately, it will cost Ronnie very little in extra overhead to sell up to $10,000 of records per month, so if she can achieve this volume, she will get to keep close to half of it.

How to Calculate Your Profit

Perhaps you're lucky enough that your break-even sales forecast shows you'll make more than you need to break even. If so, you can easily calculate your profit. Simply multiply your projected sales revenue that is over the break-even point by your average gross profit percentage.

EXAMPLE: Deborah needs $140,000 to break even in her book-keeping business. Her projected sales revenue shows that she will be bringing in $185,000 the first year—or $45,000 more than she needs to break even. To determine the profit, she multiplies her average gross profit percentage (0.692) by $45,000. Her profit will be $31,140.

Help! My Forecast Shows a Loss!

What will you do if your break-even sales forecast shows that you'll lose money? First of all, don't panic. You'll need to do some sober, serious, and meticulous thinking. Carefully check all your numbers and double-check your arithmetic. Incidentally, many people doing this exercise for the first time make some simple mistake in arithmetic that throws off the whole forecast. You might have someone with good math skills review your work.

Let's look at Antoinette's situation and see how her figures have turned out.

Break-Even Sales Revenue Forecast for Antoinette's Dress Shop		
A	B	C
Fixed costs per month (or year)	Average gross profit percentage expressed as a decimal	Break-even sales revenue (A ÷ B)
$192,600	0.382	$504,188

Antoinette needs $504,188 in sales revenue just to break even. That is $104,188 more than she expects the first year and $4,188 more than she expects for the second year. Despite her enthusiasm and determination, Antoinette's first reaction to this news is to panic and consider giving up. After some reflection, she reexamines the calculations to make sure she hasn't made a mistake in her arithmetic. Then she starts considering her options. Should she abandon her idea and work for someone else? Should she proceed with her loan application and fudge figures to show a profit? Or is there some other alternative?

In any business, only these things can improve profits:

- You can increase the sales revenue by selling more of your product or service.
- You can reduce fixed costs.
- You can increase the gross profit percentage by raising selling prices or by lowering your product cost.

Let's see how Antoinette applies that knowledge to her break-even analysis.

First, Antoinette thinks about increasing sales. Maybe she was too conservative in her original sales forecast. What would happen if she increased her annual sales forecast by $150,000 (to $550,000) and kept the same fixed costs and gross profit margin? That is more than the break-even sales and should be enough to give her a profit for her efforts. How much profit? Let's see.

Break-Even Sales Revenue Forecast for Antoinette's Dress Shop

Revision 1: Increase Sales Volume to $550,000

Annual sales	$ 550,000
Annual fixed costs	192,600
Gross profit	0.382
Break-even sales ($192,600 ÷ 0.382)	504,188
Sales over break-even ($550,000 − $504,188)	45,812
Profit ($45,812 × 0.382)	$ 17,500

Antoinette concludes that a very aggressive sales increase alone brings her a small profit, but believes that the sales increase of $150,000 is very high. The profit resulting from that sales increase is probably not enough to justify the risk of that high an increase in the sales forecast.

If a sales increase of $40,000 or $50,000 would show that profit, she would be more comfortable increasing sales. She just isn't sure she can do as well as the most established women's clothing store in the mall in her first year. After all, the range of women's clothing sales per square foot per year is $200 to $250, and she used the $250 figure to project sales of $500,000 in the second year.

As a second thought, and even though she has no idea how to accomplish it, she wonders what would happen to profits if she reduced fixed costs by $50,000 per year (about one-quarter of the current total) and left the sales forecast at $400,000 and her gross profit at 38.2%.

Let's see what would happen.

Break-Even Sales Revenue Forecast for Antoinette's Dress Shop

Revision 2: Reduce Fixed Costs by $50,000

Annual sales	$ 400,000
Annual fixed costs ($192,600 − 50,000 = $142,600)	142,600
Gross profit	0.382
Break-even sales ($142,600 ÷ 0.382)	373,300
Sales over break-even ($400,000 − $373,300)	26,700
Profit ($26,700 × 0.382)	$ 10,200

That fixed cost reduction shows a profit of $10,200, but it requires a reduction of one-quarter of the fixed costs. Antoinette believes it will be very difficult to reduce fixed costs that much. Perhaps a combination of fixed-cost reduction and sales increase will improve the profits enough and still be possible. Before she thinks about that option, though, she completes the break-even forecast analysis by seeing what will happen if she can increase the average gross profit to 50% while leaving the sales revenue and the fixed costs the same. She doesn't know if she can really do it, but wants to see what will happen to the numbers.

Break-Even Sales Revenue Forecast for Antoinette's Dress Shop

Revision 3: Increase Gross Margin to 50%

Annual sales	$ 400,000
Annual fixed costs	192,600
Gross profit	0.382
Break-even sales ($192,600 ÷ 0.5)	385,200
Sales over break-even ($400,000 − $385,200)	14,800
Profit ($14,800 × 0.5)	$ 7,400

It seems that Antoinette needs to find some combination of higher sales estimates, lower fixed costs, and higher gross profit margin that will improve profits so that she can make a living wage. But the really critical part is this: She must be absolutely sure that she can meet all the forecast changes she makes.

Antoinette was sure of her first forecasts; unfortunately, those forecasts produced a loss for the first year of business. Now, while she can manipulate the numbers to show a profit, the danger is that the numbers may not be achievable. She may be able to create a good-looking business plan but may be unable to meet those revised projections. Or, just as dangerous, she may become uneasy about the project's success. A lack of confidence may just be enough to take the edge off her drive and dedication and enough to make the project fail.

> **CAUTION**
>
> **Make sure that you have the same level of confidence in the revised forecast that you had in the first forecast.** Obviously, you can fiddle with the numbers and show good profits, but the danger lies in making the goals impossible to reach. We all have a desire to make things work, and making the numbers work is very easy to do. Just remember that you'll have to live with the numbers you write down for a very long time. Make sure they're right.

What You Have Accomplished

We'll follow Antoinette throughout her journey later in the book and see what combination of figures she settles on. For now, let's review what you've learned so far. You've decided whether to write a complete plan for your business by completing these steps:

- choosing a business you know well
- identifying a need you can fill (the customer's problem)
- describing your business and how it will fill that need
- deciding that your business is the right idea at the right time
- deciding that you like your business, and
- forecasting enough profits to make writing a complete business plan worthwhile.

In this chapter, you've been answering questions for yourself. Now that you've answered the questions positively, you can proceed to sell your idea and your answers to potential financial partners. The next few chapters show you how to write a document that sells your idea.

Potential Sources of Money to Start or Expand Your Small Business

Introduction 63

Ways to Raise Money 63

    Loans 63

    Equity Investments 67

    Loans and Equity Investments Compared 73

Common Money Sources to Start or Expand a Business 74

    Money From Your Personal Savings 74

    Friends, Relatives, and Business Acquaintances 77

    Creative Cost Cutting 79

    Equity in Other Assets 79

    Supporters 80

    Crowd Funding Online 80

    Banks 81

    Angels and Venture Capitalists 84

Now That You've Proven Yourself, How About Expanding? 86

    Trade Credit 87

    Commercial Banks 87

    Equipment Leasing Companies 88

    Accounts Receivable Factoring Companies 88

    Venture Capitalists 89

    Money Brokers and Finders 89

If No One Will Finance Your Business, Try Again 90

Secondary Sources of Financing for Start-Ups or Expansions 91

    Small Business Administration 91

    Small Business Investment Companies (SBICs) 93

    USDA Rural Development 93

Economic Development Administration (EDA)..94

Federal, State, and Local Programs...94

Overseas Private Investment Corporation (OPIC)...94

Insurance Companies and Pension Funds 95

Advertising Your Project and Selling Stock to the General Public........................95

Conclusion..96

Introduction

This chapter helps your writing process because it gives you an idea of what lenders and investors want to see in a finished plan. Your ability to understand your financiers' motives can mean the difference between getting a loan or an investment and coming up empty-handed. If you already have financial backing, you can skip this chapter.

Many people and institutions are looking for sound loans and investments. From their side of the fence, it can often seem extremely difficult to find a good one. Many potential financiers have been frightened by news stories about small business financial problems, con artists selling phony tax shelters, business bankruptcies, and so on.

What does this mean to you? Simply that you must both create a sound business plan and present it, and yourself, in a way that appeals to lenders' and investors' needs for security and profit.

If you have a good business idea and are patient and persevering, you should be able to find financing. It was Calvin Coolidge who, sometime in the 1920s, said, "The business of America is business." It's no less true today.

Ways to Raise Money

Before you can sensibly plan to raise money, you need to know how it's commonly done.

Loans

A loan is a simple concept: Someone gives you money in exchange for your promise to pay it back. The lender could be a bank, friend, family member, or anyone else willing to lend you money. The lender will almost always charge interest, which compensates the lender for the risk that you won't pay back the loan. Usually, the lender has you sign some papers (called a note and loan agreement) spelling out the details of your loan agreement. (See Chapter 10 for examples.)

While these basic concepts are simple, not everyone seems to clearly understand them. For example, some people put a great deal of energy into arranging to borrow money, but think little about the hard work that goes into repaying it. The important thing to understand is that the lender expects you to pay the money back. It's only fair that you honor your promise if you possibly can.

Your business may be so successful that you can pay back the loan sooner than the original note calls for and save some interest expense in the process. Some state laws allow repayment of the entire principal at any time with no penalty. However, laws in some states allow the lender to charge a penalty of lost interest if the borrower pays the loan back sooner than called for. Make sure you read the loan documents and ask about prepayment penalties. Your lender may be willing to cross a prepayment penalty clause out of the agreement if you ask.

As for the manner in which loans are repaid, there are about as many variations as there are loans. Here are the most typical:

- **Fully amortized loan.** This type of loan repayment provides for principal and interest to be paid off in equal monthly payments for a certain number of months. When you've made all the payments, you don't owe anything else. The amount of the interest rate and the number of years or months you agree to make payments can change your monthly payments a great deal; pay close attention to these details. For example, if you borrow $10,000 for five years at 10% interest, you will agree to make 60 monthly payments of $212.48, for a total repayment of $12,748.80. That means you will pay $2,748.80 in interest. Now let's say you borrow $10,000 for five years at 20% interest. Your monthly payments will be $264.92 and you will end up paying $15,895, including $5,895 in interest.

- **Balloon payment loan.** This loan (sometimes called an interest-only loan) calls for repayment of relatively small amounts for a preestablished period of time. You then pay the entire remaining amount off at once. This last large payment is called a "balloon payment," because it's so much larger than the others. Most balloon payment loans require interest-only payments for a number of years until the entire principal amount becomes due and payable. Although this type of repayment schedule sounds unwieldy, it can be very useful if you can't make large payments now, but expect that to change in the near future.

Problems With Cosigned Loans

Bankers sometimes request that you find a cosigner for your loan. This is likely if you have insufficient collateral or a poor or nonexistent credit history. Perhaps someone who likes your idea and has a lot of property, but little cash, will cosign for a bank loan.

A cosigner agrees to make all payments you can't make. It doesn't matter if the cosigner gets anything from the loan—she'll still be responsible. And if you can't pay, the lender can sue both you and the cosigner. The exception is that you're off the hook if you declare Chapter 7 bankruptcy, but the cosigner isn't. Cosigning a loan is a big obligation, and it can strain even the best of friendships. If someone cosigns your loan, you might want to consider rewarding your angel for taking this risk.

From my own experience, I cosigned a car loan for an employee once, and I'll think twice before I do it again. I didn't lose any money, but the bank called me every time a payment was 24 hours late, and a couple of times I thought I might have to pay. I didn't like being financially responsible for a car that I had never driven and might never see again.

Secured Loans

Lenders often protect themselves by taking a security interest in something valuable that you own, called "collateral." If you pledge collateral, the lender will hold title to your house, your inventory, accounts receivable, or other valuable property until the loan is paid off. Loans with collateral are called "secured" loans.

If you don't repay a secured loan, the lender sells your collateral and pockets the unpaid balance of your loan, plus any costs of sale. Not surprisingly, if you have valuable property to secure a loan, a lender will be much more willing to advance you money. But you also risk losing your house or other collateral if you can't pay back the loan.

A lender will expect you to maintain some ownership stake in the asset. This will normally be 10% to 30%, depending on the type of asset and the type of lender. That means you can't expect to get a loan for the same amount as your collateral is worth.

If you default on a loan and proceeds from the sale of the collateral are not enough to pay off the loan, the lender can sue you for the remaining amount. The best advice is this: Be very cautious when considering a secured loan. Make sure you know your obligations if the business fails and the loan can't be repaid.

Lenders like collateral, but it never substitutes for a sound business plan. They don't want to be selling houses or cars to recoup their money. In fact, lenders often only accept real property, stocks and bonds, and vehicles as collateral. Items of personal property, such as jewelry, furniture, artwork, or collections usually don't qualify. All lenders really want is for you to pay back the loan, plus interest. If they have to foreclose on your house, it makes them look, and probably feel, bad. Here's an example of a loan secured by real estate and used to open a business.

> **EXAMPLE:** Mary needs to borrow $50,000 to open a take-out bagel shop. She owns a house worth $200,000 and has a first mortgage with a remaining balance of $100,000. Uncle Albert has offered to lend Mary the amount she needs at a favorable interest rate, taking a second mortgage on Mary's house as collateral for the loan. Mary agrees and borrows $50,000, obligating herself to repay in five years with interest at 10%, by making 60 payments of $1,062.50. If Mary can't make all the payments, the second mortgage gives Uncle Albert the right to foreclose on Mary's home and sell it to recover the money he loaned her. Uncle Albert feels secure, since he is confident the house will sell for at least $150,000, and the only other lien against the house is the $100,000 first mortgage. If a foreclosure did occur, Mary would, of course collect any difference between the selling price and the balance of the two mortgages.

Unsecured Loans

Loans without collateral are called "unsecured" loans. The lender has nothing to take if you don't pay. However, the lender is still entitled to sue you if you fail to repay an unsecured loan. If he wins, he can go after your bank account, property, and business.

Lenders typically don't make unsecured loans for a new business, although a sound business plan may sway them. Remember, the lender's maximum profit from the loan will be the interest he charges you. Since he won't participate in the profits, naturally he is going to be more concerned with security.

Equity Investments

An equity investor buys a portion of your business and becomes part owner. The equity investor shares in your profits when you succeed. Depending on the legal form of ownership, she only shares in your losses up to the amount of her initial investment. Put another way, most equity investors' risk is limited to the money they put up, which can be lost if the business fails.

Investors expect you to think of their money as a tool; you will use their tool for a while, and then you will give it back. Your business plan should include a forecast of when and how that will happen. Failing to discuss a repayment strategy in your plan can cause a potential investor to wonder about your motives.

To understand a little more about your potential backers, let's look at the dilemma they face when they consider investing in a small business like yours. On one extreme are the very safe investments that produce a low profit. At the other extreme lie investments that promise a very high profit but that also carry a high risk of losing the entire investment.

Your new business proposal will be far less safe than an insured bank deposit. This means that to attract money, you must offer investors the possibility of fairly high returns. While investors will not find your proposal as risky as casino gambling, the smart ones will know that, statistically, putting money into a new small business isn't a whole lot safer. In addition to the possibility of a big gain, investors will want to minimize their risks by looking for any security-enhancing feature your investment proposal offers, such as your skill at making businesses succeed or your business's profitable track record.

You will want to offer investors the possibility of a good financial return, a sense of security, and, if possible, a little more. Often, this is a vision of engaging in a business designed to enhance some particularly worthwhile objective such as health, education, or environmental concerns. Or it can be simply an opportunity to help someone with enthusiasm and drive. One of the best ways to convince a potential lender or investor that his money is secure is to convince him that you are an honest, sincere person. At least as many businesses fail to get financed because potential investors don't like the person making the sales pitch as those that fail because investors don't like the pitch itself.

In fact, when they like you and your idea, some investors and banks want to make sure that you have something to lose other than just your pride if the business fails. They will want to see that you are backing your ideas with your hard-earned dollars. Be prepared to put up most of your own money to get the business open. This lets them know that you will do everything in your power to make the business work; sometimes, your dollar commitment can take the place of any other guarantees.

Return on Equity Investments: What's Fair

Every investor has her personal requirements and every deal is different. The important thing is that both parties understand the risks and think it is a good deal. Here are some suggestions that have worked well for others in situations where the potential investors weren't well acquainted with the entrepreneur. Obviously, if your investors are family members, close friends, or people who wish to support your business for political or personal reasons, they may be willing to accept a lower rate of return.

If you are starting a new business and do not plan to guarantee the return of the investment, you'll almost always need to offer investors a high possible return. If you don't put up any money, investors may expect as much as 75% of the profits. You, the promoter, may get as little as 25% of the profits plus a reasonable salary for your work to make the project go. Of course, it is rare that a person who starts a business doesn't invest at least some of his own money, so the investors' percentage would normally be adjusted downward.

Should You Guarantee a Return?

Very few investment proposals offer the investor any guarantees. Nevertheless, some equity investors want a guaranteed return in addition to a share of the profits. If you guarantee a return, you will pay back the original investment plus a profit on the investment, even if the deal goes sour. Doing this is great if the project makes the profit you think it will. But it's a risk for you since you'll have to get the money to pay off the investor from some other source if your business fails.

If you are willing to guarantee the repayment and the profits, you may be able to get an investor to accept the return of her investment plus a reasonable profit of 20% or 30% on her investment, within a year or two time frame.

Guaranteed investments are rare, and I suggest you avoid the temptation to offer a guarantee. Most entrepreneurs with the ability and assets to offer a guarantee can secure financing at a lower cost from more conventional sources. Perhaps they can pledge their assets for a straight bank loan or sell their assets and obtain money that way.

Another alternative for a start-up business where investors bear the entire risk of loss is for the founder to work in the business on a daily basis and receive a small wage as a project expense. The first profits are used to pay back all the money advanced. Profits are split on an agreed percentage. If the investor puts up all the money, this might be 50/50; if the investor puts up less, his share should also be less. Sometimes these profit splits terminate after a specific number of years, and sometimes they continue indefinitely. Occasionally, the parties agree on a formula to establish a price for which one party may buy out the other party in the future.

If you're expanding an established business, the returns can be adjusted toward normal bank loan rates if the expansion appears conservative. Investment profits will have to be considerably higher than bank rates if the project appears risky. The main thing that increases risk for an established business is changing its normal course of business. For example, an established employee leasing company that plans to expand its receivables in the face of increasing demand is more conservative than the same company that plans to open a new office in another state. It's a higher risk if the same company plans to enter a completely new line of business, such as management consulting.

Legal Forms of Owning Equity Investments

An equity investor chooses among three options in sharing ownership in your small business. These are the only options available, even if the consideration for the ownership share is something other than cash, such as labor, materials, and so forth:

- **General partnerships.** A general partner joins you in owning the business. He shares in your profits and losses in proportion to his partnership share. General partnerships work best when all partners work full-time in the business. Equity investors normally prefer not to become general partners, because they don't want day-to-day involvement in your business. Also, by law, if the partnership loses money, the investing general partner must pay back part or all of the losses. Everybody has heard stories of partnerships that went sour, with dire consequences. These were usually general partnerships. If you are interested in forming a partnership, limited or general, or learning more about them, see *Form a Partnership: The Complete Legal Guide,* by Denis Clifford and Ralph Warner (Nolo).

- **Limited liability companies (LLCs).** LLCs are becoming more popular for small business owners. They offer the liability protection of a corporation, but are cheaper and easier to create and maintain. The relationship of you (as the entrepreneur) to your investors is similar in many ways to the relationship in the corporate form (discussed below). Limited liability partnerships (LLPs) offer similar benefits but are usually reserved for professionals like doctors and dentists. If you are considering either an LLC or LLP, consult with your accountant or attorney before proceeding.

- **Corporations.** One of the most popular methods of selling equity investments is to form a corporation and sell shares of stock. The shareholders' potential losses are typically limited to the purchase price of their shares. A corporation is a legal entity that is separate from you. You form a corporation by paying fees and filing forms at a state office. A corporation lets you keep management control of the business; as long as you retain 51% of the shares of stock, you can call the shots.

  How much people are willing to pay for your stock depends mostly on what they think of your prospects. If you have a firm, exclusive contract to sell a popular, new type of computer peripheral and only need money to build a showroom, potential buyers will probably find you. However, if you're trying to build a factory to mass produce a new and relatively untried type of pooper-scooper, you will almost certainly have more difficulty.

  If you conduct business in a legal and ethical manner, the corporation can shield you and your shareholders from personal liability for business losses. However, officers and directors of a corporation can be held personally liable for any corporate acts that break the law or breach their duty to the shareholders to act responsibly.

  If you are interested in forming a corporation, I recommend *Incorporate Your Business: A Legal Guide to Forming a Corporation in Your State,* or *How to Form Your Own California Corporation,* both by Anthony Mancuso (Nolo). These books show you how to set up your own small profit corporation and also go into considerable detail on limited liability, electing Subchapter S tax status, issuing shares, holding your first Board of Directors' meeting, and so on.

By the way, Nolo (www.nolo.com), the publisher of this book, provides many ways to assist you when it comes to corporations and LLCs—including assistance with state filings, helpful books, and lots of free information. Visit the site and click "Business Formation" under "Get Informed."

Corporations and Red Tape

Corporations bring several complications—but most entrepreneurs consider the costs and inconvenience a small price to pay for the ability to raise the capital they need. I only summarize a few issues here:

- **Record keeping in corporations.** Keeping your shareholders informed and your corporation in good standing means that you have to perform certain legal acts and pay various taxes and fees. It's more complicated and expensive than doing business as a sole proprietor.

- **Taxes and corporations.** You can take money out of your corporation in only two ways: salaries and dividends. Both payments have to be approved by your board of directors and entered into the minutes of the company. Salaries become your personal income and are taxed at your personal rates. Dividends are payments to shareholders made only after corporate taxes have been paid. Dividends then become personal income to the shareholders and are taxed at personal rates.

- **Selling shares in your corporation.** Both federal and state regulatory authorities have many rules and regulations governing sales of corporate shares or limited partnership interests. The bottom line of all these regulations is this: You can't take any money into your venture until you comply with the appropriate rules. These rules try to protect investors from crooks and con artists and also try to make it relatively easy to raise money for legitimate ventures. Before selling any security, or soliciting for the sale of any security, make sure you have complied with the appropriate regulations.

CAUTION

Lenders and landlords normally require that corporate officers personally guarantee any loans or leases that the corporation enters into until it has a several-year track record and a strong financial position. So, you can expect to be held personally responsible for company debts even though you form a corporation and are protected from routine business losses.

Loans and Equity Investments Compared

To raise money for your new business, you must decide whether you prefer to borrow money or sell part of your project to an equity investor. Often, you may not have many options. The person with money to lend or invest will obviously have a lot to say about it. But you should know the trade-offs you normally make by preferring one to the other:

- **Loan advantages.** The lender has no profit participation or management say in your business. Your only obligation is to repay the loan on time. Interest payments (not principal payments) are a deductible business expense. Loans from close friends or relatives can have flexible repayment terms.

- **Loan disadvantages.** You may have to make loan repayments when your need for cash is greatest, such as during your business's start-up or expansion. Also, you may have to assign a security interest in your property to obtain a loan, thereby placing personal assets at risk. Under most circumstances, you can be sued personally for any unpaid balance of the loan, even if it's unsecured.

- **Equity investment advantages.** You can be flexible about repayment requirements. Investors sometimes are partners and often offer valuable advice and assistance. If your business loses money or goes broke, you probably won't have to repay your investors.

- **Equity investment disadvantages.** Equity investors require a larger share of the profits. Your shareholders and partners have a legal right to be informed about all significant business events and a right to ethical management; they can sue you if they feel their rights are compromised.

Loans are better for businesses if the cash flow allows for realistic repayment schedules and the loans can be obtained without jeopardizing personal assets. Equity investments are often the best way to finance start-up ventures because of the flexible repayment schedules.

If you don't already know an accountant specializing in small business affairs, you will be wise to find one. Your personal tax situation, the tax situation of the people who may invest, and the tax status of the type of business you plan to open are all likely to influence your choice.

Common Money Sources to Start or Expand a Business

Most small businesses are started or expanded with money from one of seven readily available sources. They are in order of frequency:

1. the savings of the person starting the business
2. money from close friends and relatives
3. scaling back cash requirements and substituting creative cost cutting for financial equity
4. selling or borrowing against equity in other property
5. money from supporters or others interested in what you are doing
6. bank loans, and
7. venture capital.

I recommend never financing a business with only borrowed money, even if it's possible. If you're starting a new business and use your own money or sell equity, you can make your inevitable start-up mistakes cheaply and survive to borrow money later, when you know how better to use it.

My general rule is that you should borrow less than half of the money you need, especially if you're starting a new business. If you're expanding an existing business, make sure that you can handle the cash payments necessary to repay the loan even if business isn't as good as you hope. In other words, it's usually more dangerous to borrow too much than too little. If you have to raise nearly all the money from others, I recommend selling equity instead of borrowing.

Now let's look at each of the most likely funding sources for new and expanding businesses in more depth.

Money From Your Personal Savings

Most businesses are financed, at least in part, with personal savings. Sure, it's hard to save money, but this form of financing has so many advantages, it's worth some effort. Incidentally, savings don't necessarily come from a bank account or piggy bank. Lots of entrepreneurs sell or refinance a house or some other valuable property to come up with cash.

Starting a business with your savings is the quintessence of the capitalist idea. As the entrepreneur with capital, you hire people, purchase equipment, and ideally create profits. It's a long and honored tradition. Henry Ford, John D. Rockefeller, and, more recently, Steve Jobs of Apple Inc. all started with at least some money from their own pockets and ended up creating industrial empires. While chances are your goals are more modest, the idea is pretty much the same.

If you finance a business with your own money, you won't have to worry about making loan payments or keeping investors happy. Think of it this way: The more you borrow, the more you increase your fixed operating costs—making it more difficult to survive the slow periods and mistakes almost every business faces.

Another reason to start a business with savings is that you enhance your borrowing capacity for the future. The inventory, fixtures, and equipment you purchase with your cash investment are treated as assets should you later apply for a business expansion loan.

Of course, not everybody is lucky enough to be able to start or expand a business entirely from savings. But there are at least two ways you may be able to increase the amount of money you can put into your business.

Living Expense Deferral

People who need just a little more cash than they have sometimes take a risky—but not unheard of—step. This might more appropriately be called "borrowing from the future," as it involves deliberately falling behind in monthly living expenses or taking cash advances from credit cards. This way of getting extra money involves risk, and it's not for everybody.

You may have a credit card or two that has more credit available; by running your credit line to the maximum, sometimes you can obtain some cash from an unexpected source or buy material for the business. Of course, the interest rates are high, and you flirt with bankruptcy if you can't make payments. Still, several people I know have used this method to help start a business.

If you have a good payment record with the telephone company, gas and electric company, landlord, bank, and so forth, you should be able to skip several months' payments without seriously damaging your credit rating. Of course, you'll have to catch up again fast. In the meantime, you can use the money to help get your business going.

You may be able to fall behind a month or two on your mortgage payments and generate some quick cash that way. However, the mortgage holder will take the property back from you after a few months. Don't use this method unless you're very sure that you can become current again quickly.

> ⓘ CAUTION
> **This scheme should be tried only if you're sure you'll be able to come up with the money when you need it.** As with everything else, common sense should be applied to living expense deferral plans. Otherwise, you may find yourself trying to read a foreclosure notice in a dark room.

Trade Credit

Arranging for trade credit involves borrowing from the companies from whom you will buy your merchandise or raw materials. This form of borrowing rarely works for service businesses, because salaries are the biggest expense and employees are usually not interested in lending you their salaries. However, I do know of a number of new businesses where friends and family members pitched in for free in the early days; it never hurts to ask.

If you're in a retail, wholesale, or manufacturing business, arranging for trade credit can help considerably. In most businesses, you typically order supplies and pay for them 30 to 60 days after you receive them. The problem for new businesses is that it's also standard practice for suppliers to demand cash up front from start-ups. This policy isn't immutable, however. Often, if you present your business plan to potential suppliers, you can arrange to order at least some supplies and merchandise on credit. After all, your supplier has an interest in helping you succeed so that you will buy his merchandise for many years to come.

The key to maintaining good relations with suppliers while borrowing from them is to keep them informed of what you're doing and why. This communication rule is particularly important for new businesses. If you arrange credit and can only pay a part of your first bill in 30 days, pay that amount and ask the supplier for a short extension.

Some suppliers may offer extended payment terms to get your business. Occasionally a supplier will ship merchandise in a slow part of the season and let you pay for it several months later, in the busy season. Before you try any of this, check with your suppliers' sales reps about company policies. Your suppliers are invaluable to your business, and you want to keep them on your side.

Friends, Relatives, and Business Acquaintances

The type of financing provided by close friends and relatives does not normally vary much from that provided by strangers. The help may be in the form of a gift, a loan, or an equity investment. The big differences are usually the availability of money in the first place and the interest rate or investment return.

With friend- or relative-provided financing, however, the commercial model isn't the only one. A common alternative is the loan-gift hybrid. Here a relative or friend lends you money at either a low interest rate, or with no interest at all, telling you to pay it back when you can and to treat it as a gift if you can't. Obviously, this type of help is invaluable if it's available. It gives you time to get your business established with a minimum of pressure. If you've any doubt about your angels' financial position, make sure they consult their bankers, attorneys, or financial advisers before advancing you the money. Also, check with a tax adviser if you receive a substantial gift in one year from any individual, since there may be tax implications. Generally, property you receive as a gift, a bequest, or an inheritance is not included in your income. However, if property you receive this way later produces income such as interest, dividends, or rentals, that income is taxable to you. For additional information, refer to IRS Publication 17, *Your Federal Income Tax (For*

Individuals). You can find this publication online at the IRS website www.irs.gov.

Finally, write down the terms of the loan or transaction and make sure everyone thoroughly understands them. After all, you want to feel like you can go to family reunions even if your business fails.

> ⓘ **CAUTION**
>
> **Think twice before you accept.** Think about what a business reversal could do to your personal relationship, even if your relative or friend says they don't need the money. I know families that have been torn apart because a borrower didn't meet the agreements she made with a lender. Besides, a loan from a relative or close friend that comes with emotional strings probably isn't worth the cost.

Your Money Machine

Here is a task you can start right now that will save you time and frustration. Begin writing a list of all your relatives, friends, business acquaintances, supporters, professional advisers, and so on. This list will be one of the primary sources of money for your new or growing venture, since people who know you already are most likely to be interested in your business.

One advantage of dealing with your relatives and friends is that they already know your strengths and weaknesses. They are likely to be more understanding than a banker if you have start-up problems and make a few late loan payments. Nevertheless, you'll be wise to treat people close to you in a businesslike manner.

Don't make the money a test of whether they love you or not. If your close relatives feel they can decline the investment opportunity without hurting your feelings, both of you will be happier in the long run. Pay attention to criticism and suggestions, especially if they come from people with business experience. If they don't wish to invest or lend you money, accept their reasons at face value—you might not like their hidden reasons.

Some people looking for business financing will write a business plan and loan package and then show it only to the bank, assuming relatives or friends don't need to see it. This is a mistake. Make sure those people close to you get the benefit of all your hard work. A good business plan may even help them see you in a new light and encourage them to make a financial commitment.

Creative Cost Cutting

Although not really a funding source, one of the most effective ways to finance a small business is to make do with less. If your initial business proposal calls for $50,000, think about how you can reduce spending on nonessential items. Perhaps you can begin your consulting business in your home or share expensive equipment with an established business rather than buying it.

Of course, there will be many situations where you will need a fair amount of money to get started—it's hard to cook without a stove, paint without a ladder, or program without a computer. The important principle is not that you should avoid raising outside money, but that you should borrow or raise equity capital only if you absolutely can't do without it. For more on this concept, I recommend *Honest Business,* by Michael Phillips and Salli Rasberry (Shambhala Publications).

Equity in Other Assets

You may choose to raise money by selling existing assets or by pledging your equity in them as collateral for a loan. Remember, collateral is something you own that you give your lender title to until you pay back all the money you borrowed, plus interest. If you fail to repay the loan, the lender keeps the collateral. Basically, equity is the difference between the market value of property you own and what you owe against it, plus any costs necessary to turn the asset into cash.

EXAMPLE: Eric owns a car worth $9,000, but owes the bank $4,000. His equity in the car is $5,000. To convert the equity to cash, he could try to sell the car for $9,000 cash and pay off the bank loan, leaving him $5,000. If he borrows against the car, he'd probably be lent less than $5,000, since banks don't like to finance 100% of an asset's value.

Supporters

Many types of businesses tend to have loyal and devoted followers—in many ways, their customers care about the business as much as the owners do. Examples are as myriad and varied as the likes, loves, and desires of the human community. A health food restaurant, an exercise club, a motorcycle shop, a family counseling facility, a solar heating business, a religious bookstore, or a kayak manufacturing shop all could work, assuming you can find your audience.

As with the discussion about family members, people who care about what you do may well be willing to support you on better terms than would a commercial investor. No matter what your business or business idea, think about whom you know or can get to know and who really cares about what you plan to do. Share your idea with these people and be ready to listen to them. You'll surely get lots of good ideas, and you may be surprised at how easy it is to raise money for what people perceive as an honest and needed endeavor.

Crowd Funding Online

The Internet offers new ways of raising money for new ventures. This field is undergoing rapid development with daily changes.

For example, at this writing, President Obama has signed a new law permitting start-up companies to raise money over the Internet. But, be aware that any funding has to go through a funding portal—read, "new company that will take a fee." And, the SEC has up to 270 days to write the rules and regulations for this new process. You can track their progress at www.sec.gov.

In the meantime, there are other funding portals that are already up and running. The portals listed below are basically introduction services, and the hard work to convert a potential interest into a viable investment is up to you.

- **Startups.co** (www.startups.co) offers funding for start-ups and claims that 300,000 companies have used their services.
- **Kickstarter** (www.kickstarter.com) and **Indiegogo** (www.indiegogo.com) offer people with creative projects the ability to raise money from small investors while retaining complete ownership. "Creative project" refers to innovative artistic projects as opposed to profit-making companies. Donors may receive trinkets but cannot receive ownership shares.
- **Prosper** (www.prosper.com) is a lending portal that facilitates person-to-person loans, but no equity is allowed.

As with any supplier, do your homework to be sure that the company has a positive track record and that they offer what you want, on terms you can afford.

One potential disadvantage is that selling small numbers of shares to several early investors may interfere with your ability to ramp up to bigger investors if your venture is very successful.

Banks

When asked why he robbed banks, Willie Sutton said, "Because that's where the money is." For the same reason, banks are high on the list of potential sources people ask about for business funding. Unfortunately, as far as a small business is concerned, banks act cautiously when lending out money. This makes sense when you remember that it isn't their money.

This discussion applies to financial institutions that lend to businesses and individuals. Recent banking deregulation has made it more difficult to locate which of the various departments of institutions such as the

Bank of America, Wells Fargo, and others actually make loans, but the same fundamentals apply when you finally locate the right department and person.

Banks always want to see a written business plan along with your loan application. Banks are financial intermediaries. They pay interest to account holders to attract deposits, which they lend out to people like you. When lending, they charge enough interest to pay for their cost of funds and produce a profit. While many banks buy stocks or underwrite stock offerings, those activities usually target larger businesses; any transaction you have with a bank will probably be a loan and will come with a repayment schedule. Banks try to minimize risks by making sure you have enough assets to pay them back, even if your business does badly. They don't make equity investments in businesses.

Some commercial banks work closely with the Small Business Administration (SBA) (www.sba.gov) in offering loan guarantee programs. If you want a loan but don't qualify under the bank's normal guidelines, the banker may suggest that you apply for an SBA guaranteed loan. If you're approved, the SBA guarantees the bank that you will repay the loan and the bank lends you the money. While this program can work for start-ups, it is most used by business owners wanting to expand a successful business. Ask your banker if he knows about the SBA guarantee program. (See below for background on the SBA.)

Commercial banks sometimes lend to a start-up business, but they almost always ask for collateral to secure the loan. The most banks will usually lend a start-up is half the cash needed. In addition, they usually require that you do not borrow all or most of your cash from someone else; they want you to have as much to lose as they do.

The good news about banks is that money generally costs less from banks than from other professional lenders, such as mortgage loan brokers. If the bank lending officer likes your business plan and loan application, and you have sufficient collateral, she may give you an interest-only loan for a short time, with the option of converting it to an amortized loan later. That means you can delay larger principal payments until your business has a chance to generate a positive cash flow.

EXAMPLE 1: Katherine O'Malley Pertz-Walter has saved $20,000 to start the Rack-a-Frax Fastener Company, but she needs an additional $10,000. After a careful study of her business plan, a banker grants her an interest-only loan with payments to be made quarterly for one year and takes a second mortgage on her home as collateral. At the end of the year, she must repay the entire principal. Her interest rate will probably be something like the prime rate (the interest rate charged the bank's favored customers) plus 3%. If the prime rate is 12%, she'll be paying about 15% interest, and her quarterly interest payment will be $375. At the end of the year, she will be obligated to repay the $10,000 in one lump sum.

EXAMPLE 2: To continue this story, let's assume that at the end of the first year, Ms. Pertz-Walter asks the bank to convert the loan to a three-year payment schedule, including principal and interest. Based on her favorable first-year results, the bank agrees to amortize the loan rather than demand immediate repayment. She now has to make 36 equal monthly payments of $341.75. After she makes those 36 payments, the loan will be paid off completely.

EXAMPLE 3: Now let's forget about Rack-a-Frax and switch to the story of a friend of mine. Peter Wong wanted to start a garage specializing in Italian cars in Santa Fe, New Mexico. He estimated that he needed a total of $50,000 to get his business started. He had $25,000 cash saved from his job as chief mechanic at an independent Ferrari garage and $30,000 equity in a house. He thought he was home free and confidently walked into a local bank to ask for a $25,000 loan.

An hour later he walked back out with his head spinning. The banker asked him a number of questions about monthly sales projections, cash flow, and cash for a parts inventory. Peter hemmed and hawed. It came down to this: The banker didn't want to talk to Peter seriously until he produced a written business plan demonstrating that he understood how his business would work. After the initial shock of his bank interview wore off, Peter went to work. Putting his plan down on paper and doing a budget encouraged him to deal with a number of details he had never thought about before. When he did, he changed his plan considerably.

Finally, Peter presented his plan to the bank loan committee. This time they offered to lend him $25,000, provided he put up the other $25,000 and give the bank a second trust deed on his house and title to all equipment purchased for the shop. The bank also asked that Peter buy a life insurance policy for $25,000, naming the bank as beneficiary. He negotiated the second trust deed on his house out of the requirements and then agreed to take the package. The terms were 36 monthly payments at a floating interest rate that was calculated at the prime rate plus 3%.

By this time, Peter and the banker, whose name was Fred, had established a good relationship. When the business got off to a slow start, Peter kept Fred informed of the problems and his plans to deal with them. Fred let Peter delay three payments in a row with no penalty. Eventually, when the business began to do well and Peter wanted to expand, Fred worked out a financing package, this time taking as collateral Peter's accounts receivable and inventory.

Angels and Venture Capitalists

Angels and venture capitalists can be anyone who invests equity money in a business in the hope of future profits. While this can include any business investor, from your Aunt Rose to the largest investment banker in New York, the term often connotes a group of businesses that look for hot companies in which they can make large profits. Typically, this group won't consider any investment smaller than $500,000 and prefers companies specializing in the emerging technological fields, where a lot of money is needed to get started and where it's possible to achieve enormous returns. Computers, genetic engineering, and medical technology are familiar examples.

Most readers of this book will be interested in starting or expanding small or medium-sized service, retail, wholesale, or low-technology manufacturing businesses. Large-scale venture capitalists traditionally do not invest in these areas. Fortunately, relatives, friends, business acquaintances, and local businesspeople with a little money to invest can all be pint-sized venture capitalists. Many do very well at it.

> **EXAMPLE:** Jack Boots loved to ride dirt motorbikes on the weekends. He was frustrated that no retailer in his county carried either a good selection of off-road bikes or the right accessories. He and his friends sometimes had to drive 200 miles to buy supplies.
>
> Eventually, it occurred to Jack to quit his job and open a local motorcycle store. He talked to several manufacturers and was encouraged. The only problem was, he would need $50,000 to swing it. As he only had $20,000, he was about to give up the idea when some of his biker buddies offered to help raise the cash. Jack found six people willing to invest $5,000 each in a limited partnership. Each of these friends was, in reality, a small-scale venture capitalist, betting a portion of his savings on the notion that Jack would succeed and they would participate in his financial success.
>
> Jack's Cycles opened for business and is doing well. All the limited partners were paid back their initial investments plus the agreed-upon return set out in their limited partnership agreement, and Jack is now the sole owner. The only sad part of it is that Jack is too busy to ride much anymore.

Many cities have venture capital clubs, comprising groups of individual investors interested in helping businesses start and grow. These clubs often serve as an introductory service—you receive a few minutes to discuss your business at a club meeting. If any investors want to pursue the discussion further, they make an appointment with you privately. You can use these groups to expand the list you are making of investment prospects.

You may also be able to obtain computerized lists of venture capitalists and investor magazines in which you can advertise your proposition. Often, these clubs are formed and disbanded rapidly; ask the local Chamber of Commerce or your local bankers if there is an active club in your area.

When thinking about raising money by selling a share in your business, it's important that you have a hardheaded picture of what you're getting into. Amateur venture capitalists or equity investors gamble on your idea for your expansion or new venture. They invest money hoping that you'll make them rich, or at least richer. If you intend to look for equity investors, your business plan needs enough economic and marketing research to show investors that your idea has the potential of making a substantial profit. You'll also need to show potential investors exactly how they'll profit by investing in your business.

> **EXAMPLE:** Jack Boots spelled out his profit distribution plans in his limited partnership document: Investors received 50% of the profits paid monthly according to their relative share of investment after he paid himself a nominal, agreed-upon salary for running the store. In addition, they qualified to buy merchandise at a substantial discount. They also owned a share of the assets of the business. Jack estimated that a $10,000 investor would receive a monthly cash flow of $200 for an annual return of 24%. When added to the partner's investment share in the inventory of the shop, this would make a $10,000 investment worth $20,000 in three years.

Now That You've Proven Yourself, How About Expanding?

If you've been in business for at least three or four years and can show a history of profitable operations, a whole new world of financing options opens up to you. The major advantage you have over a start-up is that you can prove what you say, whereas a start-up can't. Be careful if you've been in business for less than three years or can't show a profitable history—financing sources may consider you a start-up and put you in a higher risk category.

Take your latest two or three years' financial statements with you as part of your business plan when you talk to any financing source. That way, the lender or investor can see where you've been and where you're planning to go.

Discussed below are readily available financing sources for expanding your small business. Consider each potential source of money carefully— each has unique advantages and disadvantages as they apply to your business. Approach whatever source makes the most sense for your business first; you can try others if the first one doesn't work.

Trade Credit

After you establish a reliable record of prompt payment with your suppliers, normally they will consider extending additional credit for your expansion plans. Let them know of your plans well in advance; if you begin delaying your payments to finance your expansion without notifying them, they may get annoyed. They have an interest in seeing you grow; after all, you'll be buying more from them in the future. Sometimes they will even introduce you to their bankers and investors if you approach them with a well-thought-out business plan.

Commercial Banks

Remember those banks that were so hard to get money from when you started your business? Well, once you can show a profitable history, they become a lot more friendly. As an established businessperson you can often secure flexibility from banks that you might not expect. For example, they may lend you money and take a security interest in your accounts receivable. Or they may take a security interest in your inventory, equipment, or other business assets.

Equipment Leasing Companies

Leasing companies own equipment that they rent to businesses and individuals. Some leasing companies are similar to rental yards in that they have a supply of equipment on hand that they rent out. Sometimes these companies offer repair and trade-in privileges in addition to short-term rentals.

Other leasing companies—called full-finance leasing companies—do not take physical possession of any equipment. You find the equipment you want, and they buy it for you. Full-finance leasing companies have no equipment inventory and offer no return or repair services. They borrow money from a bank, so you'll have to pay back the equipment cost plus interest and a leasing company service fee over a fixed time. Normally, you have the option of buying the equipment for an additional price at the end of the lease term. Full-finance leasing companies base their credit decisions on your company's financial condition. They will want to see lots of financial records from your company and may request that you pledge some of your personal assets to guarantee the lease. Of course, make sure you understand what you agree to before you sign anything.

Accounts Receivable Factoring Companies

Factoring companies—also called factors—buy your accounts receivable at a discount. Then, they collect your accounts at full face value. This can be a very expensive way to raise cash—I only recommend it as a last resort. Some factors require that your accounts pay them directly instead of paying you. This can cause problems with customers, who'll assume that you are having serious cash flow problems. Approach a factor with caution and make sure you understand the implications of the agreement before you sign it.

Factors can buy your receivables with or without recourse—that is, your guarantee of payment to the factor. Factoring with recourse means that the factor pays you a higher percentage of the receivable in cash and makes raising cash less expensive. But you can be seriously damaged if a big account fails to pay its bill and you have to make good on your guarantee.

Venture Capitalists

Some venture capitalists specialize in funding businesses after they have a track record and are willing to take a smaller return as a result. The industry is changing, and more venture capitalists are looking at a wider range of possibilities and client companies. Often a venture capitalist will specialize in a market area and company size or stage of growth. The possibilities have increased, and so has the work involved in finding just the right backers.

Money Brokers and Finders

Money brokers and finders develop and maintain lists of investors and lenders interested in businesses. For a fee, they will circulate your financing proposal to potential money sources. A legitimate broker or finder can look at your business plan and know if he has a good chance of finding money for you.

Finders simply introduce you to possible backers; they cannot negotiate on your behalf, and they are not licensed. Money brokers are licensed and can negotiate on your behalf. Fees for both finders and brokers are comparable. I recommend that you work with people who work on a contingency fee basis only and do not require up-front fees. While some worthwhile finders and brokers require an up-front fee, there are some nonlegitimate people who take the up-front fees and disappear. Also, I recommend that you obtain references from any broker or finder and that you verify the references.

Total fees, including both up-front and contingency, can range up to 10% or 15% of the money raised, so be cautious and remember that everything is negotiable. You can contact finders and brokers in the financial section of your newspaper's classified advertising section.

If No One Will Finance Your Business, Try Again

Let's say that you've been unsuccessful in your attempts to raise money for your business from the primary sources listed above, or you have raised some money, but still need more. What do you do next? The first step is to go back to the people who initially seemed interested but ultimately turned you down and find out why. This is not a waste of time. If you get the same answer from several people, you will know what you have to work on. And then there is the possibility that someone's circumstances have changed and they have more funds now. Remember, it took the man who invented dry paper copying 21 years to raise the money to get the first photocopier made.

If a bank lending officer, or even two or three, turned you down but you still think borrowing is a good way to fund your business, try other lending officers at other banks. A friend of mine got a $15,000 unsecured loan to improve some agricultural property just by going to five different banks. The first banker laughed him out of the office, the second banker listened to his story for five minutes and the third for ten minutes. By the time he got to the fifth bank, he knew what questions the banker was going to ask and was ready with some solid answers. The banker was impressed and he got the loan. In fact, for this very reason, it's not a bad idea to try a longshot bank first and the most likely one last. (See Chapter 10 for ideas on how to present your business plan to bankers.)

> EXAMPLE: Sue Lester tried all the usual sources to get the $20,000 she needed to open a piano school. One person she talked to was her Aunt Hillary, who had loaned her money to go to school several years before. This time Aunt Hillary said, "Sorry, but no." One afternoon a few months later Sue ran into Hillary at her niece's birthday party. Hillary asked how she was doing with plans for the school. Sue told her she was still short $10,000 and was going to try the Small Business Administration as soon as

she made one or two changes in her business plan. Aunt Hillary asked about the changes. Sue told her that an experienced teacher had suggested she charge slightly more per hour, start with a good secondhand piano instead of a new one, and try to work out a referral arrangement with a local piano store. This way she could pay herself more salary and wouldn't need to take another job to make ends meet. Hillary asked to see the changes when they were complete.

After Sue showed the revised plan to her Aunt Hillary, she offered to lend her the money. Sue was both delighted and curious. When she asked, Aunt Hillary said there were two reasons for her change of heart. First, she was pleased that the more realistic sales projections left Sue enough money to live on so she would be able to keep her enthusiasm for the hard job of creating a new business. Second, she had sold a small piece of land for more than expected and now had the money to lend.

Secondary Sources of Financing for Start-Ups or Expansions

Let's assume you have tried all of the primary sources of financing small businesses at least twice, and have been turned down each time. Is it time to head for the showers? Not if you really want to start your business. If everyone turns you down, you have no choice but to get creative. Remember Knute Rockne's exhortation, "Winners never quit and quitters never win." Here are some suggestions.

Small Business Administration

Many years ago, Congress recognized both that small businesses provide most of the employment and growth in the country and that they have a great deal of trouble borrowing money because large corporations tend to hog too much of the loan money from banks. As a result, Congress created the Small Business Administration (SBA) and several other government organizations specifically to help small businesses compete with larger corporations for loans.

While the SBA can make direct loans to small businesses, it usually guarantees loans from commercial banks. The SBA will guarantee 85% of a bank loan up to $750,000 if the loan meets SBA criteria. These criteria are not as difficult as some readers may think. Typical requirements include that the borrower show profits for at least two years, that the borrower work in the business full-time, and that the borrower have some real or personal property available to offer as collateral.

Some bankers are strongly interested in working with loans guaranteed by the SBA since the bank can make a fee by processing the loans and later selling them to other financial institutions. Since the bank's fee is based on the size of the loan, such banks are typically only interested in processing loan requests for more than $50,000.

Many banks treat SBA loan origination as a profit center and aggressively seek out borrowers. Some of these banks offer assistance in completing the SBA forms for a fee and offer quick turnaround on decisions. If any banks in your area offer this service, make an appointment with a loan officer specializing in SBA loans. Chances are, he will be able to estimate your chances of success based on reading your business plan. Loan approvals sometimes take place as soon as a week or so after you complete all the paperwork. The SBA's past reputation of being hard to deal with and not very cooperative seems to be changing! That's true for the guarantee program, at least.

Your chances of receiving a direct loan in a reasonable time from the SBA will be greatly enhanced if you qualify for a preference category. For example, if you are disabled or a veteran, requirements are slightly less restrictive. Ask your local SBA bank or SBA office about some of the direct loan programs.

There are also small private business lending companies that perform a function similar to a bank's function in assisting small businesses obtain SBA financing. To get names and addresses of organizations in your area, write the SBA, Financial Assistance Division, Office of Lender Relations, Non-Bank Lender Section, 409 3rd Street, SW, Washington, DC 20416, or check the SBA website at www.sba.gov.

Small Business Investment Companies (SBICs)

A Small Business Investment Company (SBIC) is a corporation established with the assistance of the SBA to lend money to small businesses. Some SBICs serve minority enterprises, and are called Minority Small Business Investment Companies (MSBICs). An SBIC can borrow up to four times its invested capital from the SBA. It then lends out these funds to other businesses, aiming to make a profit on each loan transaction. There are some 400 of these across the country, each with different investment goals and objectives. For more information on business financing, click "Loans & Grants" on the SBA home page (www.sba.gov). The SBA now partners with an entity called BusinessUSA. You can start finding financing at this URL: http://business.usa.gov/access-financing#.

USDA Rural Development

This loan program is aimed at businesses that provide jobs in rural America. Business loans through the U.S. Department of Agriculture's Rural Development program (formerly the Farmers' Home Adminis-tration or FmHA) are guaranteed in towns with a population of 50,000 or less or in suburban areas where the population density is no more than 100 per square mile. Use of the loans varies considerably; loans have been made to enable a grocery clerk to buy the store he worked in and for someone to buy a McDonald's fast food franchise. Rural Development loans are normally made through a local bank. For information on these loans click "Loans" at the USDA Rural Development website (www.rurdev.usda.gov). At the website you can also locate the nearest USDA Service Center. Loans under this program often take months to complete, so allow plenty of lead time.

Economic Development Administration (EDA)

The EDA, which is part of the Department of Commerce, makes or guarantees loans to businesses in redevelopment areas—city areas with high unemployment. Eligible areas are listed in a publication available quarterly from the regional EDA director. Contact your local SBA office to locate the regional EDA director. If you're in one of the designated redevelopment areas, this program bears looking into. For more information, check online at www.eda.gov.

Federal, State, and Local Programs

Other federal programs are published online at the Catalog of Federal Domestic Assistance (CFDA), which can be accessed at https://www.cfda.gov/. There always seems to be a variety of programs available from the federal government, so this directory is worth checking if you're interested in government money.

All states and many local governments have a number of aid programs available to help businesses create jobs. These are normally called development agencies or development administrations. You can find out about them by contacting your local Chamber of Commerce or by asking a banker.

Overseas Private Investment Corporation (OPIC)

OPIC is a self-funded U.S. government agency that makes direct loans and loan guarantees and insures private businesses against political risks in developing countries. The ideal candidate for assistance is an American company that enters into partnership with a well-established foreign business. To learn more about this agency, check online at www.opic.gov or call 202-336-8400.

Insurance Companies and Pension Funds

You may have heard about the possibility of borrowing money from insurance companies or pension funds. Normally, neither is a viable lending source for small businesses. Some insurance companies have a small fund they can invest in businesses, especially if you can offer a combination of loans and investments. However, most small businesses will find money from less restrictive sources long before they make an application to an insurance company.

Advertising Your Project and Selling Stock to the General Public

Advertising and selling corporate stock to the general public through a public offering is very different from selling stock to your friends, relatives, and business acquaintances. Unless your corporation qualifies for an exemption, you must register every issuance of corporate stock with the federal Securities and Exchange Commission (SEC) and the state securities agency. Registration takes time and costs money. Following any of these procedures requires a knowledgeable attorney—don't try it without help. It can be an expensive, time-consuming process that can easily cost $200,000 in attorneys' fees, accountant fees, and printing expenses just to meet government filing costs.

Fortunately, however, smaller corporations usually qualify for state and federal securities laws exemptions. For example, SEC rules permit the private sale of securities without registration if all of the shareholders reside in one state and all of the sales are made in the state. This is called the "intrastate offering" exemption. Another federal exemption allows a "private offering" of shares without registration. A private offering can be a sale, without advertising, to a limited number of people (35 or fewer is often used as a yardstick even though the federal statute does not mention a number). Another way to qualify for a private offering exemption is to only sell, without advertising, to persons who, because of their net worth or income-earning capacity, can reasonably be expected to take care of themselves—that is, they can adequately assess the risk and bear the cost of investing in the business, without needing the protections afforded by the registration procedures of the securities laws. Most states have enacted their own versions of these popular federal exemptions.

For more information about SEC small business exemptions, visit the SEC website at www.sec.gov. The question and answer portion of the small business information section contains a great deal of useful information, in easy-to-understand language.

Conclusion

There you have it—the primary and some secondary sources of finding money to start your business. If you really believe in your idea, complete the business plan outlined in the rest of this book. Then contact all the sources listed above. If you have a good plan and refuse to take "No" for an answer, you will find the money you need. The Chinese say the longest journey begins with a single step. Let's get started.

Your Résumé and Financial Statement

Introduction 98

Draft Your Business Accomplishment Résumé 98

Draft Your Personal Financial Statement 108

Determine Your Assets 109

Determine Your Liabilities 115

Determine Your Net Worth 118

Determine Your Annual Income... 118

Determine Your Annual Living Expenses 122

Complete Your Personal Financial Statement... 125

Verifying the Accuracy of Your Financial Statement..................................... 125

QUICK PLAN

If you've chosen the quick plan method to prepare a business plan (see Introduction), you need to read and complete only this section of Chapter 5: "Draft Your Business Accomplishment Résumé."

Introduction

In this chapter, you'll draft two important documents for your business plan:

- **a special business accomplishment résumé** that focuses on those abilities you'll need to start or expand your business, and
- **a financial statement,** which details the value of your material possessions.

Draft Your Business Accomplishment Résumé

Investors and lenders want to be certain that you have the experience, education, and desire to make your business a success. Your résumé shows your backers that you can achieve your objectives. This isn't a traditional résumé that lists past jobs and the years or months you held each. More correctly, you'll develop a statement of everything you have accomplished that has a direct bearing on your business objectives.

Although you may not have owned or expanded a business before, you have accomplished some demanding tasks that are similar to the tasks you'll undertake when you begin your business. But don't fool yourself into thinking that good credentials alone will get a loan from the first person you approach. When it comes right down to it, few people will part with their money unless they also have a positive feeling about you as a person. Your task is to get them to trust and like you as a businessperson.

If you're like most people, your glowing accomplishments are sprinkled with past mistakes and failures. Everybody makes mistakes, including your backers. Be honest in your résumé but don't go overboard. You don't need to give a litany of every sin you have committed, including the time you skipped algebra class in the seventh grade. Only provide details of your errors when they're relevant to your business plan. For example, if you ran a business for five years and eventually went bankrupt, you'll need to mention that.

Be prepared to talk with prospective investors and lenders about everything you present in your résumé. The best way to build trust in a financial relationship is to communicate with full disclosure. The worst thing you can do is to lie about or try to cover up a negative. (See Chapter 10 for suggestions about how to discuss your past mistakes.)

Now that that's out of the way, let's deal with the important, positive information: How do you demonstrate that you're qualified to run a business? As with anything else, there are some tricks to writing a résumé that will interest a potential investor.

First, make a list of every job and experience in which you produced positive accomplishments for any organization, even if you were a volunteer or working for yourself. Since you're not writing a standard résumé, dates of employment are optional. You may be able to create this list by cutting and pasting old résumés, or you might just start from scratch. Also, it's okay to include personal information about your hobbies and family status in this résumé. Your financial backers want to know you as a person.

Under each organization, list the business areas you worked in—for instance, sales, management, delivery, credit, and so on. Now, set out the specific things you accomplished for that organization while carrying out your responsibilities. This information will become the raw material from which you choose the accomplishments most likely to support your proposal.

Remember, this isn't the place to be humble. Getting a new business off the ground is no project for the meek. Maybe you reduced costs for your employer by redesigning a delivery route. Perhaps you designed a better canoe or came up with a new marketing strategy that increased sales of tortilla chips. Maybe you figured out how to improve the efficiency of a computer system or revised a recipe to make brownies taste better.

Once you've completed your first list of accomplishments, write a statement that shows how your specific accomplishments relate to your ability to run your business. Include experiences and achievements that support your case and exclude those that are too general or off the point. Emphasize your knowledge of how your potential business works and your knowledge of and respect for financial realities.

Now that you understand the process and the objective, write a first draft of your business accomplishment résumé. You may have to rewrite it several times to get the right perspective. Depending on your experience, your résumé probably should be between one and three pages long. Ask someone to read your drafts to make sure you're convincing the reader that you're the right person for the job. You needn't prove you can walk on water, but you should show a good understanding of business realities.

EXAMPLE 1: Here's an example of an inadequate statement for a credit manager's job. This description doesn't give a potential investor any information about the credit manager's ability to run a business:

> **Credit Manager, XYZ Company:** Supervised two clerks and the accounts receivable and billing sections.

EXAMPLE 2: Here is a much better version that details the credit manager's positive accomplishments for the company. It shows that the credit manager understands and can improve critical business factors:

Credit Manager, XYZ Company: Managed a credit department of ten people, consisting of an accounts receivable section, a billing section, and a delinquent accounts section. Reorganized both our collection department and our credit-granting process to accomplish the following:

- Collected $200,000 in delinquent accounts that had previously been consigned to the "unlikely to ever collect" category. This was a result of my decision to keep in closer contact with customers.
- Reduced accounts receivable from an average of 90 days to an average of 38 days, considerably below the industry norm, again primarily by getting to know our customers better.
- Reduced bad debt losses from 4% of sales to 0.5% of sales in two years by streamlining the credit application process and credit checking procedures as well as requiring our sales reps to personally vouch for customers' creditworthiness. Maintained the 0.5% loss percentage in the following years. As part of this, we successfully brought 15 lawsuits with no new staff.
- Through sales conferences, newsletters, and frequent phone contact, worked closely with the sales force to ensure that new accounts were creditworthy. During this time, XYZ sales grew from $3 million to $7 million.

The following two résumés—Jim Phillips's and Sally Baldwin's—share two important attributes:

- knowledge of the particular business the individual wants to start, and
- specific business accomplishments.

In this respect they are somewhat different from many typical job application résumés. For example, a potential employer might be concerned about whether your independent personality will fit in well in a job environment, where these résumés focus on concrete accomplishments.

Jim Phillips wants to start a retail computer store. Here's how he drafts his résumé.

Résumé
James T. "Jim" Phillips

WORK EXPERIENCE

Manager, The Computer Store, San Jose (20xx to present)

Manager of chain retail computer and electronic store with annual sales of three million dollars.

- Hired, managed, and fired sales and support staff of 15–20 to meet sales goals established by chain management.
- Developed promotional plans and merchandising strategy, which resulted in the store exceeding sales and profitability goals by at least 10% each year.
- Created a computerized inventory plan used by all stores in the 62-store chain. Received Manager of the Month award seven times.
- Conceived and implemented a quarterly newsletter (Compufacts) that was mailed to all 62 stores' customers. Enabled us to maintain close contact with customers as well as directly market to them.

Self-employed Software Sales Representative (20xx to 20xx)

Acted as independent sales representative for three software developers: Softy, Inc. (Cupertino, CA), Biosoft (Colorado Springs, CO), and Playtime (San Jose, CA).

- Increased sales of all three, enabling them to expand and hire more programmers.
- Developed a comprehensive knowledge of the software marketing process. Helped organize a money-back, no-questions-asked warranty program.

Computer Programmer, Southern Atlantic Railroad Company (20xx to 20xx)

Worked in FORTRAN, COBOL, and BASIC languages on IBM mainframe computer doing real-time applications on freight car locations as well as miscellaneous business programming.

- Saved the company approximately $2.3 million by designing a better program to handle both automatic banking and collection of receivables.
- Helped design a new freight car location computer program, which resulted in an increase in car utilization from 60% to 65%.

Bookkeeping

I had several part-time jobs doing bookkeeping while attending programming school.

EDUCATION

Bachelor of Arts Degree, History, San Jose State College, 20xx

Master of Arts Degree, History, University of California, Berkeley, 20xx

Certified Programmer, ACME Programming School, 20xx

HOBBIES

Active in Boy Scouts and United Way; handicap golfer.

The next résumé typifies people who see their potential business as offering a chance for self-expression as well as profit. Individuals in an art or craft field often want to begin a business primarily to work in an area they love. Normally this sort of business starts and stays small because the business owners want to keep their hands on a cherished activity rather than achieve big profits or learn the business skills needed to handle fast growth.

Sally Baldwin loves to work with fabric and color and has become expert at helping people create a pleasant living and work environment. She needs money to open her own small interior decorating business.

The statement for Stephen Brinkle is typical of a person with good general business experience but no work history in the particular business he wants to start. Stephen Brinkle is an attorney who wants to start a gourmet, vegetarian, and low-fat hot dog stand in downtown Chicago. He needs to convince a lender that his general business experience substitutes, at least in part, for his lack of frankfurter finesse. He accomplishes this by demonstrating that he knows enough to hire a manager with enough experience to squeeze the mustard and shake the ketchup.

If you don't possess all the skills needed to run your business, you'll also want to hire people to fill in the gaps. If possible, those résumés should be included in your plan. Because Stephen Brinkle doesn't have experience in selling food, he includes a résumé for his key employee, who happens to be his nephew.

Résumé
Sally Baldwin

Commission Sales, Martha's Interior Design Studio (20xx to present)
Work on commission for a full-line interior design studio. Prospect for people who wish to redecorate, prepare a design plan for the project, purchase the supplies and materials necessary, hire workers to install the design, and collect payments from customers.

- Last year I sold over $500,000 worth of projects. The projects consisted of seven complete remodeling jobs, including three offices, one house, two apartments, and a small pet hospital.
- Keep up with all aspects of the business such as new trends, materials, and suppliers. I take continuing education courses at the Design Institute in New York City, and attend at least a dozen textile, furniture, and appliance trade shows per year.
- Maintain a substantial list of contacts in the design field, including potential customers, contractors, and suppliers.

Commission Sales, J.C. Dollar Interior Design Company (20xx to 20xx)
Sold drapes and furniture for J.C. Dollar on commission. I was responsible for design, installation, purchase of noncompany products, and account collection.

- Sold nearly one million dollars' worth of company merchandise and won Salesperson of the Year award.
- My sales normally required several visits to the customer's home or place of work and I became expert at dealing with all sorts of people.

EDUCATION
Graduated high school in 20xx, followed by one year at Mount McKinley Junior College.

HOBBIES
Decorating on a low budget; collecting Raggedy Ann Dolls.

Résumé
Stephen Brinkle

ATTORNEY IN PRIVATE PRACTICE

Specialize in business law matters, along with some general civil law practice.

BUSINESS INVESTMENTS

I have successfully invested in a variety of small businesses, including an auto tune-up shop and a sporting goods store, which I currently own (Bill's Track and Court, 11 Van Renseller Blvd., Chicago).

In some of my small business investments, I took an active role in management. For example, in the tune-up shop, I had to fire the manager and locate more qualified mechanics. After doing that, the business became profitable and I sold it at a profit. In Bill's Track and Court, the manager and I agreed to concentrate on tennis and running equipment. As a result, the store became considerably more profitable.

EDUCATION

B.A., Northwestern University, History, 20xx
J.D., Northwestern Law School, 20xx
Passed Illinois bar exam, 20xx

HOBBIES

Squash

COMMUNITY INVOLVEMENT

Active in various charitable organizations specializing in relieving worldwide hunger.

Jonathan "Johnny" Brinkle

5678 Palatine Boulevard
West Chicago, IL
(312) 556-1314

CAREER PLANS
Manage hot dog stand, become area manager if franchise plans develop.

WORK HISTORY
MANAGER, BURGER WORLD RESTAURANT (20xx to date)
Supervised three shifts (20 employees in all). Before I took over, Unit 211 had sales of less than two-thirds the Burger World national averages. In two years I brought Unit 211 up to surpass the national averages. My main strategy was to maintain tight quality control and to improve the cleanliness and general appearance of the unit. Within six months after I took over, we began getting top ratings for general appearance and cleanliness from Burger World and many compliments from customers.

MANAGER TRAINEE, JACK IN THE BOX RESTAURANTS (20xx to 20xx)
I was trained in fast food management at a number of Jack in the Box locations. The principal training method was to rotate me through every job in the operation. I learned to adjust cooking to demand so that customers always received freshly cooked food. I also learned that the cleaner the restaurant, the more food you sell.

EDUCATION
Graduated Northside High School, 20xx

PERSONAL
Single, no dependents

HOBBIES
Restoring a 1968 Ford Mustang; playing softball

Draft Your Personal Financial Statement

You can skip the rest of this chapter unless you are seeking a loan or investors for your business.

Your personal financial statement will list your personal assets, liabilities, income, and expenses. It tells your backers a lot about your ability to handle money. Don't be discouraged if your financial condition is weak. Your backers want to know about you, the good and the bad, and they understand that you need money.

Preparing this statement in a form lenders are used to seeing involves several steps, which this chapter will take you through step by step. As you'll see, the task is not much harder than filling out a credit application.

Drawing up a good personal financial statement isn't difficult, but it does involve attention to detail. I recommend that you do a rough draft first.

If you already own or have an interest in an existing business, you may wish to include a separate statement of the business's net worth or balance sheet and profit and loss statement. If you own all or a portion of a business and don't plan to submit a separate statement on the business, include your share of the business on this personal financial statement.

TIP

Co-owned property note: If you own an item with others and the other owners will not sign for the loan, enter only the value of your share of the assets and corresponding liability. If all parties will sign for the loan, enter the full amount. Describe the ownership type (joint tenancy, community property, tenants in common, partnership, or separate property). If you're not sure how you own property, look at the deed or other title document.

Determine Your Assets

Your task is to briefly describe and estimate the current value of everything you own, even if you owe money against it. If you're not sure how much a particular item is worth, make an estimate now and verify it later. Give the market value—the price for which you could sell the particular piece of property today.

FORM

You'll find a copy of the Personal Financial Statement on this book's companion page on Nolo.com; see Appendix D for details on accessing this form and all others in this book. Note that formulas have been embedded in the spreadsheet document so that it will automatically calculate relevant totals.

CAUTION

Keep assets separate from income. An asset is a money item or something that you could sell, like a car or a house. Income is money you receive periodically, such as a paycheck. Some assets produce regular income—for example, stocks and bonds that pay dividends, patents with royalty agreements, and promissory notes you own. Only list your assets here; you'll list your income later.

Cash and Cash Equivalents: List the approximate cash balance in each of your financial accounts. Include accounts in banks, savings and loans, thrifts, credit unions, or any other institutions. Identify each by institution name, account type, and number. Also list money market funds, certificates of deposit (including maturity date), and cash in your safe deposit box, buried in the backyard, or any other place you keep cash.

Marketable Securities: List any stocks, mutual funds, and bonds you own that are publicly traded. Show the number of shares or the amount (face value) of bonds, the exchange on which they are listed, and the current market value. The value of stocks is the number of shares owned multiplied by the bid price per share listed in a newspaper business section.

The current cash value for savings or bank bonds is listed on the table printed on each bond according to the number of years since it was issued.

Corporate bonds are listed in the newspaper in relation to their face or par value, with a price of 100 being equal to par. To calculate the value of your corporate bonds, multiply the price listed by their face value and divide by 100.

If you can't find the listing for your securities in your local paper, check online, read *The Wall Street Journal* at your library, or call your broker and ask.

TIP

Note about unlisted securities: Call your broker for the value of any stocks that are not publicly traded and enter them under Other Assets, below.

Cash Value of Life Insurance: If you own whole life insurance policies, they may include a cash surrender value, which will probably be less than the face value of the property. Obtain the value from your insurance agent. If you own term insurance, there will be no cash value, so don't list the policies.

Accounts and Notes Receivable: List only those business assets and other assets that are not shown on a separate financial statement for your business or secured by real property. List each note (loan) people owe you and show the unpaid balance and payment schedule, as well as a description of any property securing the note. Briefly state your relationship to the payer and indicate if the payment of the loan is questionable.

Trust Deeds and Mortgages: Itemize any properties you have sold or lent money against for which you are carrying back a mortgage (deed of trust). Also list notes you hold that are secured by real property. Loans against property you own will be listed under Liabilities, below. Show the street address of the property, type of improvements (house, duplex, and so on), name of payer, payment terms, and the current unpaid balance. State your relationship to the payer and the status of the note.

Real Estate: Describe each piece of real estate you own. State whether it is unimproved, a personal residence, a rental, or whatever. Include the street address or parcel number of each property. Estimate the market value of your property by checking newspaper listings for your neighborhood, calling a local realtor, or comparing the recent sale prices of similar property. If you own valuable property other than your house, it's best to include a written appraisal.

If you own real estate with others and the co-owners are not going to cosign your business loan, describe how title is held, such as, "John Jones as separate property" or "John Jones and Mary Smith in joint tenancy."

Personal Property: Personal property is anything you own that is not real estate. Separately itemize each of the more valuable items like cars, boats, and collections, describing each item in as much detail as possible. Less-valuable property can be grouped together, such as "household furniture," "appliances," or "power tools." You don't need to be overly detailed. Don't forget household items, valuable clothing, jewelry, electronic equipment, musical instruments, and sports equipment.

Estimate the current market value. For cars, start with the high *Edmunds* (www.edmunds.com) or *Kelley Blue Book* (www.kbb.com) price. Jewelry, antiques, and other collectibles should be appraised if you plan to show them as a significant part of your assets. Make a ballpark figure of less-valuable groups of property; garage sale prices should suffice.

Other Assets: List any assets that weren't covered elsewhere. Items such as annuities, IRAs, vested portions of pensions or profit sharing retirement plans, business interests (value of partnerships, etc.), unlisted securities, trusts, life estates, copyrights, patents, trademarks, and so forth should be listed in this section.

Remember not to list the income generated by your assets.

Total Assets: Finally, add up the values of all your property listed on the form. The result is your total assets.

Personal Financial Statement

ASSETS

Cash and Cash Equivalents

Checking and Savings Accounts (Include Money Market Accounts)

Institution Name	Account Type and #	Current Balance
Bank of Centerville	Checking Acct. #1114443231	$ 1,876
Thrift Savings	Savings Account #556472	3,000
	Total Checking and Savings Accounts	$ 4,876

Time Deposit Accounts (Include Certificates of Deposit)

Institution Name	Account #	Maturity Date	Current Balance
Charles Chubb Co.	00-12345	1-25-20	$ 2,000
		Total Time Deposit Accounts	$ 2,000

Cash on Hand/Miscellaneous Cash (Drawers, Safety Deposit Box, Etc.)

Cash at home, travelers checks	$ 500
Total Miscellaneous Cash	$ 500
Total Cash and Cash Equivalents	$ 7,376

Marketable Securities (Include Mutual Funds)

No. of Shares/ Amt. of Bonds	Name of Stock/Bond	Exchange Listed	Current Market Value
50 sh.	General Computer Stock	NYSE	$ 3,250
100 sh.	Consolidated Radio	NYSE	1,200
5,000	IMB Bonds		6,250
	Total Value of Marketable Securities		$ 10,700

Cash Value of Life Insurance

Policy Description and Company	Cash Surrender Value
Reliable Life Company; whole life insurance policy	$ 2,457
Total Life Insurance Cash Value	$ 2,457

Accounts and Notes Receivable

Note/Account Description	Current Balance
Jack Sprate, nephew; unsecured note, payable monthly	$ 2,356
Total Accounts and Notes Receivable	$ 2,356

Trust Deeds and Mortgages

Note Description	Current Balance
Second deed of trust on former personal residence, single-family home at 4445 Karma St., Modesto, CA, payable monthly. Borrower is son-in-law, Dan Carnegie. Loan is current.	$ 9,786
First mortgage on unimproved lot, payable monthly. Borrower is my mother, Gertrude Hubbard. Loan is current.	2,098
Total Trust Deeds/Mortgages	$ 11,884

Real Estate

Description	Market Value
Personal residence, three bedrm, two bath frame/stucco house,	$ 140,000
33324 Being St., Modesto, CA (Approx. 15 years old)	
Unimproved lot, New City, IL; Parcel #811-2-849. Owned in joint	15,000
tenancy with my mother, Gertrude Hubbard. Total current	
market value is $30,000.	
Total Value of Real Estate	$ 155,000

Personal Property

Description	Current Value
1958 Buick Century hardtop, good condition	$ 2,500
2005 Honda Accord	4,000
Stamp collection	2,000
Household furniture	3,500
Total Value Personal Property	$ 12,000

Other Assets (Include interests in Partnerships and Private-Held Stock)

Description	Current Value
N/A	$ 0
Total Other Assets	$ 0
Total Assets	$ 201,773

Determine Your Liabilities

In your Personal Financial Statement—Liabilities and Net Worth, you'll write down everything you owe to others. To a considerable degree, the information on this form will be the flip side of what you just did. That is, if you showed a house as an asset, you will now list the mortgage on that same house as a liability.

Credit Cards and Revolving Credit Account: List bank cards and revolving accounts at stores and with gasoline companies, and fill in the outstanding balances.

Unsecured Loans: List any unsecured notes to banks, individuals, credit unions, savings and loans, or any other person or institution. These are commonly called signature loans because all the lender gets is your signature on your promise to repay the loan—you don't pledge any collateral. Examples include student loans and loans from relatives. State the lender and terms of payment, including any balloon payments and when the loan will be paid in full, as well as the outstanding balance.

Loans Secured by Real Estate: List each note and deed of trust you owe. State the property by which it is secured and the terms of payment, including any balloon payment and when the note will be paid in full, as well as the unpaid balance.

Loans Secured by Personal Property: List any loans secured by equipment, vehicles, business inventory, or anything other than real estate. Show the payee, unpaid balance, security, terms of payment, including any balloon payment, and when the note will be paid in full.

Loans Against Life Insurance Policies: If you borrowed against a whole life insurance policy, list the insurance company, terms, and outstanding balance.

Other Liabilities: List whatever else you currently owe. This may include unpaid medical bills, tax liabilities, unpaid lawyer bills, unpaid alimony or child support, and debts to bookies.

Total Liabilities: Add up all the amounts you owe others. The result is your total liabilities.

Personal Financial Statement

LIABILITIES & NET WORTH

Credit Cards and Revolving Credit Accounts

Name of Creditor	Amount Owed
VISA (Bank of Centerville)	$ 1,600
American Local	290
Total Credit Cards and Revolving Credit Accounts	$ 1,890

Unsecured Loans

Bank (or other lender)	Terms	Amount Owed
Merchant's Bank	interest only quarterly at prime + 2%, due 9/1/xx	$ 5,000
Total Unsecured Loans		$ 5,000

Loans Secured by Real Estate

Bank (or other lender)	Terms	Amount Owed
Bank of Centerville	First trust deed and note on personal residence: Fixed rate (10%); 30 years ending 20xx	$ 87,583
Abner Small	Mortgage on unimproved lot; monthly interest only at 18%, to be paid off January 1, 20xx	10,000
Total Loans Secured by Real Estate		$ 97,583

Loans Secured by Personal Property

Bank (or other lender)	Terms	Amount Owed
Merchant's Bank	Secured by 1989 Honda: 48 mos; will be paid off Sept. 20xx	$ 1,000
	Total Personal Property Loans	$ 1,000

Loans Against Life Insurance Policies

Insurance Company	Terms	Amount Owed
Reliable Life	$5,000 against policy; 60 mos. at 6% interest	$ 3,987
	Total Insurance Policy Loans	$ 3,987

Other Liabilities

Name of Creditor	Terms	Amount Owed
Mother-in-law	Whenever I can repay—no worry	$ 1,000
	Total Other Liabilities	$ 1,000

	Total Liabilities	$ 110,460
Total Net Worth (Total Assets Minus Total Liabilities)		$ 91,313
Total Liabilities and Net Worth		$ 201,773

> ⓘ CAUTION
>
> **Check for consistency.** Before you go on, carefully compare the information on your assets and liabilities lists. Make sure they are consistent. For instance, make sure that you show assets for which you show liabilities and vice versa.

Determine Your Net Worth

To calculate your net worth, simply subtract your total liabilities from your total assets. (If you are using the Personal Financial Statement form available on this book's companion page—see Appendix D for instructions on accessing this form—the spreadsheet program will automatically calculate this amount.)

In the last blank, add together your total liabilities and net worth. This figure should match your total assets. If it doesn't, you've made a mathematical error.

> ⓘ CAUTION
>
> **If your total liabilities are more than your total assets, your net worth will be a negative figure and you'll need to place brackets around the number.** Of course, people with a negative net worth frequently have difficulty borrowing money and may have to consider another form of financing, such as selling equity in the business. (See Chapter 4 for information about raising money.)

Determine Your Annual Income

The next part of the Personal Financial Statement shows your income from all sources. These figures show the annual total of each income source, so don't confuse this with the asset section completed earlier. However, if you show any income from an asset in this section, make sure you also list that asset in the asset section. This form should reflect your current situation and show your present salary, even if you'll quit your job to start the new business.

> **TIP**
> **Note about cosigners:** If someone else will guarantee the loan with you—such as your spouse—fill in the requested information for that person as well.

Gross Salary and Wages: List all the sources of your income, including wages, earnings from your business, and independent contractor work.

Income From Receivables and Loan Repayments: If anyone owes you money, list the annual payments you receive. If you have substantial income from loans, you may list interest income and principal repayments separately. Otherwise show the entire repayment amount.

Rental Property Income: If you rent out real property or valuable personal property like a truck or piano, list the annual rental payments here. Include relevant details, such as your plans to raise the rent in six months.

Dividends and Interest: List the source and annual amount you expect to receive. Make sure that the information shown here corresponds to information you have shown in the Assets portion of your Personal Financial Statement. For example, if you list dividend income from several stocks and bank accounts here, they must be listed in the Assets portion.

Income From Business or Profession: If you already own a business, list the annual income.

Other Income: Describe any other source of income, such as payments from judgments, payments from business investments other than your main business, trust fund payments, and so forth. It's generally a good idea to list alimony and child support payments you receive, since it increases your ability to repay any loan.

Total Annual Income: Add up the income you receive from all sources and fill in the total.

Personal Financial Statement

ANNUAL INCOME

Gross Salary and Wages

Source	Annual Amount
Consolidated Console, Inc.	$ 35,000
Primavera Community College	4,500
Pine Tree Unified School District	20,000
Total Gross Salary and Wages	$ 59,500

Income From Receivables and Loan Repayments

Person Owing	Terms	Annual Amount
Jack Sprate, nephew	8% interest; unsecured, $106.25/mo.	$ 1,275
Total Receivable and Loan Repayment Income		$ 1,275

Rental Property Income

Source	Annual Amount
27 Fruitvale St., New City, IL	$ 3,600
Total Rental Property Income	$ 3,600

Dividends and Interest

Source	Annual Amount
General Computer (50 shares)	$ 780
Thrift Savings (interest on savings account–$3,000 at 5%)	150
Total Dividends and Interest	$ 930

Income From Business or Profession

Description	Annual Amount
N/A	$
Total Income From Business or Profession	$ 0

Other Income

Description	Annual Amount
Child Support (former husband)	$ 2,500
Total Other Income	$ 2,500
Total Annual Income	$ 67,805

Determine Your Annual Living Expenses

The goal of this part of the form is to make an accurate estimate of how much it costs you to live. Business expenses should be covered under a separate profit and loss statement for the business.

Real Estate Loan Payments or Rent: List your mortgage holder or landlord and your monthly payment. Indicate whether you rent or own. Fill in the annual total of all your rental or real estate loan payments, including principal and interest.

Property Taxes and Assessments: List your yearly liabilities if you own real property. Also list business non-real-estate property, such as inventory or equipment, if it is taxed every year and the taxes are not shown on statements for your business.

Federal and State Income Taxes: Show your totals from last year's income tax forms. If this year's taxes will be very different from last year's, make an estimate. Especially if you're an independent contractor, you may want an accountant to help you prepare your estimated taxes for the year.

Other Loan Payments: List payments for all of the non–real-estate loans, notes, charge accounts, and credit cards you listed in the Liabilities part of the form. Use last year's numbers unless they have changed substantially; if they have, append a sheet and explain.

Insurance Premiums: List everything you expect to pay for the year that won't be covered through your job. Common types of insurance include life, health, disability, property, and automobile.

Living Expenses: Estimate your other regular personal living expenses that weren't covered earlier, such as utilities, child care, medical and dental costs, transportation, food, clothing, entertainment, and travel. Either provide an itemized list or a general category of expenses.

Other Expenses: List child and/or spousal support obligations and any other expense not listed above, like art collection purchases or vacation trips. Include professional associations that have continuing education expenses and club membership fees.

Total Annual Expenses: Now add up all your expenses. (If you are using the Personal Financial Statement form included on the companion page on nolo.com—see Appendix D—the spreadsheet program will

Personal Financial Statement

ANNUAL EXPENSES

Real Estate Loan Payments or Rent

Mortgage Holder/Landlord	Rent or Own?	Annual Payment
Bank of Centerville, 1st deed on residence, monthly payment $895	Own	$ 10,740
Abner Small, 1st deed on unimproved lot, split $380 monthly payment with my mother, co-owner	Own	2,280
Total Real Estate Loan Payments or Rent		$ 13,020

Property Taxes and Assessments

Property Taxes/Assessments	Annual Payment
Winchester County real estate taxes	$ 1,250
Total Property Taxes and Assessments	$ 1,250

Federal and State Income Taxes

Description	Annual Payment
IRS	$ 3,000
State	898
Total Income Taxes	$ 3,898

Other Loan Payments

Creditor	Annual Payment
VISA (Bank of Centerville)	$ 1,600
American Local	290
Total Other Loan Payments	$ 1,890

Insurance Premiums

Insurance Company	Type of Policy	Annual Payment
Reliable Insurance	Whole life	$ 1,164
	Total Insurance Premiums	$ 1,164

Living Expenses

Description	Annual Payment
Food, clothing, entertainment, etc.	$ 22,000
Total Living Expenses	$ 22,000

Other Expenses

Description	Annual Payment
Child support payments per year	$ 3,150
Total Other Expenses	$ 3,150
Total Annual Expenses	$ 46,372

Date:_____ Signature: _____

automatically calculate your expenses.) If your total is greater than your annual income total above, examine the information carefully before you consider borrowing money with a fixed repayment schedule.

Complete Your Personal Financial Statement

If you have not already done so, print out your spreadsheet. Make sure you sign and date your completed form; you'll be surprised at how fast things change.

As noted above, many financial institutions prefer their own forms, which they will supply you. However, chances are that you won't have to redo your Personal Financial Statement or, if you do, it will be easy.

Verifying the Accuracy of Your Financial Statement

Potential lenders probably will want to verify your financial statements. Tax returns for the last two or three years are normally adequate to back up your income and expense statements. If your actual income is somewhat greater than your tax returns show, be ready to verify your assets in some other way. But don't worry too much about this sort of disparity unless it is large. In an age of overly high taxation, your lender will not be surprised if your actual income is a shade higher than your reported income. His probably is, too.

In addition, lenders usually obtain a personal credit check from a credit information agency on your track record in making payments. That shows what bills you pay and when, as well as any unpaid bills. Credit reports also list your current employment, lawsuits in which you're involved, and bankruptcies filed in the last ten years. It's a good idea to request your own copy of your credit report before you meet with any prospective lenders. That way, you'll know what they will see and will be prepared to discuss it. If your credit file contains some inaccurate or misleading information, you have the right to challenge that information. (For information on how to go about this, see *Solve Your Money Troubles: Debt, Credit & Bankruptcy,* by Robin Leonard and Margaret Reiter (Nolo).)

Most of the time, lenders will accept your estimates of your personal assets and liabilities on your Personal Financial Statement, since it is a crime to knowingly make false financial statements.

Banks will also verify your cash deposits by contacting the relevant institutions. Also, lenders will want evidence of your title to property they take as security for a loan.

Your Profit and Loss Forecast

Introduction 128

What Is a Profit and Loss Forecast? 129

Determine Your Average Cost of Sales 130

Complete Your Profit and Loss Forecast 134

Review Your Profit and Loss Forecast 150

    Your Profit and Loss Forecast and Income Tax Return 151

QUICK PLAN

If you've chosen the quick plan method to prepare a business plan (see Introduction), you need to read and complete the section "Complete Your Profit and Loss Forecast," below.

If you have any difficulties completing your Profit and Loss Forecast, go back to Chapter 3 and read the section entitled "Break-Even Analysis: Will Your Business Make Money?" before completing this step. If you've chosen a quick plan, you should be able to complete this step easily.

Introduction

Your next job is to forecast how much money you'll need. You can't make realistic financial projections in a vacuum; they must be integrated into a thought-through plan. As a result, you'll need to make a number of decisions about how your business will operate and forecasts of financial results. But don't let this intimidate you. You've probably been thinking about the financial side of your business for some time. You will inevitably need to make some assumptions and even a guess or two. Of course, you should make your projections as accurate as possible; shoot for an accuracy rate of plus or minus 10%.

TIP

Project development note: If you plan to do a project development, skip the rest of this chapter and go on to Chapter 7. Then turn to Appendix C, where you will find a project development example.

As you begin dealing with all the details inherent in financial projections, it is easy to lose perspective and forget the larger picture—that is, what all your work is supposed to prove. If this happens, pause for a moment and remember that, for yourself and your potential backers, you're simply figuring out:

- how much money you need
- what you will spend it on, and
- how you will pay it back.

What Is a Profit and Loss Forecast?

A profit and loss forecast is a projection of how much you will sell and how much profit you will make. This is the foundation of your business plan. It gives you and your potential backers the basic information necessary to decide whether your business will succeed. Basically, a profit and loss forecast forces you to estimate how many dollars you will take in and how many dollars you will spend for some future period. While other extremely important factors affect your business, such as your cash flow (Chapter 7), you'll be in good shape if you can confidently predict that the money coming in will exceed the money going out by a healthy margin.

In Chapter 3, you completed a rough break-even analysis for your business. That analysis helped you decide whether you chose the right business. Now we are going to take a closer look at those numbers and develop them into a comprehensive forecast of your business's future profits. (If you did not complete or don't remember the work you did then, review the section in Chapter 3 entitled "Break-Even Analysis: Will Your Business Make Money?")

Your business's profits result from three specific dollar figures:

- **Sales revenue.** This is all the money you take into your business each month, week, or year. It is also called "gross sales," "sales income," or simply "sales."
- **Cost of sales.** This is your direct cost of the product or service you sell. Sometimes it is called "direct product cost," "variable cost," "incremental cost," or "direct cost."
- **Fixed expenses.** These are sometimes called "overhead," and you must pay them regardless of how well you do. Fixed expenses don't vary much from month to month. They include rent, insurance, and other set expenses. They are also called "fixed costs," "operating expenses," "expenses," or "discretionary costs" (discussed in the section in Chapter 3 entitled "Break-Even Analysis: Will Your Business Make Money?").

In a given period, you make profits when sales revenues exceed your total cost of sales and fixed expenses. To put it another way, sales revenue minus both cost of sales and fixed expenses equals profits or losses for a given time period.

Our job here is to examine closely all the above numbers and, once you are convinced they are right, to present them on a month-by-month basis for two years. Two years is enough time to see if any short-term problems or long-range trends begin developing. Of course, you can change the time frame if necessary. For instance, if you are starting a beer stand for the annual county fair or a vineyard with a five-year growing cycle, a different time frame will make sense for you.

FORM
You'll find a copy of the Profit and Loss Forecast on this book's companion page on Nolo.com; see Appendix D for details on accessing this form and all others in this book. Note that formulas have been embedded in the spreadsheet document so that it will automatically calculate relevant totals.

Determine Your Average Cost of Sales

Your first step in your profit and loss projection is to determine your average cost of sales—that is, your direct cost of the products or services you sell. You'll use the Sales Revenue Forecast you completed in Chapter 3 to make this estimate.

One way to derive your average cost of sales is to estimate your annual sales revenue for each product or service. Then calculate each product's annual cost of sales. Finally, add up the numbers to get an annual average.

More Detailed Method to Determine Average Cost of Sales

Another way to calculate your average cost of sales is to make a separate monthly sales revenue and cost of sales forecast for each of your major product or service lines. If you complete a separate monthly forecast for each of your product or service lines, you will have a very detailed forecast. However, many people balk at this level of detail in forecasting and wish to proceed with the less-detailed method demonstrated in this section. Either way is acceptable.

CAUTION

Whether you make one annual cost of sales forecast or a number of detailed forecasts, don't forget about the inevitable percentage of merchandise you will have to move at marked-down prices. Whether you're in the book business, bake cookies, or are a child psychologist, chances are you will commonly sell some of your product or services for less than standard prices. This may be because you need to move out last year's styles or because you need to sell broken cookies or because you provide counseling cheaper to low-income groups.

EXAMPLE: Antoinette Gorzak plans to sell dresses for an average price of $250, and her research shows they will cost $125 each. Her cost of each sale for dresses before she allows for labor and other overhead will be 50% of the selling price. If she plans to give her customers anything with the purchase, say a specially printed shopping bag and an imprinted dress box, she should include the cost of these items as part of her cost of sales. Maybe this will make her cost of each sale 51% or 52% instead of 50%. Since Antoinette sells accessories in addition to dresses she needs to allow for different gross profit margins for the additional merchandise.

A cost-of-sales averaging chart for Antoinette's Dress Shop might look like this:

Annual Average Cost of Sales Chart: Antoinette's Dress Shop

Item	Forecast Sales Revenue	Cost per Sale*	Total Cost of Sales
Dresses	$ 200,000	50.4%	$ 100,800
Accessories & sale items	200,000	73.3%	146,600
TOTAL	$ 400,000		$ 247,400

Total Average Cost of Sales = 61.8% ($247,400 ÷ $400,000)

*These percentages come from Chapter 3, where she calculated gross profit. To get cost of sales percentage, simply subtract gross profit percentage from 100%. The remainder is cost of sales. (You already calculated this on line 5 of the table on page 53.)

Here's how Antoinette completed this chart. First, she estimated how much sales revenue for each of the product categories the shop would receive in the first year; that enabled her to complete the first column of the chart.

Next, she obtained her cost of sales percentage by using the figure she developed in Chapter 3. She then multiplied the sales revenue for each product category by the cost of sales percentage for that category; that enabled her to complete the total cost of sales column of the chart.

The average total cost of sales figure (61.8% in Antoinette's example) is not an average of the cost per sale percentages. Instead, it is weighted according to the amount of expected sales revenue and is derived by dividing the total cost of sales by the expected sales revenue ($247,400 ÷ $400,000).

An average cost of sales of 60% is reasonable for many profitable retailers. Even though it is wise to be a little conservative, Antoinette uses 60% as her cost of sales when forecasting profits.

You can use the procedure in the example above to estimate your average cost of sales if you're in the retail, manufacturing, or wholesale businesses. Simply modify the item categories to fit your business. For example, a restaurant would have categories for food, nonalcoholic drinks, liquor, beer/wine, and possibly take-out orders. Another example, for a bar and restaurant, is shown below.

Annual Average Cost of Sales Chart: Bar and Restaurant

Item	Forecast Sales Revenue	Cost per Sale	Total Cost of Sales
Food	$ 300,000	38%	$ 114,000
Liquor	60,000	29%	17,400
Beer/wine	40,000	75%	30,000
TOTAL	$ 400,000		$ 161,400

Total Average Cost of Sales = 40% ($161,400 ÷ $400,000)

By definition, service businesses sell services or labor and do not sell merchandise. Occasionally they may bill a client for a service they purchase outside the firm or bill for a service that has some incidental costs. The cost of sales portion of a service business's total costs will be low. For example, a consulting firm may incur outside typing, photocopying, and report binding expenses that will vary somewhat with every sale. Most expenses, such as salaries and rent, will be fixed costs and won't appear on this chart. Service businesses should follow the example below of the consulting business.

Annual Average Cost of Sales Chart: Consulting Firm

Item	Forecast Sales Revenue	Cost per Sale	Total Cost of Sales
Publications, phone, travel	$ 100,000	20%	$ 20,000
Contract services (typing, etc.)	50,000	75%	37,500
Studies, consultations	527,000	0%	0
TOTAL	$ 677,000		$ 57,500

Total Average Cost of Sales = 8.5% ($57,500 ÷ $677,000)

> **CAUTION**
>
> **Include piece-rate and commission costs.** Note that some businesses pay workers on a piece-rate or commission basis. All your costs that vary with each sale should be in cost of sales instead of fixed expenses.

When you've completed your cost of sales calculations, you are ready to prepare your Profit and Loss Forecast.

Complete Your Profit and Loss Forecast

Follow the line-by-line instructions below to complete your form.

> **FORM**
>
> **You'll find a formatted copy of the Profit and Loss Forecast on this book's companion page on Nolo.com;** see Appendix D for details on accessing this and all other forms in this book.

1. Sales Revenue. You have completed this estimate already. Simply enter the total sales revenue dollars for each month for two years from the Sales Revenue Forecast you completed in Chapter 3.

CAUTION

Here's another chance to revise the sales revenue numbers in case you think they need work. However, be sure you really believe that you can generate all the revenues you forecast. Make sure you don't do it backwards by writing down enough sales revenue to show the profits you want. Otherwise, you'll have to explain to your backers each month why things aren't as good as you said they would be.

2. Cost of Sales. Enter your monthly dollar cost of sales. To get these figures, multiply your monthly sales revenue forecast by the average cost of sales percentage. Returning to our dress shop example, Antoinette would multiply her monthly sales figure estimate by 60% (or 0.6). For example, if March sales are forecast at $30,000, the cost of sales for March would be $18,000 (0.6 × $30,000 = $18,000).

FORM

If you are using the Profit & Loss Forecast form on this book's companion page, you can enter the Cost of Sales percentage in Column B in the spreadsheet (where it is marked "(%here)" in red). Then enter the relevant Sales Revenue in Column C. The spreadsheet program will automatically calculate your Gross Profits. Note, if a series of #### symbols appear in a box in a spreadsheet that means that you need to widen the column in order to display the numbers. See Appendix D for details on accessing the companion page.

CAUTION

If you made separate forecasts of sales revenue, cost of sales, and gross profit for each product line, then add together all the gross profit numbers and enter them on a summary form Line 3. You will have prepared separate forms for each product line for the first three lines (sales revenue, cost of sales, and gross profit) and a summary sheet showing total gross profit, operating expenses, and profit.

3. Gross Profit. Subtract cost of sales (Line 2) from sales revenue (Line 1) to get gross profit. It's the amount of money that remains after you've paid your direct costs of the products sold. This money is available to pay the business's fixed expenses and your profits. If gross profit is larger than fixed expenses for that month, you will have a profit. But if gross profit is smaller than fixed expenses, you will have a loss that month.

For example, looking at the dress shop example for March, Antoinette arrives at gross profit by subtracting the cost of sales of $18,000 from the forecast sales revenue of $30,000 and entering the result of $12,000. She'll do the same thing for each subsequent month.

4. Fixed Expenses. The categories listed on the form are the most common fixed expenses, but feel free to add or modify items to suit your business. All fixed expense items reduce your profit so that you pay less business income tax.

4a. Wages/Salaries. Most small businesses keep some employees on a fixed weekly or monthly work schedule regardless of how business fluctuates. Many businesses call in some temporary employees as needed. All such wages are a fixed expense. To fill out Line 4a, you'll need to know how many people you'll hire, how many hours per month each will work, and how much you'll pay each person. If you plan to pay yourself a regular wage, regardless of how profitable the business is, include your salary as well.

Fill in the gross amount, before employee withholding deductions, you will pay every month for wages and salaries. (If you don't know, or aren't sure how this works, turn to Chapter 8 for a complete discussion.)

CAUTION

Certain wages aren't fixed expenses. Some small manufacturing businesses pay workers on a piece-rate basis or hire employees when orders are high and lay them off when business is slow. Others don't pay a salary at all, but compensate workers with a commission for each sale. In all of these situations, the portion of the wages that changes with each additional unit of production should be considered a variable cost of sale. Those costs belong in the cost-of-sales category and not the fixed-expense category.

4b. Payroll Tax. As an employer, you'll pay the federal government taxes of approximately 14% of your employees' wages and salaries. It is your contribution to your employees' Social Security program. Multiply each month's dollar figure for wages and salaries by 14% (0.14). For example, if employees receive $4,560 in wages and salaries in May, the payroll tax is $638 ($4,560 × 0.14 = $638). In other words, the employees in this example cost the employer $5,198 in May ($4,560 + $638 = $5,198) even though the employees' gross pay is only $4,560.

These tax rates change from time to time. You can call the IRS for current rates. Most states have additional taxes not included here that vary from state to state. (Workers' compensation insurance is covered in Line 4e, below.)

4c. Rent/Lease. Rent is the next major item to consider, unless you plan to operate out of your home or some other space that will not result in additional out-of-pocket costs. If you're not renting commercial space, however, bear in mind that local zoning laws may affect you. You'll want to check out zoning ordinances before going ahead with your plans.

If you don't already have a spot in mind, check building availability and costs by talking to a commercial real estate broker and people who occupy space similar to the one you have in mind. You should know what kind of location you want by now—for instance whether you need high visibility or whether an obscure, low-cost location is just as good. You should also know how large a space you need, what plumbing, electrical, and lighting you want, and how much storage you need. Sometimes cheap rent doesn't turn out to be such a bargain if you have to build walls or install a bathroom and a loading area, or if a poor location means you get few customers.

Profit and Loss Forecast: Year One

for   Antoinette's Dress Shop

Month	1	2	3	4	5
	Mar	Apr	May	Jun	Jul
1. Sales Revenue	$ 30,000	$ 33,800	$ 45,000	$ 37,500	$ 33,800
2. *Less:* Cost of Sales (___%)	(18,000)	(20,300)	(27,000)	(22,500)	(20,300)
3. Gross Profit (___%)	12,000	13,500	18,000	15,000	13,500
4. Fixed Expenses:					
a. Wages/Salaries	3,168	3,168	3,168	3,168	3,168
b. Payroll Tax	432	432	432	432	432
c. Rent/Lease	3,850	3,850	3,850	3,850	3,850
d. Marketing & Advertising	1,000	1,000	1,000	1,000	1,000
e. Insurance	500	500	500	500	500
f. Accounting/Books	200	200	200	200	200
g. Interest Expense	0	0	0	0	0
h. Depreciation	0	0	0	0	0
i. Utilities	800	800	800	800	800
j. Telephone	600	600	600	600	600
k. Supplies	200	200	200	200	200
l. Bad Debts	100	100	100	100	100
m. Freight	200	200	200	200	200
n. Miscellaneous	1,000	1,000	1,000	1,000	1,000
5. *Less:* Total Fixed Expenses	(12,050)	(12,050)	(12,050)	(12,050)	(12,050)
6. Profit/(Loss)	$ (50)	$ 1,450	$ 5,950	$ 2,950	$ 1,450

Date Completed: ___1/25/xx___

6	7	8	9	10	11	12	Year Total
Aug	Sept	Oct	Nov	Dec	Jan	Feb	
$ 33,800	$ 41,200	$ 41,200	$ 45,000	$ 52,500	$ 26,200	$ 30,000	$ 450,000
(20,300)	(24,700)	(24,700)	(27,000)	(31,500)	(15,700)	(18,000)	(270,000)
13,500	16,500	16,500	18,000	21,000	10,500	12,000	180,000
3,168	3,168	3,168	3,168	3,168	3,168	3,168	38,016
432	432	432	432	432	432	432	5,184
3,850	3,850	3,850	3,850	3,850	3,850	3,850	46,200
1,000	1,000	1,000	1,000	1,000	1,000	1,000	12,000
500	500	500	500	500	500	500	6,000
200	200	200	200	200	200	200	2,400
0	0	0	0	0	0	0	0
0	0	0	0	0	0	0	0
800	800	800	800	800	800	800	9,600
600	600	600	600	600	600	600	7,200
200	200	200	200	200	200	200	2,400
100	100	100	100	100	100	100	1,200
200	200	200	200	200	200	200	2,400
1,000	1,000	1,000	1,000	1,000	1,000	1,000	12,000
(12,050)	(12,050)	(12,050)	(12,050)	(12,050)	(12,050)	(12,050)	(144,600)
$ 1,450	$ 4,450	$ 4,450	$ 5,950	$ 8,950	$ (155)	$ (50)	$ 35,400

> **TIP**
>
> **Leasehold improvements note:** Any time you build something like a wall or a bathroom, it is considered a capital outlay, not a fixed expense. (Capital expenses are covered in Chapter 7.) Do not show the expenditure as a current operating expense. Only the depreciation is a fixed expense. You can write off or depreciate leasehold improvements over the term of the lease in most cases. (If you don't know what depreciation is, look at Line 4h, below. For more help, check with your CPA.)

Normally you will want to sign a lease for a business space rather than to accept a month-to-month tenancy. Business leases generally protect the tenant more than the landlord, although it may not seem so if you read all those fine print clauses. You'll be sure that you can stay at the location long enough to build your business around it, and you'll know what your rental costs will be. But what happens if your business fails or you discover the location is poor? You'll be responsible for paying the rent until the space is rented to someone else, which could take a long time in some areas. Assuming someone else will pay at least as much as you do, you'll have no further obligation once the new tenant begins paying rent.

Be sure you know exactly what your rent will include. Commercial leases often require the tenant to pay for a number of things that a landlord commonly pays for in residential rentals. For example, some shopping center leases require you to pay a pro rata share of property taxes, building maintenance, and fire insurance on the building, as well as a pro rata share of the parking and common area charges. A friend of mine who rented a small building for a retail nursery business put it this way: "That blankety-blank landlord sold me the building; he just kept the title." So, as part of making your financial projection, be sure you know exactly what charges, if any, the realtor or landlord expects you to pay in addition to the rent. By the way, no matter what you determine the rent to be, expect to put up the first and last month's rent and often a security deposit when you sign the lease. Don't include those deposits here. (See Chapter 7 for treatment of preopening expenses.)

Many leases that last longer than a year contain a method to protect the landlord from inflation. Some are tied to a cost-of-living index, which means your rent goes up each year at the same percentage as the inflation rate. Others contain a percentage of sales clause, where you pay a set rent or a percentage of your gross sales, whichever is higher.

> **EXAMPLE:** Bob Smith signed a shopping center lease for his optometry office. His lease called for a base rent of $2,400 or 6% of monthly sales, whichever was more, plus a set charge of $400 for taxes, maintenance, and insurance. If sales exceeded $40,000 per month ($2,400 ÷ 0.06), he would be obligated to pay the landlord more rent. Bob was pleased to sign the lease because his sales projections ($32,000 per month) indicated he would be making a healthy profit if his sales volume reached $40,000 a month, so he would not mind paying a higher rent. Of course, this sort of lease is not a good idea if the amount of sales needed to trigger a substantially higher rent is too low. In Bob's situation, for example, if he was required to pay more rent if monthly sales reached $28,000, he probably would have looked elsewhere.

When you have figured out your total monthly rent from a lease quotation from your expected landlord or from a survey of market rents, fill in that amount.

4d. Marketing and Advertising. Here's a story about advertising. Back in the early 1930s, John Axelrod opened a hot dog stand on the main road into Pine Valley. Business was fair. When he put up a small sign, business got a little better. Then he added several more signs and things got a lot better. Finally, he put up a dozen big signs. Business became so good, he had to expand his seating area and hire more cooks. He was feeling pretty happy about life when his son, who he thought was a positive wizard, came home from college. The son, an economics major, was appalled at all the new signs and seating.

"Dad, what are you doing spending so much on advertising? Don't you know there's a depression going on and everybody's going broke? If you don't pull in your horns a bit, you will never make it."

"No kidding," John replied, and took down the signs and stopped the construction program. Soon business dwindled away to nothing and John went broke.

The lesson of this story is simple: When the signs went up, business improved. When they came down, there wasn't enough income to buy ketchup. One way or another, successful businesses get the word out. (Incidentally, the son went on to get his degree and opened his own business consulting firm.)

There are small libraries full of books about how to market a business or product. Such books used to focus almost exclusively on paid advertising. I recommend especially *Marketing Without Advertising*, by Michael Phillips and Salli Rasberry (Nolo). More recently, broader concepts of marketing have come into prominence. Network marketing, or selling to friends and acquaintances, has become an identified alternative to more traditional selling methods. In addition to your own business website, social network marketing using social media like Twitter and Facebook has become an accepted method of getting out word on your business. Guerrilla marketing involves getting the word out to the people and groups who are most apt to need your goods or services, rather than advertising your product or service to the community as a whole. "Guerrilla" refers to the use of unconventional methods to spread product or service information. For example, guerrilla marketers may pay students or part-time workers to hang out in bars or coffeehouses and talk about their product in a favorable way.

If you get creative, there are all sorts of ways you can reach the people most likely to want your product or service, for little or no cost. For example, if you invent a better software program (or develop a consulting business in your special field), you could advertise on the radio—or you could target your market by finding a computer bulletin board of people who need your product. Your next step might be to get someone to write about your business for a computer magazine or newsletter. Similar opportunities exist in every business. If you open an oboe repair shop, for example, one of the first jobs is to figure out inexpensive ways to let every oboist within a hundred-mile radius know of your existence. One way might be to contact every wind instrument instructor, school bandleader, and music store in the area and supply them with free literature on oboe cleaning.

Many successful businesses allow a set percentage of gross sales for promotion, often 3% to 5% of sales revenue as a budget figure. They allocate half that amount for a continuing, low-level effort to let people know about their product or service and schedule the other half to advertise sales and special events.

Think about what you will need to do to tell people about your business. In today's world, a business website is obligatory; see Nolo's website as an example of a complex, professionally developed site: www.nolo.com. Be aware that most potential customers will find your website only if they encounter it in a search engine like Google, while they are looking for similar products or services; there is an entire industry of consultants who may be able to improve your placement on those search engines—they are called Search Engine Optimization (SEO) consultants.

In addition, think about the more traditional ways of getting out the word. Will your business need cards? Flyers? Newspaper ads? A good-sized ad in the yellow pages? Sample merchandise sent to media outlets so they can review your product? Window displays? Mailings? A part-time marketing expert to help you pull this together? Avoid expensive promotions that you haven't tried before. For example, if you get an idea that involves mailing out 100,000 flyers, plan for a test by mailing only 5,000. If it works, go for the rest. If not, use the money you saved for something else.

A great deal of money spent on conventional advertising is wasted. New businesses especially are prone to spend too much in the wrong places. So use your common sense. Talk with friends in business. Check with trade associations to see what they suggest as a good budget number for telling potential customers about your business. Once you've set a budget for special promotions and continuing low-level advertising, write both amounts in the Profit and Loss Forecast.

RELATED TOPIC

For more help, look ahead to Chapter 8. In that chapter, you'll write a detailed marketing plan for your business that includes both preopening promotions and continuing marketing costs.

4e. Insurance. You must have at least some insurance in this litigation-happy society. Your lease may require you to keep fire, flood, or earthquake insurance on the building. If the public comes into your business, public liability and property damage insurance is a necessity. This will protect you from the person who slips and falls on your floor mat. If you employ anyone, you also need workers' compensation insurance, since you are absolutely liable if one of your employees injures herself while at work. You will probably also want to carry insurance on your valuable inventory and fixtures. And if you manufacture any product that could possibly harm anyone, such as food or machinery, you will want to consider product liability insurance.

Talk to an independent insurance broker who specializes in business insurance to get an idea of what coverage you'll need and how much it will cost. Then shop around warily. Lots of over-enthusiastic insurance people will try to sell you far more insurance than you need. Although you need some insurance to protect against obvious risks, you don't need to starve to death trying to raise enough to pay your premiums.

CAUTION

Some people try to avoid the responsibility of paying workers' compensation insurance or payroll taxes by calling their employees "independent contractors." This can cause serious problems with back taxes if the IRS rules against you. Also, if the independent contractor is injured while working for you, the workers' compensation appeals board will almost always rule in favor of the employee and against independent contractor status, unless your worker genuinely has her own business. This means you may end up paying huge sums if one of your workers becomes disabled while you don't have insurance. In other words, trying to save a few pennies on this insurance is just not worth the risk.

Once you arrive at a good estimate for your total insurance bill, inquire about deferred payment programs. Most companies that offer them often require that you pay 20% of the total premium up front each year and the balance in ten payments. For purposes of your Profit and Loss Forecast, divide the total annual insurance payment by 12 and enter those figures.

4f. Accounting/Books. You can do your own books if you like working with numbers. Chances are, however, you'll be so busy with the business, you won't have time.

One good approach is to budget for a CPA to set up your books initially and to hire a part-time bookkeeper to do day-to-day upkeep. If you are starting small, your initial cost should be under $500 and your monthly cost under $200 to keep the records up to date and to prepare routine employee withholding tax returns, statements, etc., assuming you close the register each day. Once a year you will pay the CPA another few hundred dollars to review this work and help you prepare your yearly returns. If your business is going to be fairly good-sized from the start, your figures will be larger.

If you're interested in keeping your own books, you'll probably want to look into reliable accounting software such as Intuit's *QuickBooks* (www.quickbooks.intuit.com), or *M.Y.O.B. Plus* (www.myob.com.au). The program you need depends on how big your business might grow to be, what extra features like statements or payroll you want the computer to provide, and so forth. Many accounting programs—including Quickbooks and MYOB—can be run as online services where you subscribe to the service and do your work online instead of installing software onto your own computer; both methods have advantages and disadvantages. You can research the different programs yourself, but remember to keep in mind the features you may need later on after your business has grown. Or you can look into an outside service, which may recommend a program to fit your business and computer, set up the books, and run parallel for a month or two to make sure that you don't lose any data. The systems can be very handy and timesaving if you have no strong attachment to a paper record, or are willing to print out the documents you may want.

When designing a bookkeeping system for your business, remember that it costs a lot of time and money to change it—make sure it really fits you and your business. (See Chapter 12 for a further discussion of computers in business.)

Make as good an estimate as you can and enter this figure on your Profit and Loss Forecast. You can take the year total and divide it by 12, or you can enter the amounts when you think they will be paid.

4g. Interest. This line of your Profit and Loss Forecast concerns the interest portion of the payments you make on any money you borrow. Unless you have an interest-only loan with a balloon payment at the end, your interest payment will vary from month to month even though you pay the same monthly amount.

> **EXAMPLE:** Joanie Ricardo borrows $50,000 from the bank to open a Gelato's Ice Cream store in Providence, Rhode Island. She agrees to repay it in 36 equal monthly installments of $1,660.80, including 12% interest on the unpaid balance. While Joanie's monthly payments remain equal, the portion of the payment that is credited to principal increases every month, while the portion of her payment going toward interest decreases.

Loan Interest Calculation Chart

A	B	C	D	E	F
Month	Balance (from column F above)	Monthly payment	Interest paid (B × ___% ÷ 12)	Principal Paid (C – D)	New balance (B – E)
				Starting amount:	$ 50,000.00
June 20xx	$ 50,000.00	$ 1,660.80	$ 500.00	$1,160.80	$ 48,839.20
July 20xx	48,839.20	1,660.80	488.39	1,172.41	47,666.79
Aug 20xx	47,666.79	1,660.80	476.67	1,184.13	46,482.66

But, let's say that you don't know how much money you'll borrow at this time. After all, one of the main reasons for doing a business plan is to decide how much money you'll need to finance your business. In that case you have three choices:

- You can complete the Profit and Loss Forecast in this chapter, and the Cash Flow Forecast in the next chapter, making your best guess about how much you'll borrow and what your payments will be.
- You can complete the forecasts without showing any loans or payments. Then use the results to decide how much money you'll borrow and revise the forecasts to include loan payments.
- You can complete both forecasts without showing any loans at all. Then you can include a discussion about how much money you'll need to borrow and the cash flow available to make repayments. (See your Plan Summary discussion in Chapter 9.)

There are loan progress charts and computer programs that show approximately how much of any payment is interest and how much is principal.

RESOURCE

Nolo, the publisher of this book, provides a calculator that will create a chart similar to the one shown above. You can access it at www. nolo.com/legal-calculators. Click on "How much will my loan payments be?" and enter the information in the form, and the program will calculate interest payments over the loan period.

CAUTION

You can't write in the entire loan payment amount on your Profit and Loss Forecast, because the IRS does not consider principal repayments fixed expenses that can reduce your taxable income.

TIP

Note of sanity: You don't need to be perfect in forecasting your interest costs. Just make your best informed guess. You can also check with your banker, CPA, realtor, or bookstore for loan repayment tables. Make sure the sum of your interest payments here and the principal payments from Chapter 7 equal the total loan payment.

4h. Depreciation. Depreciation is a gift to the businessperson from Uncle Sam. Ask not what your country can do for you—this is it. Depreciation is an amount you can subtract from your profits when you pay taxes. It compensates you for the fact that your business equipment and buildings are wearing out. The government allows you to assume that your fixed assets wear out over some period of years, meaning that for tax purposes, your assets are worth less at the end of that period. Your depreciation allowance simply lets you show a percentage of this wear as an expense on your tax return each year. In a sense, it is a sinking fund for equipment replacement, or would be if you put the depreciation amount in the bank. In actuality, the stuff usually lasts longer than your depreciation shows, which is why depreciation can be seen as a friendly federal gesture.

Often, equipment is depreciated over three to five years and buildings over 15 to 30 years for tax purposes. It's not your choice, however; the IRS publishes very explicit rules and lists of what can be depreciated and how fast. These lists and rules change frequently, so you'll probably need to check with your tax adviser about depreciation and fixed assets.

You can depreciate all fixed assets that last longer than one year. Remember, you don't show the purchase price as an expense on the Profit and Loss Statement if you depreciate an item.

If the asset will last less than one year, you simply show the entire purchase price in the expense column for the year you bought the equipment and do not depreciate it. Inventory of goods available for resale and consumable supplies are examples of purchases that are expensed immediately because they last less than one year.

> **EXAMPLE:** Chuck Leong expects to spend $20,000 for fixed assets to open his business. Items include a new toilet, several new walls, a cash register, a small computer, and store fixtures. Assuming Chuck's accountant agrees that five years is the proper time frame to use for depreciation, he can take $333 as an expense for depreciation each month ($20,000 ÷ 60 months).

Common Expenses

Here are some of the more common expenses that businesses incur on a regular basis:

- attorneys, consultants, tax advisers
- auto and truck expenses
- bad debts
- commissions (probably should be placed in cost of sales or as a deduction from sales revenue if commissions are paid regularly; if paid only occasionally, include them in fixed expenses)
- dues and publications
- employee benefit programs
- equipment rental
- freight in on merchandise acquired (also sometimes placed in cost of sales; freight out to customers is usually paid for by the customer)
- janitorial
- laundry
- licenses and taxes including permit fees (not income taxes, which are calculated after profits are known)
- office supplies
- payments to investors
- postage, fax, telephone
- repairs and maintenance
- security and alarm systems
- travel and entertainment, and
- utilities.

4i.–4n. Other Expenses. Inevitably, you will encounter a number of other expenses, depending on your business. Spend some time thinking about these using the accompanying list as a starting point. Then list all the other costs you expect to incur on Lines 4i to 4n. If you expect any of these to be recurring expenses, include your monthly estimate for each. For expenses that occur once or twice a year, divide the annual total by 12 and enter an amount each month.

Total Fixed Expenses. Add up Lines 4a through 4n and fill in the total for each month.

Profit/(Loss). From the Gross Profit (Line 3), subtract the Total Fixed Expenses (Line 5) and fill in the result. Make sure that you place brackets around each negative number to identify it as a loss.

Year Total. Finally, add up each of the rows (Lines 1 through 6). Enter the yearly totals under the Year Total column. Check your arithmetic by seeing if the monthly profit figures add up to the same figure you get for your yearly total. If they don't match, double-check your addition to find the error. If they match, congratulations!

Review Your Profit and Loss Forecast

You've now completed your first run through a Profit and Loss Forecast. Date it so you won't get confused if you do another draft. I hope it looks positive. However, if like many people you find you need to increase profitability to make the business a good economic idea, go back through all your assumptions. How can you realistically reduce costs or increase volume? Incorporate into your forecast only those changes you're sure are sound. Now look at the profit figures again. Do they show enough profit to make a good living, pay back your money source, and leave some margin for error? If they do, and you're sure the figures are right, you will want to go ahead with your business idea. If the adjusted figures still do not show enough profit, it may be wise to look for another business idea or change your basic business assumptions.

Notice that Antoinette's business looks more profitable in her Profit and Loss Forecast than it did in her preliminary analyses in Chapter 3. That's because she increased her first year's sales estimate from $400,000 to $450,000 and reduced her fixed costs from $16,050 to $12,050 per month. The net effect of these changes was a slight increase in profit. She knows these numbers will be hard to achieve, but she is confident that she can make her goals.

How much profitability is enough to justify going ahead with your business? That's both a good question and a touchy one. Or, put another way, there are almost as many answers as there are businesspeople. My personal response is, I look for a yearly profit (including my wages and return on investment) equal to the amount of cash needed to start the business. If I need $40,000 to start a business, a conservative profit forecast would show a yearly profit of at least $40,000.

One way to approach the issue of profitability is to look at your profit forecast from an investor's viewpoint. A $35,400 profit for the dress shop won't seem like much to them. They will be concerned that the dress shop owner will have a difficult time earning a living and making it through the inevitable slow times. An investor or lender will probably want her to be able to convincingly demonstrate she has a plan to increase sales enough to raise the profit forecast to a more respectable level—say, the $46,200 she shows in the second year.

Your Profit and Loss Forecast and Income Tax Return

Figuring out your business's income tax return involves more calculations than we have shown so far. One major difference involves cost of sales, which we have viewed as a simple percentage of sales for forecasting purposes. You'll need to follow more complicated rules when computing your business income tax return. Read below to learn how to spot employee theft. You can skip this discussion if your business has no inventory.

Here's how to do it the right way. First, take a physical count of all your merchandise for resale every year or every few months. Even if you have a computerized inventory system that can tell you how much inventory you have at any time, it's a good idea to take a physical inventory every six or 12 months to reconcile the real inventory with the computer inventory. Once you have a complete listing of the description and count of all the goods in your store at a particular date, then you apply the best figures you have for what the merchandise cost you when you bought. Multiplying the unit cost of each item on your shelves by the number of items you have and adding purchases during the period gives you the cost of the goods available for sale. While there are a number of different theories on which cost figure to use (the latest or the earliest), the critical thing is to make sure you do it the same way every time. Then, you can make accurate comparisons from year to year. Of course, if you have a service business or business with no inventory, the inventory valuation discussion is moot.

After you have developed a total dollar value of the goods you have on hand, you can calculate your real cost of sales this way:

1. Add together the goods you purchased during the period and the inventory amount at the beginning of the period. (This total represents the dollar value of the goods you had available to sell during the period.)
2. From that amount, subtract the dollar value of the inventory at the end of the period.
3. The difference is the cost of sales for the period.

Here's an example that demonstrates how you do this:

Cost of Sales

Beginning inventory from physical count	$ 10,000
Add: Purchases during period	+ 30,000
Subtotal: Goods available for sale	40,000
Less: Ending inventory from physical count	− 15,000
Cost of Goods Sold during period	$ 25,000

This calculation has more use than merely filling out IRS forms: It can let you know when someone is stealing from you. Suppose you have a good estimate of what the cost of sales percentage should be, either from past statements or from a good understanding of your business. Suppose further that you expect a cost of sales of 61.5% and that you actually had a cost of sales of 77.3%. What does that mean? It could mean that some of the merchandise you buy for resale is leaving the store without any money entering your register. At any rate, it means that you need to do some serious research to find out what is really happening.

Your Cash Flow Loss Forecast and Capital Spending Plan

Introduction 154

Prepare Your Capital Spending Plan 157

Prepare Your Cash Flow Forecast 159

Required Investment for Your Business 172

Check for Trouble 172

　　Antoinette's Inventory Problem 173

　　Typical Problems Retailers Face 175

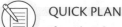

QUICK PLAN

If you've chosen the quick plan method to prepare a business plan
(see Introduction), you need to read and complete these sections of Chapter 7:
- "Prepare Your Capital Spending Plan"
- "Prepare Your Cash Flow Forecast," and
- "Required Investment for Your Business."

Introduction

In Chapter 6, you drafted your estimated Profit and Loss Forecast.
While it tells you a lot about the big financial picture, it leaves you
ignorant of many details. If you overlook one critical detail, you may go
broke, even though your business seems profitable viewed from afar.

The crucial detail a business owner must manage is called "cash flow."
Cash flow is another term for the money coming into and going out of
your business. Positive cash flow occurs when the money coming into
your business exceeds the money flowing out, and negative cash flow
is the opposite. In the day-to-day world of starting and operating your
business, you will be at least as concerned about short-term cash flow as
you will be about long-term profitability. After all, you don't want your
creditors to sue you because you can't pay your bills even though your
sales are increasing rapidly. One new business owner I know even wears
a T-shirt that says: "Happiness is positive cash flow."

Your Cash Flow Forecast is different from your Profit and Loss
Forecast because money comes into and flows out of your business at
different times than your Profit and Loss Forecast shows. A formal Cash
Flow Forecast is required by most potential backers, who want to know
that you understand and can manage that time difference.

> EXAMPLE: Rita Singh plans to open a small tie-dye manufacturing
> business. Since several of her likely customers are chain stores, Rita
> knows that she will have to sell and ship their orders before the
> stores pay her. The stores often can take several months to pay their
> bills. Wisely, Rita carefully prepares a Cash Flow Forecast to make
> sure she can afford to sell on credit.

In your Cash Flow Forecast, you'll refine any guesses you've made about how much money you need to start or expand your business. You'll develop an amount of money you are comfortable with—an amount you can explain to prospective investors. In other words, you need to be as accurate as you can be in this forecast.

The money you need to start or expand your business can be separated into two categories:

- **Capital investment.** This is the cash you need to spend before you begin or expand your business.
- **Initial working capital.** This consists of the cash reserves you need to keep your business afloat before you begin to show profits every month.

Commonly, cash flow from monthly sales is not enough to cover monthly expenses for the first few months after a new business opens. If your Cash Flow Forecast shows a negative picture for this period, you need to have extra money set aside for initial working capital. Your initial working capital keeps the doors open until cash flow from monthly business becomes positive. If your Cash Flow Forecast shows you'll run a cash deficit for several months, don't be too concerned. Just be sure you have enough initial working capital to cover it. But if your Cash Flow Forecast shows a continuing cash deficit, or a deficit that rises over time, your business may have some fatal flaw and you should reexamine the whole idea before making any commitments.

Growth, too, can create problems. Many businesses that grow quickly suffer severe cash flow shortages because money from sales does not come in fast enough to cover the investment needed to expand. If you find yourself in this situation, you will need to reduce your growth rate or find extra sources of money. (See the cash flow discussion below.)

So, let's put a close-up lens on our camera and focus on cash forecasting. Here again, it's necessary to get out your calculator or computer and play with some numbers.

Common Items in a Capital Spending Plan

Here's a list of common items businesses need to buy before opening. Note that they fall into two categories—capital items and expense items.

Capital items generally have a useful life of more than one year and can be depreciated for tax purposes. They include:

- permanent signs, heaters, air conditioners, and cooking and refrigeration equipment
- equipment, including machinery, large tools, and other expensive items
- racks and display fixtures for retail selling areas
- office furniture
- leasehold improvements or any alterations you make to the building, including walls, bathrooms, and carpeting, and
- computers, typewriters, fax machines, adding machines, cash registers, phone systems, and other small equipment you purchase.

Expense items generally are shown as either fixed expenses or costs of sale at the time they are purchased because they last less than one year. They include:

- opening inventory (sometimes you can get a deferred payment schedule from suppliers, but you will usually have to pay for many, if not most, goods before you sell them)
- lease deposits
- tax deposits
- business licenses and permits
- opening marketing and promotion
- insurance
- telephone installation
- utility deposits
- office supplies and stationery
- legal fees, costs to incorporate, and CPA fees to establish your business, and
- a contingency reserve.

Prepare Your Capital Spending Plan

Your capital spending plan includes all the things you have to buy before your business begins bringing in sales revenue, including opening inventory, fixtures and equipment, business licenses, deposits for the building lease, and whatever else you need.

Open a computer file or take out a clean sheet of paper and write "CAPITAL SPENDING PLAN" at the top. Now, make a list of all the things you'll have to buy before you open. This will enable you to make a good estimate of the cash you need to open your doors.

The list shown on the preceding page sets out many common items businesses need to purchase before they are ready to open. Some of the items you'll buy will be considered capital items, which depreciate over their useful lives. All preopening expenses represent your capital investment in the business, regardless of whether they are treated as capital items or expense items. If you have doubts about whether an item can be depreciated, ask your accountant.

Now assign specific dollar amounts to each item on this list. If you're unsure about the cost of an item, ask the person from whom you'll buy the item for an estimate or a quote. Try for plus or minus 10%. Remember that you're trying for an accurate estimate here, so use the numbers you think are right. Most experienced businesspeople will add another 10% to 20% of the total as a contingency to allow for poor guesses and other foul-ups. If you think you need such a contingency and haven't included it already, add it in now. Add up all the items you've listed to get an estimate of the cash you need to open your business.

Your capital spending plan should reflect as accurately as possible the exact amounts you will spend. For example, it was okay for Antoinette to use estimates of costs when she thought about her business in general terms, but now she needs to be precise. She should have shopped around for the best deals by now and know them. If a potential lender asks her why she's spending $3,000 each for dress racks, she can say, "The used ones from the auctioneer are terminally rusty and the discount ones are shoddy. I want my image to be high quality, and this is the best deal on good racks." As the accompanying example shows, Antoinette knows the business she is about to open.

Although she doesn't include an itemized list of fixtures, office equipment, and leasehold improvements in her summary, she has detailed lists available.

Capital Spending Plan: Antoinette's Dress Shop

Item	Amount
Fixtures in selling area include cash registers, sewing machines, dress racks (see list)	$ 30,000
Leasehold improvements, bid from Jones Construction includes signs, lights, decorations	80,000
Rent deposit, two months' rent	7,500
Opening inventory	30,000
Contingency	15,000
Total capital required to open	$ 162,500

For a second example, here's a one-man consulting firm's opening cash needs. As you can see, he plans to start with extra cash; he has allocated $10,000 for working capital.

Capital Spending Plan: Jeffers Associates Consulting

Item	Amount
Desk, conference tables, chairs	$ 6,000
Fax machine	1,000
Computer system: PC, laser printer, software	4,000
Copy machine	2,000
Typewriter	700
Telephone system	1,000
Misc. decorative accessories	500
Misc. deposits for utilities, business license	2,000
Opening marketing and advertising	2,000
Supplies, stationery	1,000
Working capital estimate	10,000
Total capital required to open	$ 30,200

Prepare Your Cash Flow Forecast

Once you complete your capital spending plan, you'll know how much money you need to open your doors. The next step is to estimate how much additional money you'll need to survive the first lean months.

The basic process we'll use to make a Cash Flow Forecast is to start with the monthly profit (or loss) figures you developed in your Profit and Loss Forecast in Chapter 6. You'll then make adjustments each month to the monthly profits to account for the time differences in collecting and spending money.

Open the blank Cash Flow Forecast forms included on this book's online companion page (see Appendix D for details) and follow the step-by-step instructions below. You'll be completing a forecast for the first two years of your business. Complete every line for each of the 24 months before going on to the next line.

Cash Flow Forecast: Year One

for   Antoinette's Dress Shop

Cash In/(Out)

Month	1	2	3	4	5
	Mar	Apr	May	Jun	Jul
1. Profit/(Loss) [P & L line 6]	$ (50)	$ 1,450	$ 5,950	$ 2,950	$ 1,450
2. *Less:* Credit Sales—____% on credit × Sales Revenue [P & L line 1]	(7,500)	(8,450)	(11,250)	(9,375)	(8,450)
3. *Plus:* Collections of Credit Sales _____ months after sale	0	0	7,500	8,450	11,250
4. *Plus:* Credit Purchases—____% of purchases on credit × Cost of Sales [P & L line 2]	9,000	10,150	13,500	11,250	10,150
5. *Less:* Payments for Credit Purchases _____ months after purchase	(0)	(0)	(9,000)	(10,150)	(13,500)
6. *Plus:* Withholding ___% of total wages (if paying taxes quarterly)	0	0	0	0	0
7. *Less:* Quarterly withholding payments (if paying taxes quarterly)	(0)	(0)	(0)	(0)	(0)
8. *Plus:* Depreciation	0	0	0	0	0
9. *Less:* Principal Payments	(0)	(0)	(0)	(0)	(0)
10. *Less:* Extra Purchases	(0)	(0)	(0)	(0)	(0)
11. Other Cash Items in/(out)	0	0	0	0	0
12. Monthly Net Cash	1,450	3,150	6,700	3,125	900
13. Cumulative Net Cash	$ 1,450	$ 4,600	$ 11,300	$ 14,425	$ 15,325

Date Completed: __1/25/xx__

6	7	8	9	10	11	12	Year Total
Aug	Sept	Oct	Nov	Dec	Jan	Feb	
$ 1,450	$ 4,450	$ 4,450	$ 5,950	$ 8,950	$ (1,550)	$ (50)	$ 35,400
(8,450)	(10,300)	(10,300)	(11,250)	(13,125)	(6,550)	(7,500)	(112,500)
9,375	8,450	8,450	10,300	10,300	11,250	13,125	98,450
10,150	12,350	12,350	13,500	15,750	7,850	9,000	135,000
(11,250)	(10,150)	(10,150)	(12,350)	(12,350)	(13,500)	(15,750)	(118,150)
0	0	0	0	0	0	0	0
(0)	(0)	(0)	(0)	(0)	(0)	(0)	(0)
0	0	0	0	0	0	0	0
(0)	(0)	(0)	(0)	(0)	(0)	(0)	(0)
(0)	(0)	(0)	(0)	(0)	(0)	(0)	(0)
0	0	0	0	0	0	0	0
1,275	4,800	4,800	6,150	9,525	(2,500)	(1,175)	$ 38,200
$ 16,600	$ 21,400	$ 26,200	$ 32,350	$ 41,875	$ 39,375	$ 38,200	

FORM

A formatted copy of the Cash Flow Forecast is available on this book's companion page on Nolo.com (please see Appendix D for details on accessing this form and all others in this book). The spreadsheet program will automatically calculate your Monthly Net Cash, Cumulative Net Cash, and Yearly Totals. Note, if a series of #### symbols appear in a box in a spreadsheet that means that you need to widen the column in order to display the numbers. If you use a spreadsheet program that cannot convert the *Excel* format, set up the form in your program using the same categories as the completed Cash Flow Forecast in this chapter. (Make sure that the column and row headings are the same.)

1. Profit/(Loss). To begin, take out the Profit and Loss Forecast you completed in Chapter 6 and copy the monthly profit/(loss) from Line 6 onto the first line of the Cash Flow Forecast form. The profits or losses you show have already taken into account the normal expenses of running a business like rent, wages and salaries, and so forth. You won't have to worry about those costs in this forecast.

CAUTION

If any of your figures are losses, place brackets around them. Otherwise, your entire Cash Flow Forecast will be seriously inaccurate.

2. Credit Sales. Skip ahead to Line 4 if you don't plan to sell merchandise or services on credit. If you sell merchandise or services on credit, the customer receives the goods or services right away. Even though you incur costs, you don't get paid right away. Credit sales create bills people owe you; they are called your "accounts receivable" because you will receive the money soon. (When you buy goods on credit, you create bills you owe others. These are called your "accounts payable" because you will pay them soon.)

Most businesses that sell to other businesses should plan for some sales on credit. Most businesses that sell only or primarily to retail consumers can plan to sell mostly for cash, including checks and credit cards.

TIP

Credit card note: For purposes of this discussion, sales on credit cards are the same as cash sales, except for the processing fees the bank charges you. If you use an electronic terminal, the money is credited to your bank account right away, and if you use a paper imprinter, the money is deposited to your account in a few days.

It takes more money to start and run your business if you offer credit to your customers than it would if you received cash for every sale. Here's how to figure out how much cash you'll need. First, estimate what portion of your total sales will be for credit. For example, if you think that about one-third of your sales will be for credit, that means that about 33% of your monthly sales dollars will not be collected in the month in which the sale is made. Make a note of that percentage now on the Cash Flow Forecast form in the heading for Line 2.

Look at the Profit and Loss Forecast you completed in Chapter 6. Multiply each month's Sales Revenue dollars (Line 1 of the Profit and Loss Forecast) by the credit percentage that you forecast for your business. Then enter each of those monthly figures on Line 2 of your Cash Flow Forecast.

EXAMPLE: Mickey and Michele run a photocopy and fax service. They estimate that about 40% of their total sales revenue will be on credit and the remaining 60% will be for cash. On Line 2 of the Cash Flow Forecast, they'll enter these credit sales: $4,400 for January; $4,400 for February; and so forth throughout the forecast.

M & M Copy Shop Cash Flow Forecast Credit Sales Calculation, Six Months ($000s)

	Jan	Feb	Mar	Apr	May	Jun
Forecast sales revenue	$ 11.0	$ 10.9	$ 12.6	$ 13.1	$ 15.6	$ 16.8
% sales on credit	40%	40%	40%	40%	40%	40%
Forecast credit sales	$ 4.4	$ 4.4	$ 5.0	$ 5.2	$ 6.2	$ 6.7

3. Collections of Credit Sales. Skip this item if you don't plan to sell merchandise or services on credit. Your cash receipts are reduced when a sale is made for credit instead of cash. On the other hand, your cash receipts increase when you collect the money from a credit sale you made earlier. This Cash Flow Forecast shows you exactly how much your receipts will be reduced and increased as a result of your credit policies. Even though your customers don't pay you right away, they eventually pay you. Your job is to figure out when they'll do so. If you grant your customer your normal 30-day terms, it usually takes 60 days to get paid. Here's why. You make a sale on Day One, then write a statement at the end of the month and mail it to the customer. He pays it 30 days after he gets the statement. Of course, some people pay sooner and some people pay later. In a well-run business with good paying customers that grants 30 days to pay bills, the average turnaround will be 45 to 60 days.

Make an estimate of the number of months you anticipate as an average lag time between a sale and the collection of the bill. Most businesses use two months. It's easier to use whole months for this purpose than to use portions of months. If you think 45 days is the likely answer, use two months—don't use one and one-half months. Enter the number of months in the heading for Line 3.

> **EXAMPLE:** If Mickey and Michele collect bills in an average of two months, the credit sales that were just subtracted from monthly sales will be added back two months later. In this example, the business starts up in January and there are no outstanding accounts from the previous year. As you can see, the delay in collections means that the M & M Copy Shop will have an $8,800 cash flow reduction in January and February. This means they need at least $9,000 in working capital to sustain them during the first two months.

M & M Copy Shop Cash Flow Forecast Credit Sales and Collections, Six Months ($000s)

	Jan	Feb	Mar	Apr	May	Jun
Credit Sales	$ 4.4	$ 4.4	$5.0	$5.2	$6.2	$6.7
Collections of credit sales	0	0	$ 4.4	$ 4.4	$5.0	$5.2

Now that you see how it works, complete your monthly Cash Flow Forecast for two years, writing in the cash collections in the month you collect the money on Line 3.

4. Credit Purchases. Make an estimate of how the timing of your purchases will affect your cash flow. Most businesses buy merchandise from their suppliers on credit and delay paying them for a time. Most suppliers will grant you 30 days to pay your bills on a fairly routine basis, if they approve your credit application. That way, you get to use their money for a while, just like your customers use your money if you sell on credit.

Here's how to complete this section of the Cash Flow Forecast. First, make an estimate of the percentage of your total goods and services you expect to buy on credit. (See the section entitled "Break-Even Analysis: Will Your Business Make Money?" in Chapter 3, on how to make educated guesses, or SWAGs.) Write the percentage figure in the heading for Line 4.

Next you'll calculate the dollar costs of purchases your business will buy on credit each month. To derive that figure, multiply each month's cost of sales by the estimated percentage of credit purchases. And write the answer on Line 4. Note that they increase cash flow.

EXAMPLE: Mickey and Michele estimated that they'd buy approximately 60% of their purchases on credit. Their January cost of sales is $3,600, so the credit purchases come to $2,160 ($3,600 × 0.6 = $2,160). They round this figure to $2,200. Here's how it looks for a few months at the M & M Copy Shop. On Line 4 of their Cash Flow Forecast, they'll enter their credit purchases: $2,200 for January; $2,200 for February; $2,500 for March; and so forth.

M & M Copy Shop Cash Flow Forecast
Credit Purchases, Six Months ($000s)

	Jan	Feb	Mar	Apr	May	Jun
Forecast cost of sales	$ 3.6	$ 3.6	$ 4.2	$ 4.3	$ 5.1	$ 5.5
% bought on credit	60%	60%	60%	60%	60%	60%
Credit purchases	$ 2.2	$ 2.2	$ 2.5	$ 2.6	$ 3.1	$ 3.3

5. Payments for Credit Purchases. Here you show when you pay for the purchases you've made on credit. These payments are subtracted from profits on the Cash Flow Forecast. Make an estimate of how long you will take between the time you sell merchandise and the time it is reordered and paid for. Write your estimate of how many months will elapse between selling your merchandise and paying for the replacement in the heading for Line 5.

If you're in doubt, figure it this way: It usually takes about 60 days to make an inventory of what you've sold, reorder the merchandise, receive and restock the merchandise, and pay the invoice or statement. If that's true for you, then the merchandise you sell in January will be reordered and paid for by March. Here's a word of caution, though: Many suppliers have tightened their terms considerably. It is not unusual for suppliers to expect payment within ten days of the date you receive the merchandise.

CAUTION

Know suppliers' credit policies. If you're not sure of your suppliers' policies, it's a good idea to check them out before you complete this forecast. A mistake here can result in a dramatically incorrect cash forecast.

EXAMPLE: Here's how it works for the M & M Copy Shop, which expects a two-month delay between ordering and paying for merchandise:

M & M Copy Shop Cash Flow Forecast Credit Sales and Collections, Six Months ($000s)

	Jan	Feb	Mar	Apr	May	Jun
Line 4: Credit purchases	$ 2.2	$2.2	$2.5	$5.2	$ 3.1	$3.3
Line 5: Paying for credit purchases	0	0	$2.2	$2.2	$2.5	$2.6

Now, enter the dollar amount of credit purchases you entered on Line 4, but in a later month, in a similar fashion to the M & M Copy Shop.

6. Withholding Taxes. Most businesses must pay their employees' taxes every month. That means that every month you send the IRS the amount of wages you've withheld from your employees' paychecks plus the amount you're required to contribute to their Social Security. If you make these tax payments every month, they don't affect your cash flow, so they won't show up on your Cash Flow Forecast.

Some businesses qualify to pay withholding taxes every three months rather than every month. To qualify for the quarterly payment program, you must owe the IRS less than $2,500 every quarter. If you do not qualify for the quarterly option or wish to pay every month, skip ahead to Line 8. If you wish to explore the quarterly option, read the following discussion of withholding taxes.

When you completed the Profit and Loss Forecast, you added at least 14% to the total wages and salaries you pay each month as an additional expense (Profit and Loss Forecast, Line 4b, Withholding Taxes). That's your approximate mandatory contribution to your employees' Social Security fund and federal unemployment insurance. You'll write a check to the government to pay that amount.

RESOURCE

These are approximate tax figures, for your planning purposes. Later, you'll need to learn more about the tax rules. Some good information resources include *Tax Savvy for Small Business*, by Frederick W. Daily and Jeffrey A. Quinn (Nolo), and IRS Publication 15 *Circular E, Employer's Tax Guide*, available, along with other publications, at the IRS website (www.irs.gov).

In addition, the government also expects you to collect money from your employees for their portion of income and Social Security taxes and pay the government directly. While every employee is different because of his or her individual tax situation, the average employee has about 15% of total wages or salary withheld from every paycheck for federal withholding. This is money that belongs to the employee that you must mail to the IRS.

If you will pay a total withholding of less than $2,500 every quarter, you may choose to pay taxes quarterly rather than monthly. Make sure you verify your employees' actual withholding rates before deciding on this option.

> **EXAMPLE:** Let's say that you plan to hire one full-time sales clerk in your business for a total salary of $1,500 per month or $4,500 per quarter. Multiplying 29% by the quarterly salary (0.29 × $4,500 = $1,300) gives an answer of $1,300, which is less than $2,500. In that case, you qualify for and may choose the quarterly option.

CAUTION

Please note that paying these taxes every three months instead of every month is a dangerous option because it means that you will be using your employees' money in your business. By far the simplest, safest, and best way to pay the government is to pay the total withholding amount every month.

7. Withholding Tax Payments. Skip this item if you'll be paying your employees' taxes monthly instead of quarterly. Otherwise, add together three months' worth of withholding from Line 6 and enter the total amount every third month on Line 7. That is the amount you must pay every three months to the IRS. If this little exercise seems confusing to you, take your confusion as a sign that you should not attempt this option. You'll be much better off simply paying the withholding taxes every month.

8. Depreciation. As discussed previously, depreciation is a fictitious expense you charge the business for using up fixed assets. Look at your Profit and Loss Forecast, which you prepared in Chapter 6. If you included an amount for depreciation in Line 4h of your Profit and Loss Forecast and reduced your profits accordingly, you must enter the same numbers here to get your monthly cash flow.

If you wrote nothing in Line 4h of your Profit and Loss Forecast, you can leave this line blank and skip to Line 9.

9. Principal Payments. In your Profit and Loss Forecast, you calculated how much interest you'd pay every month. You'll also make regular payments on the principal of your loan, which are shown in your Cash Flow Forecast. To get the amount of the principal payment, just subtract the interest payment, taken from Line 4g of your Profit and Loss Forecast, from the total loan payment. (Review the chart in Chapter 6, Line 4g, if you have trouble.)

If you have a loan with interest-only payments and a large principal payment every few months or at the end of the loan, it's essential that you write in the scheduled principal payments. That way, you'll be able to plan for them and avoid the nasty surprise of having to make a large loan payment you forgot about.

CAUTION

Interest and principal. Be sure that the interest expense from the Profit and Loss Forecast (Chapter 6, "Profit and Loss Forecast: Year One," Line 4g) and the principal repayment line from your Cash Flow Forecast add up to your total monthly payment.

10. Extra Purchases. Let's say that you plan to have a big sale sometime during the year and need to buy extra merchandise for the sale. These extra purchases are above and beyond normal inventory replacement, so they won't be covered by the amounts you have written for purchases resulting from your cost of sales. Include those extra purchases here.

11. Other Cash Items. Here is where you place any cash receipt or expenditure that is not covered in the Profit and Loss Forecast or elsewhere in your Cash Flow Forecast. For example, perhaps you anticipate an investment in your business in a few months and you need to show the positive cash infusion. Or you might plan to buy a new piece of equipment sometime down the road. If your total is negative, make sure you put brackets around it. Otherwise, your Cash Flow Forecast will be incorrect.

12. Monthly Net Cash. Take a moment to review your work to make sure you have understood the cash flow effect of each of the entries and that they are all on the right lines. Make a final check to be sure that any negative numbers have brackets around them.

Then add and subtract the various entries on the Cash Flow Forecast form to derive the monthly net cash for each of the 24 months. Positive cash numbers represent additions to your bank account, while negative cash numbers represent money you'll have to add to the business. Remember that numbers with brackets around them are subtracted from the total and that numbers without brackets are added to the total.

If the monthly cash flow figure is a negative figure, make sure you place a bracket around it. Do that as you complete each month's calculations; otherwise, you'll forget which numbers are positive and which are negative and you'll have to do all the arithmetic again.

Year Total. Add up each of the rows (Lines 1 through 13). Enter the yearly totals under the Year Total column. Check your arithmetic by seeing if the total monthly net cash figures add up to the same figure as your yearly total. If your answer is the same whether you add vertically or horizontally, your math is correct. If not, you've made a mistake somewhere.

CAUTION

Don't use Line 13 to check your math. It won't work in the second and later years because those years start with a previous balance.

13. Cumulative Net Cash. This line shows how the monthly negative or positive monthly net cash numbers add across to derive the total cash required for working capital. Most businesses will show several months of negative cash flow followed by months of positive cash flow. By adding the monthly figures together, you'll see the maximum negative cash—that's the amount you'll need for working capital.

For Month One, simply copy the net cash amount listed in Line 12 for that month. To get Month Two's cumulative net cash, add together Month One's cumulative net cash (Line 13) and Month Two's net cash (Line 12). For Month Three, add Month Two's cumulative net cash (Line 13) to Month Three's net cash (Line 12). Continue that process for the entire 24 months. Remember that when you add two negative numbers together, you get a larger negative number—you do not get a positive number.

> EXAMPLE: The M & M Copy Shop chart shows how to accumulate these figures. Note how the cumulative cash flow increases the negative amount when each individual month's net cash flow is negative. Then, when the individual monthly figures turn positive, the cumulative negative figure becomes smaller as the positive cash flow reduces the cumulative negative figure. Finally, in the fifth month, the cumulative figure becomes a small positive. This means that the fourth and fifth months of positive cash flow have offset the first three months of negative cash flow.

M & M Copy Shop Cash Flow Forecast Cumulative Net Cash ($000s)					
	1	2	3	4	5
Line 12: Monthly Net Cash	(2.5)	(1.8)	(0.2)	1.9	3.9
Line 13: Cumulative Net Cash	(2.5)	(4.3)	(4.5)	(2.6)	1.3

Required Investment for Your Business

This chapter's objective is to develop the amount of money you need to start or expand your business. That amount of money is the sum of two numbers:

- the total dollars you developed from the Capital Spending Plan, and
- the largest negative figure you developed on Line 13 (Cumulative Net Cash) of the monthly Cash Flow Forecast.

Make this calculation for your business. You'll use this figure later, when you write your plan summary and spell out your need for funds to start or expand your business.

EXAMPLE 1: For the M & M Copy Shop, the maximum negative cash flow of $4,500 was reached in the third month (assuming that future individual monthly cash flow figures continued to be positive figures). That is the amount of working capital that M & M Copy Shop needs to begin operation. Mickey and Michele add together the amount listed in their Capital Spending Plan to $4,500 to derive the amount of cash they need to open their business.

EXAMPLE 2: Antoinette's Cash Flow Forecast shows a positive cash flow from the beginning because her sales revenue starts out high. That means her total cash investment will be limited to the amount from her Capital Spending Plan or $162,500. She chooses not to reduce that amount by subtracting any of her first year's cash flow from the total so she can have a salary for herself.

Check for Trouble

You have completed most of the foundations on which your business will be built. The Cash Flow Forecast ties together all the previous work and allows you, or your backers, to see exactly how your business will function. I hope that you have gained an understanding of the relationship between sales, expenses, cost of sales, profits, and cash flow by completing your Cash Flow Forecast. If so, that understanding will help you a great deal in the future.

If you still aren't clear about those relationships, it is worth a little time to review your forecasts. It's important that you understand where the money comes from and where it goes. If necessary, take your forecasts to a business adviser or a friend who understands cash flow analysis and ask her to explain them to you.

Don't be surprised if the answers you develop aren't the ones you expected. It may mean that the business won't work or that you need to polish your plans a little. It could just mean that you have made a mistake in arithmetic. It's best to let the Cash Flow Forecast rest for a day or two before looking for the problem.

No forecasting technique can ensure that your business will succeed. In addition to the problems outside your business that the future may bring (discussed in Chapter 3), you may have built into your plan some money problems that are lurking there, waiting to sabotage your efforts. Your only protection against problems like these is to know your business thoroughly. Sad to say, what you don't know can hurt you.

Antoinette's Inventory Problem

Antoinette estimated her first year's sales at $450,000 and her cost of sales at 60%. She also figured her opening inventory at $30,000. Unfortunately, this means she has to turn her inventory 9.0 times per year ($450,000 × 0.60 ÷ $30,000), just to meet her plan. This is not very likely.

> **TIP**
> **Calculate inventory turnover by dividing annual cost of sales by inventory at cost.** If annual sales revenue is $450,000 and cost of sales is 60%, then annual cost of sales is $270,000 ($450,000 × 0.60 = $270,000). Inventory of $30,000 at cost divided into $270,000 equals 9.0 inventory turns per year.

Antoinette should probably plan for a more realistic inventory turnover of 3.5 times per year, which is typical in her business. To do this and end up with $450,000 in sales, she would need an inventory of $77,000 ($450,000 × 0.60 ÷ 3.5). This would raise her initial cash requirement by $47,000. With that much cash investment needed, her business idea probably is not worth pursuing unless she can generate a good deal more profit than her Profit and Loss Forecast indicates. This would undoubtedly mean raising sales projections, and otherwise trying to force profits into a questionable business. If your retail business has an inventory turnover of three to four times per year, you'll be doing pretty well. Many retailers are able to average only one or two turns per year.

Many people who plan new retail businesses expect to start with a fairly small inventory because they don't have much capital to invest. This will very likely cause problems if the sales figures they expect this inventory to produce are too high. For example, if you plan to sell widgets, but can only buy a starting inventory of $10,000 at cost, it would seem unlikely that you could produce sales of $200,000 per year. Even assuming you doubled the price of the widgets, this would mean turning your inventory over ten times in the year. For most businesses, it simply isn't realistic to expect inventory to turn over even seven or eight times a year.

Many retailers make a similar mistake; some catch the mistake at this stage, some catch the mistake when they have a business consultant review their plan, and some never catch it. They just sink slowly into bankruptcy, wondering why sales never met projections.

What about Antoinette and her inventory problem? I shall continue with Antoinette's original assumptions, including those for inventory turnover. This book is simply not set up to go back and revise all her numbers. Second, I want Antoinette's problem (the fatal flaw in her plan) to really sink in. I hope Antoinette's predicament will give you a vague feeling of unease as you continue to read her plan. The lesson is this: Just because a business plan appears to be thorough and looks good on paper, that's no guarantee that it will be successful. It pays to be skeptical.

Typical Problems Retailers Face

You can skip the rest of this chapter if you're not planning to run a retail business. Otherwise, you'll find the following discussion extremely useful.

Here's what Antoinette should have known about inventory. Inventory management separates the professionals from the amateurs in the retail business. Inventory is usually the biggest single investment a retailer makes. Commonly, it happens that a retailer shows a high taxable income, but no cash. Why? Because all her cash went into increasing the inventory.

The goals of inventory management are:

- to have a wide enough selection of new, fresh merchandise to appeal to customers
- to quickly reduce or eliminate items that move slowly, and
- to keep the overall investment in inventory in line with profit expectations.

Good retailers keep current with the merchandise customers want now. They make it a point to always have the popular items in stock. No self-respecting popular music store would be caught dead without the top ten CDs and Blu-Ray discs in stock. Good retailers quickly mark down slow-moving items for a quick sale. They then use the cash from selling these dead items to buy new and popular ones. For example, there is nothing sadder than a small bookstore still trying to sell last year's hardcover bestseller when the drugstore down the street already has the paperback version.

A good retailer has a wide enough selection to appeal to customers. In a bookstore's case, this might mean a strong backlist in several areas of local interest. Good inventory management also means deciding that some customers just aren't worth catering to. For example, if you wear odd size clothes, you are very aware of this merchandising policy. I wear shirts with 37-inch sleeves because I'm six feet, four inches tall, and it has only been in the last 20 years that some department stores carry this size. That's because retailers used to think that 37-inch-sleeve shirts never sold. Then the baby boom generation came of age, with many men needing larger sizes, and it became economical to serve these folks.

Good retail managers accomplish all of these ends and also keep the total dollar investment in line with profit goals by carefully managing "inventory turnover"—how many times per year you completely replace the stock. For example, if your average cost of sales is 50% and your sales are $300,000 and your inventory is $40,000, you turn over your inventory 3.75 times per year ($300,000 × 0.50 ÷ $40,000). As before, many retail managers strive for three to four turns per year. Some businesses, like gasoline stations, may turn over their inventory every week. Make sure your plans reflect your industry standard and good, common sense.

Write Your Marketing and Personnel Plans

Introduction 178

Marketing Plan 178

   Review Chapter 3 Work 178

   Competition Analysis 179

   Differentiate Your Business From the Competition 180

   Describe Your Target Customer 181

   Decide How to Reach Customers 183

   Create a Marketing Budget 185

   Write Your Marketing Plan 188

   Discuss the Risks Facing Your Business 188

Personnel Plan 193

   Analyze Your Business Personality 193

   Write Your Staffing Schedule 194

   Write Job Descriptions 195

   Write Your Personnel Plan 196

Introduction

Decisions you make about marketing and personnel can spell the difference between your future success or failure. This chapter helps you answer these important questions about your business:

- Who is your competition and how are you different?
- Who are your potential customers and how can you contact them?
- Exactly what steps will you take to reach your sales projections?
- How can you hire the right people for your business?
- How can you make sure that your employees work effectively?

Marketing Plan

Marketing is a broad term that covers many specific issues. Your marketing plan will cover areas ranging all the way from determining how your business fits into the national and local economies to deciding what color your logo should be. The market plan you'll develop in this section will outline the specific steps you'll take to generate the sales dollars you forecast earlier.

Review Chapter 3 Work

In Chapter 3, you were deciding whether or not you chose the right business. As part of that work, you made some important assumptions that will influence your marketing plan:

- **Problem Statement.** This identifies the problem you'll solve for your customers and provides the underlying reason people will frequent your business.
- **Business Description.** This states exactly what your business does for your customers. After all, if you don't provide a valuable product or service, you won't have many customers.
- **Taste, Trends, and Technology: How Will the Future Affect Your Business?** This covers the developments you expect for the next few years and how they will affect your business. Even a "perfect" business can become obsolete overnight due to future developments.

- **Sales Revenue Forecast.** This shows your estimates of future sales revenue for your business. To finish your marketing plan, you'll need to spell out the specific actions you will take to achieve your forecast sales revenues.

Take a moment before proceeding any further and reread your work from Chapter 3 to decide if it still represents an accurate statement of how you view your business. If the statements are not accurate and complete, stop here and rewrite them. Make sure they correspond to your current thinking.

Competition Analysis

When customers consider patronizing your business, they first consider whether or not you can solve their problem. But they don't stop there. They also compare your business with other businesses.

It's helpful for you to make a similar comparison so that you understand how your customers think. This exercise, as any exercise in the marketing area, requires some mental gymnastics. Your job is to place yourself in your customers' frame of mind and objectively compare your business to the competition.

Sometimes business owners let their personal prejudices taint their opinion of a competitor. If your competitor provides a larger selection of merchandise or better service and lower prices than you, it won't matter much to your customers that you don't like the other business's television ads or think it has ugly delivery trucks.

Think for a moment about the decisions your customers face. What specific methods can they use or places can they go to solve their problem? Incidentally, some of these places and methods may not involve a competing business. Customers do things for themselves or get their needs solved from friends, community, and government agencies or other sources.

First, identify the most likely three ways your customers are going to solve their needs in addition to your business, and make a note of each. These are your principal competitors. To be thorough, write a short statement of each competitor's main strengths and weaknesses.

Remember to place yourself in the minds of your customers when you do this exercise.

In the accompanying example, note that Antoinette grouped her competitors instead of treating each store separately, because some stores are very similar. You might choose to group your competition or list more than three competitors.

Antoinette's Dress Shop: Strengths and Weaknesses of Three Competitors

Department stores. Bagnin's, Jerry's, Glendale's
   Principal strengths: Wide selection of merchandise
   Principal weaknesses: High prices, inconvenient hours, no alterations

Latest fashion stores. Wild Thing, Marian's, Golden Frog
   Principal strengths: Fashion conscious, frequent new styles, low prices
   Principal weaknesses: Casual wear only, don't cater to mature women, no alterations

Specialty stores. Lady Esquire
   Principal strengths: Sells our style merchandise to our type customers
   Principal weaknesses: High prices, employees have reputation as snobs, alterations take a long time

---

Differentiate Your Business From the Competition

Your next job is to describe how your business differs from the competition's strong and weak points. Again, remember to carefully look at your business from the customer's perspective.

If you're not sure how your pricing policies compare to the competition, here are some guidelines. Most people associate high prices with high quality and extra service, while they associate low prices with low or average quality and minimum service. Make sure you provide extra quality and service if your prices are higher than your competition—or make sure that your prices are lower if your quality is average and your service is minimum. Check your assumptions by making a price survey of the competition.

Remember that customers may take for granted that you have the same strong points as the competition; if so, you can leave those out of your description. Customers hope that you do not share the same weak points as the competition. But if you do share some weak points, it is probably a good idea to mention the ones you have in common.

Antoinette's Dress Shop:
How My Business Differs From the Competition

Antoinette's will offer a wide selection of merchandise to our target customers, as do the department stores and specialty shops. We will offer low prices and convenient hours for the working woman. Antoinette's will take particular pride in more efficient services such as special orders and alterations as well as a stable, helpful, and knowledgeable sales staff.

To summarize, Antoinette's takes the worry out of clothes shopping by providing a good selection, good prices, good service, and helpful people who know their field.

Describe Your Target Customer

The next step is to describe your target customer in specific, individual terms. As you know, business is a very personal endeavor. When you sell services or merchandise, you sell to one person at a time. As a matter of fact, most people don't like being treated like members of a group instead of individuals. That's why the most successful restaurants have owners or maitre d's who remember your name and ask about your family or your interests whenever you patronize their business.

Additionally, most of us are more comfortable talking with one person than making speeches to a large group. So it makes sense to address your advertising, promotions, and other marketing activities to a single person instead of a group.

Of course, no two customers are exactly the same. But if you can personalize your marketing program to a typical customer, it will be more effective because it will seem more friendly to your customers. The easiest way to do that is to create a mythical target customer and individualize that target customer so that you consider her a friend. Be as specific and as personal as you can. If you have friends you hope will be your customers, describe one of your friends. Include age, education, occupation, income, hobbies, family status, and so forth.

In the accompanying sample, Antoinette describes her friend and target customer, Terry Chen. With Terry in mind, it is very easy for Antoinette to write ads, letters, and flyers and to decide how and where to promote her business. For example, television ads are unlikely to reach Terry since she has so little time to watch TV. Radio ads during commute time can be effective, but may cost too much.

Antoinette's Dress Shop:
Target Customer

Terry is 32 years old and has a college education; she is married and has a son, Jimmy, in elementary school. She works as a salesperson for a large corporation and makes about $65,000 per year. Her husband Peter makes a little more than she does, but the family needs her income to support the lifestyle they have chosen.

Terry's work is not a hobby for her; she is very serious about it. Her work makes her travel frequently and she calls home at least twice a day when she's on the road. Since the business world is very competitive in the era of downsizing companies, she must present a good image while maintaining a strict budget.

Terry keeps current with the latest movies and enjoys dinner out with Peter once or twice a week. She watches mostly children's programs on television in order to spend time with Jimmy, whenever the TV is on. She reads business journals and economic reports and occasionally reads some fashion magazines. Mostly, she gets her fashion sense from seeing current styles in the workplace. Her greatest regret is that she has so little time for Jimmy and Peter.

Decide How to Reach Customers

Once you describe your target customer, it's easier to create a list of possible ways to reach that person. One of your jobs as a businessperson is to decide which of all the possible methods of communication will give you the most exposure for the least cost in money or time. There are an infinite number of communication methods. These methods range from personal visits to each customer to mass media advertising, with a wide range of possibilities in between. We list some in "Ways to Reach Your Target Customer," below, as a stimulus to your thinking.

Ways to Reach Your Target Customer

Here are some common methods businesspeople use to reach customers:

- Create a business Web page and/or Facebook page.
- Collect customer email addresses and send regular newsletters and updates via email.
- Take each prospect to lunch.
- Visit or telephone each prospect regularly.
- Send a personalized letter or handwritten greeting card to every prospect.
- Write a technical article in a trade journal.
- Attend or make presentations at trade or industry shows and conventions.
- Appear on radio and television shows about your field.
- Write a newspaper or magazine column about your field.
- Mail brochures or flyers to each prospect.
- Advertise in print—daily newspapers, magazines, or weekly papers.
- Advertise on radio and television.
- Place leaflets on car windshields or home doorknobs.
- Put notices on supermarket bulletin boards.
- Join service clubs and take part in community affairs.

There are lots of alternative strategies you can use to reach your market. For example, businesses with a few large-dollar customers will have different choices than businesses with many smaller-dollar customers. Technical consulting businesses tend to fall in the category of having a few customers with large contracts, whereas fast food restaurants or retail stores have many customers who make small purchases.

Above all, remember that the most effective way to reach and keep customers in the long run is by word of mouth. All the marketing and advertising you do can only entice your customer to try your business the first time. After that, she will come back to your business if she likes what she received, and she'll tell all her friends. But be aware that customers are even more likely to let friends know if a business doesn't meet their expectations.

Antoinette's Dress Shop: Costs of Reaching My Target Customers

I have about 20,000 potential customers in the greater New City trading area. I don't anticipate reaching customers beyond this area.

1. I like direct mail, since I can develop lists of active businesswomen in the area. I'd like to bulk-mail a flyer announcing our opening for about 30¢ to 50¢ each, for a total cost of $6,000 to $10,000.

2. Limited ads in the *New City Monthly* will run about $300 to $500 per month for a few months.

3. When anyone comes into the shop, I'll ask for her name and address and later I'll send notices of fashion shows and fashion tips. The cost will depend on the size of my list and the frequency of mailings.

4. I can place announcements of my fashion shows in the two daily papers serving the area at no cost.

5. I'll see if one of the local papers will carry a column I'll write for free on fashion tips.

6. I'll join all the professional women's groups in the area and become a visible spokesperson for my shop.

To complete this next exercise, write down the five or so methods you think will reach most of your customers. Remember to select methods that are appropriate for the overall number of people in your target market. For instance, if your target market is every married woman in the United States, you will probably use mass media as an effective communication method. On the other hand, if your target market is the presidents of the 100 largest companies in your trade area, you are more likely to use individual contacts than mass media.

Once you've chosen the communication methods you like best, figure out how much it will cost to reach your customers using each of the five methods.

Note that some of Antoinette's more sensible ideas don't take any money at all, just some time to convince the magazines and papers to carry her material and the time to produce it. Perhaps you can develop some similar ideas for your business.

Create a Marketing Budget

Now that you have a wish list of things you'd like to do, it's time to decide which of the promotional ideas you can afford and which are too costly. In Chapter 7, you prepared a Capital Spending Plan and estimated how much money you'd allow for an opening promotion to let people know you're in business. In Chapter 6, you prepared a Profit and Loss Forecast that took into account your monthly marketing costs. If you allowed enough money to provide the sort of promotion you want, you can finish writing your marketing plan now.

However, if you didn't allow enough money, or if you're not sure how much money is enough, you'll want to stop here for a moment and think about it. Ask yourself these questions:

- **How much money do I need for an opening promotion?** I suggest that you allow enough money to tell all your target customers one time that you are open for business. If you tell them all once, they can decide when to come see you. And if you have designed your business so that it truly addresses a customer need and is different from the competition, your target customers will be very alert to your opening. Even if they don't see your first message, they will hear about you by word of mouth.

If your opening promotion plan exceeds your budget, you'll need to go back and revise your Capital Spending Plan to allow for the promotional expense. If that's your situation, complete this chapter, then go back to Chapter 7 and revise the cash totals.

- **Are my methods of promotion cost-effective?** Once you've estimated the cost of reaching all your target customers with the first message, compare that cost with the amount of money in your budget. Your job is to get the most exposure for the least outlay. Making that final decision may mean that you have to refine your promotion cost estimates from rough guesses into bids and quotes from suppliers. Normally, unless you're really unsure of promotional costs, you shouldn't take the time to obtain those quotes for now. Just balance your wish list against your budget to develop your marketing plan.

- **Have I allowed enough money in my monthly expense budget for ongoing advertising and promotion?** Take a look at the advertising expenses you forecast in the Profit and Loss Forecast in Chapter 6. If that amount needs changing, you'll need to change both your Profit and Loss Forecast and the Cash Flow Forecast (Chapter 7). If that's your situation, do it after you complete this chapter. But, if you're not sure about how much money to allow for monthly advertising and promotion, go back and reread the discussion about advertising in Chapter 6, "Complete Your Profit and Loss Forecast" Line 4d, "Marketing and Advertising."

To create a marketing plan, start by listing each of the promotional items you decided on for your preopening promotion together with their costs. Then add up the preopening promotional costs and fill in the total.

Next, list each of the promotional items you plan to use during the first two years of your business together with the monthly cost of each.

Those two groups of specific actions and costs, preopening promotion and monthly marketing, advertising, and promotional costs, will become the blueprint for your marketing plan.

Despite Antoinette's well-thought-out marketing plan, her original budget allowed nothing for an opening promotion and $1,000 per month for ongoing advertising. She could, however, decide to take some of the $15,000 contingency and use it for preopening promotions. It looks like Antoinette needs to make some hard choices about which marketing tools to drop and by how much to increase the marketing budget. We'll leave her now to solve that problem in peace and quiet while we move along to the next step.

If you're in the same predicament, take your time to balance costs and effectiveness the best you can, and then move ahead to the next step.

Antoinette's Dress Shop: Marketing Budget

Preopening promotion

1. Mail 10,000 pieces announcing grand opening — $ 5,000
2. Advertisement in *New City Monthly*, one month (including graphics) — 500
3. Publicity from papers, *New City Monthly*, no cost—but much time to write articles and contact editors — 0

Total preopening costs — $ 5,500

Monthly advertising

1. Newsletter every two months to mailing list—approximate cost per month (Note to self: Check cost of email newsletters versus postage) — $ 650
2. Monthly column in daily paper, no cost—but time to write column — 0
3. Advertising for sale every three months, estimated monthly — 250
4. Join service clubs, estimated monthly lunch and membership fees — 100

Total monthly cost — $ 1,000

Write Your Marketing Plan

By now, you have asked some tough questions and faced some critical issues. You may wish to combine the major points of the exercises into a summary narrative, or you may wish to present the results of each exercise independently.

If you summarize the work into a narrative, your plan will read more easily and look more professional. However, the potential downside to combining the answers into a narrative format is that you may inadvertently leave out a point of major interest to your backers. If you do elect to combine the answers into a narrative, be careful to cover all the points in each exercise. Use Antoinette's marketing plan as a guide.

Discuss the Risks Facing Your Business

Every business faces risks. The people whom you will ask for money will want to see that you can not only face reality but also deal with possible difficulties. The following discussion outlines risks small business owners typically face. Once you've analyzed these factors, you'll be ready to write a summary of the risks that apply to your own business.

Competition. Most businesses have competition. How will your business differ in significant and positive ways from your competition? If your competition is strong, don't minimize that fact, but figure out ways you will adjust to or use that strength. For example, if you plan to open a restaurant next to an extremely popular one, part of your strategy might be to cater to the overflow. Another might be to open on days or evenings when the other restaurant is closed.

Pioneering. If you anticipate no direct competition, your business probably involves selling a new product or service, or one that is new to your area. How will you avoid going broke trying to develop a market?

Cycles and Trends. Many businesses have cycles of growth and decline often based on outside factors such as taste, trends, or technology (discussed in Chapter 3). What is your forecast of the cycles and trends in your business? For example, if your forecast tells you that the new electronic product you plan to manufacture may decline in three years when the market is saturated, can you earn enough money in the meantime to make the venture worthwhile?

Slow Times. Every business experiences ups and downs. Is your business small and simple enough, or capitalized adequately enough, to ride out slow times? Or do you have some other strategy, such as staying open long hours in the busy season and closing during times of the year when business is dead?

Owner's Expertise. Nobody knows everything. How do you plan to compensate for the knowledge you're short on? For example, if you've never kept a set of books, you may need to hire a part-time bookkeeper and an accountant to make sure the bookkeeping system is adequate. Or you may need to buy a computer and an accounting program and devote some time to mastering your new tools.

> EXAMPLE: Doreen Cook wanted to establish her own restaurant.
> She had cooked for other restaurant owners for years and knew
> the practical side of putting good food on the table. However, she
> had little patience with financial matters and was honest enough
> to admit she didn't want to learn how to keep books. To solve this
> problem, she invited George, her CPA, to be her junior partner,
> with full responsibility for financial management. She and George
> emphasized this connection in her business plan and loan package,
> which George designed. In addition, George was invaluable in
> lining up a list of potential lenders.

Cash Flow. Seeing the money come and go on a daily and weekly basis is very different from looking at a yearly Profit and Loss Forecast (Chapter 6). You also want to be sure that your business can survive long enough so you can enjoy your profits. If you filled out a Cash Flow Forecast such as the one set out in Chapter 7, you should be able to demonstrate that you can survive foreseeable cash flow problems.

Write your risk analysis by first thinking of the main dangers your business faces. This shouldn't be hard, as you have probably been concerned about them for some time. Some of these may be on the list set out above; others will be unique to your business. Once you have identified the principal risks facing your business, write out a plan to counter each. But don't bog yourself down worrying about all sorts of unlikely disasters.

TIP

A note of philosophy: This is the stage when remorse or jitters may set in. You may be thinking, "Am I really doing this? Think of all the things that could go wrong. I could lose everything!" Your purpose in writing a risk discussion is to force yourself to face your fears and concerns, not to scare yourself out of going into business. If your rational, intellectual analysis tells you that the risk factors are manageable, proceed as hard and fast as you can. You don't have time for useless and unnecessary worry. On the other hand, if you really do get overwhelmed worrying about potential disasters, pay attention to your anxieties. They may be telling you that you don't have either the personality or knowledge of your business to handle the risks you'll take in a small business.

The purpose of this book is to help you understand the dimensions of the risks your business faces, but you, as the potential business owner, must put your money and belief on the line. Abe Lincoln said it: "Be sure you're right, then go ahead."

Antoinette's Dress Shop: Marketing Plan

Antoinette's Dress Shop will concentrate on developing a clientele consisting primarily of working women. We are particularly interested in professional women who expect to advance in their chosen careers. These women require fashionable clothing at reasonable prices. According to the Chamber of Commerce, the greater trading areas of New City include some 20,000 women who fit this description.[1] Forecasters expect this market to continue to grow at the same 10% growth rate it has enjoyed for the past five years. We believe the trend toward a higher concentration of professional women in this county may even accelerate because of the increased concentration of professional and management industries locating here.[2]

Personal experience and market research[3] demonstrate that upwardly mobile working women prefer fashionable, but slightly conservative, clothing at moderate or sale prices. These women prefer to shop where they receive personal attention, especially prompt, free alterations that traditionally have not been provided to women. Women in this group normally prefer to shop between 5 p.m. and 8 p.m. or on their lunch hour.

Most of our target customers shop at two types of stores for their clothing:

1. Department stores such as S. Bagnin, Jerry's, and Glendale's.
2. Latest fashion stores such as Wild Thing, Marian's, and Golden Frog.

Some of our target consumers presently shop at the department stores for the type of business clothes we will sell, and others shop at fashion stores for casual clothing. However, we believe we can capture a lot of this business for a number of reasons.

Antoinette's will appeal to customers who are either shopping at one of the local stores or going out of the area to meet their needs. For instance, many professional women travel as much as 35 miles to South City to shop at Freida's because their needs are simply not being met locally.

Generally speaking, the department stores offer a wide mix of merchandise. However, it isn't easy to find a large selection of appropriate business clothing at reasonable prices in any of them. In addition, S. Bagnin and Glendale's are only open one evening a week after 6 p.m., the time most working people prefer to shop. Further, the department stores offer fairly impersonal services, with a constant turnover of personnel. Alterations are an additional charge and usually take a week or more to complete. Our policy of offering free alterations within 24 hours is sure to appeal to women who put in at least a 40-hour week in addition to maintaining their homes.

---

[1] Annual Survey of Business Conditions, New City Chamber of Commerce, January 19, 20xx.

[2] Bank of New City economic forecast for 20xx.

[3] See attached article from September 27, 20xx issue of *Woman's Monthly*.

Antoinette's Dress Shop: Risk Analysis

Like every new business, Antoinette's faces several risks. I believe I can overcome each risk with the actions discussed below.

The primary risk we face is that our concept of an entire store selling business clothing to working businesswomen is new to this area. No one else in New City is presently doing exactly what we propose. Although we believe we have identified a market niche that the competition has failed to adequately exploit, our assumption remains to be proven here in New City. On the positive side, the population base of our target customers is more than adequate to support a store of our size and we have based our volume and profit projections on average figures for the industry. In addition, the type of store we propose has been very successful elsewhere. Nevertheless, we must demonstrate that this type store will work here. It must take sufficient business away from stores with a broader line of merchandise to make a profit.

A secondary risk is that we are thinly capitalized. If our sales volume fails to meet projections in the first year, our small working capital reserve may be inadequate to meet our cash flow needs. On the positive side, however, we believe our sales projections are conservative and that we will have little trouble meeting our sales revenue goals. In addition, by starting with relatively modest capital, we will have no large loan payments. Also, we have had several potential investors express an interest in the business. If our working capital reserves are exhausted, but the business demonstrates potential, we should be able to attract investors. [*But remember, we discovered that, on the basis of the Cash Flow Forecast, Antoinette's business has a fatal flaw (Chapter 7) and her entire plan will need reworking from the beginning.*]

Finally, there is a slight risk that the population of younger working women in New City will decline. However, we do not expect this to happen. White collar jobs have doubled here in the last decade and it seems reasonable to expect that the population of working women will continue to grow and that we will profit from that expansion. This projection is based on the fact that many well-established firms have located here and more are expected to do so. Nevertheless, if for any reason general industry declines, or a significant number of local companies fail or move overseas, we could face some problems and might have to change our marketing strategy.

Personnel Plan

Chances are that you'll need some help to run your business. It's hard to overestimate the impact employees have on small businesses. First, your paperwork explodes when you hire the first employee. Many government agencies regulate your relations with your employees, and you'll need help if you've never employed anyone before. Your accountant can help with payroll forms, and your local employment development agency can help with other regulations.

Second, how to successfully hire, manage, and fire people is a fine art, which this book can't possibly cover. If you have any doubts about your abilities in this area, make sure you get guidance from employment agencies, the local employment development department, or a private consultant.

Fortunately, there are some basic steps you can take that will increase your chances of making hiring decisions correctly. Many business owners fail to be clear in their own minds about basic details affecting an employee; that's a mistake almost guaranteed to cause trouble.

Analyze Your Business Personality

Every business has a personality that customers and suppliers spot right away. Your employees help create that personality in their daily interactions with customers, suppliers, and each other. Your job as the business owner is to decide what personality you want your business to have. Once you are clear about your business's personality, you can easily look for employees who fit in well. Take out a blank sheet of paper or open a computer file and write a statement of the personality you want your business to have.

Antoinette's Dress Shop: Business Personality

The impression I want my customers to receive is that our store provides the best selection of merchandise in our clothing category. We also provide prices and service that take the worry, regrets, and hassle out of shopping. Our employees should be sincerely helpful and dedicated to solving our customers' problems. I want them to be very knowledgeable so that our customers consider us as their clothing advisers, in addition to the best store.

Write Your Staffing Schedule

Now that you know what sort of people you want to hire, your next job is to decide how many people you need. (You may have completed this already in Chapter 6, "Complete Your Profit and Loss Forecast," Line 4a.)

The following example shows how Antoinette thought through her staffing schedule. You will make your decisions a little differently, depending on the needs of your particular business.

Antoinette's Dress Shop: Staffing Schedule

My dress shop will need two people on the floor at peak times (lunch and after work). I can open the store at 11 a.m. and can usually be available to fill in if the store suddenly gets busy at an unexpected time, as well as doing the books and ordering when the store is not crowded. Therefore, I plan to hire one full-time clerk, with the title of assistant manager, to work 40 hours a week, and two full-time clerks, so that there is always one employee in the store. That's a total of 120 hours per week of labor. The assistant manager will work from 12 p.m. to 8 p.m. Tuesday through Friday and from opening to closing on Saturday. The two clerks will be scheduled so that all the open hours are covered.

Write Job Descriptions

Next, open a new computer file or take out several blank sheets of paper and title each one "JOB DESCRIPTION." Make sure you have room for a separate description for each person you plan to hire. Each job description should include several items of information:

- job title
- job duties
- skills required, personality desired
- education required
- supervisor, and
- pay rate and monthly total wages/salary, including benefits, if any.

As an example, here's how Antoinette completed a job description sheet for her sales clerks.

Antoinette's Dress Shop: Job Description for Sales Clerk

Job Title: Sales Clerk

Job Duties: Sell clothing, interact with customers, and present a good image of my shop.

Skills and Personality: The clerk must have basic retail and cash handling skills and must demonstrate good math skills before hiring. She must be friendly and well-dressed. She must know current fashions and proper accessorizing as well as basics about alterations. She must be adept at working with the occasional irate customer.

Education: She must be at least a high school graduate.

Supervisor: Since she will be supervised by both my assistant manager and by me, she must be comfortable in situations with more than one person able to give orders.

Pay Rate and Monthly Wages: The clerk will work about 40 hours per week for a total of approximately 170 hours per month. I think I can hire a suitable clerk for about $8 per hour plus payroll taxes. That brings her monthly total to $1,376 ($8 × 40 hours × 4.3 weeks).

Once you complete a job description for each employee, add together all the monthly total wages/salary amounts you'll pay each employee. Verify your calculations against the numbers you used on Line 4a of the Profit and Loss Forecast (Chapter 6).

> **EXAMPLE:** Antoinette learns that sales clerks often make minimum wage, even with one or more years' experience, and that there are lots of qualified people looking for clerk positions. Assistant managers with several years' experience make about $11 per hour. In each case, Antoinette plans to pay above the low end of the wage range to assure she'll find competent people and to minimize problems with turnover.
>
> Accordingly, Antoinette plans to pay her sales clerks $8 per hour. Although she could probably hire an assistant manager for $10 per hour, she decides to pay $11 because she knows an excellent person whom she really likes and trusts. If each of her two sales clerks and her manager work 40 hours per week, her weekly wage cost will be $1,020 ($8 + $8 + $11 = $27, which she multiplies by 40). Multiplying these weekly figures by 4.3 weeks to get an average month results in an average monthly wage cost of $4,644. Extra costs for mandatory employers' contributions to Social Security, unemployment insurance, and so forth will average out to about 14% of each person's salary. She uses this 14% figure since she plans no extra benefits, like health insurance or vacations, until the business is a success and she can afford them.

When you work out these numbers for your business, check them against your entries on Lines 4a and 4b of your Profit and Loss Forecast.

Write Your Personnel Plan

As we discussed before under the marketing plan section, you may wish to summarize the information in these exercises into a narrative personnel plan. Just make sure you don't forget some important information when you do that. Here's Antoinette's written summary of her personnel plan.

Antoinette's Dress Shop: Personnel Plan

Antoinette's Dress Shop will employ a full-time assistant manager and two full-time clerks.

The assistant manger will be Sally Walters (resume attached). I have known Sally for several years and believe we will work well together. Until recently, she was the assistant manager of the dress department of a large department store, where she helped modernize the merchandise line. Her department increased sales by 25% in two years.

Sally will be paid $11 an hour to start, with a raise to $12 as soon as the business pays the owner $3,000 per month and shows a profit. My goal is to fully involve Sally in the business so that I will feel comfortable leaving her in charge when I take time off or have obligations outside the store.

Sally will work a 40-hour week primarily assisting customers. She will also assist in ordering decisions. Sally will sometimes open and close the shop and make bank deposits, although she will not have to do so regularly. She will work from 12 p.m. until 8 p.m. Tuesday through Friday and all day Saturday.

The sales clerks will be paid slightly above prevailing wage. They must be personable, presentable, and have some prior retail sales experience. They will work evening hours Thursday through Saturday and be available to help Sally and me during peak selling times. They will also assist in keeping the store attractive by stocking, cleaning, and developing window displays. Sally and I know several acceptable candidates and the local unemployment office indicates that many more are available.

I will work six days a week at the start, but will consider closing the store on Mondays if that proves to be a slow day. I will act as seamstress until business expands significantly. If business expands more rapidly than forecast, additional part-time clerks and a part-time seamstress will be hired as appropriate.

Antoinette's will not offer health insurance or other employee benefits until the profit picture warrants them.

Editing and Finalizing Your Business Plan

Introduction 200

Decide How to Organize Your Plan 200

Quick Plan (One-Day Plan)—Suggested Outline 200

Complete Plan—Suggested Outline 201

Write Final Portions of Your Plan 202

Write Your Plan Summary 202

Section Introductions 207

Personal Goal Statement 208

Create the Appendix 209

Create Title Page and Table of Contents 211

Complete Your Final Edit 211

Let Your Plan Rest 212

Final Details 212

Consider Using a Business Consultant 213

QUICK PLAN

If you've chosen the quick plan method to prepare a business plan (see Introduction), you need to read and complete these sections of Chapter 9:
- "Decide How to Organize Your Plan"
- "Write Your Plan Summary"
- "Create the Appendix," and
- "Create Title Page and Table of Contents."

Introduction

Lenders and investors see lots of business plans. You'll want to make sure your plan gets the attention it deserves by presenting it in the best possible manner. This chapter shows you how.

Decide How to Organize Your Plan

Each business plan has a unique structure that to some degree is determined by the particular business and fundraising needs.

Although you'll be writing a few more short sections in this chapter, you'll probably want to take a few minutes now to get organized. Take out all the work you've completed so far using this book. Then arrange the various components in the order suggested below for a complete plan or a quick plan, whichever you've chosen. (See the Introduction for an explanation of these different methods.) Of course, you can vary the sequence if a different order makes more sense to you. If you're happy with the order in which the various parts appear, chances are that your readers will be also.

Quick Plan (One-Day Plan)—Suggested Outline

Title Page: See: "Create Title Page and Table of Contents" of this chapter
Plan Summary: See: "Write Your Plan Summary" of this chapter
Table of Contents: See: "Create Title Page and Table of Contents" of this chapter

Problem Statement: Chapter 3

Business Description: Chapter 3

Business Accomplishments: Chapter 5

Sales Revenue Forecast: Chapter 3

Profit and Loss Forecast: Chapter 6

Capital Spending Plan: Chapter 7

Cash Flow Forecast: Chapter 7

Appendix: Table of Contents: See: "Create the Appendix" of this chapter

Appendix: Supporting Documents: See: "Create the Appendix" of this chapter.

Complete Plan—Suggested Outline

Title Page: See: "Create Title Page and Table of Contents" of this chapter

Plan Summary: See: "Write Your Plan Summary" of this chapter

Table of Contents: See: "Create Title Page and Table of Contents" of this chapter

Problem Statement: Chapter 3

Business Description: Chapter 3

Business Accomplishments: Chapter 5

Marketing Plan: Chapter 8

Sales Revenue Forecast: Chapter 3

Profit and Loss Forecast: Chapter 6

Capital Spending Plan: Chapter 7

Cash Flow Forecast: Chapter 7

Future Trends: Chapter 3

Risks Facing Your Business: Chapter 8

Personnel Plan: Chapter 8

    Business Personality: Chapter 8

    Staffing Schedule: Chapter 8

    Job Descriptions: Chapter 8

Specific Business Goals: Chapter 2

Personal Financial Statement: Chapter 5

Personal Background: (Your Strong and Weak Points, General and
Specific Skills, Your Business Needs, Your Likes and Dislikes):
Chapter 2
Appendix: Table of Contents: See: "Create the Appendix" of this chapter
Appendix: Supporting Documents: See: "Create the Appendix" of this
chapter.

Length of Your Plan

Some of you probably wonder how long a business plan should be. Should
it be five pages or 500 pages? The best answer is that your plan should
completely and concisely cover all the issues that we raise in this book. You
may be able to place all that information on 15 to 20 pages or you may
need more, especially if you provide several appendixes.

The key is to include all the information you need to tell your story
and exclude any information that isn't needed. Remember, more isn't
necessarily better. If you have any doubts about this, have a consultant
review your plan's length.

Write Final Portions of Your Plan

Now that you have an overview of what your finished plan will include,
it's time to begin writing the final sections. Every business plan needs a
summary, which is covered below. In addition, you may choose to write
several short statements that will improve your plan and make it more
cohesive. Those optional statements are also covered below.

Write Your Plan Summary

The plan summary introduces and emphasizes the high points of your
plan. It includes a statement of the total amount of money you seek.
Because the summary is based on the rest of your plan, we've waited

until now to cover it. Your job is to tell your readers who you are, what you want to do, how much money you need, and how much money you expect to make, all on one page.

> CAUTION
>
> **Pay attention!** Many people will never read your entire package. They will make their preliminary decision about lending you money or investing in your project on the basis of their first impression of your plan summary. Others will decide to read the rest of your materials only if your summary engages their interest. So put all your strong points in the first few paragraphs, saving the details for later. Absolutely follow these rules:
> - Keep it short.
> - Be specific.

Your plan summary needs a statement of the total cash you need to begin or expand your business. This is the sum of the preopening costs and the maximum negative cash flow. (See Chapter 7.)

> EXAMPLE: This summary introduces Juanita's Waffle Warehouse.
>
> "My Waffle Warehouse requires $45,000 in preopening costs, which are detailed on the following pages. I have researched my equipment costs carefully, resulting in a potential savings of $15,000 by buying secondhand (reconditioned and guaranteed) cooking equipment. Also, my grand opening costs are firm estimates resulting from verbal quotes from the ad agency recommended by the Waffle Warehouse franchising company. I am confident that these are accurate estimates and I look forward to proceeding."

> CAUTION
>
> **Businesses seeking investors.** If you will solicit equity investors instead of applying for a loan, you'll need a statement delineating what investors will receive for their money rather than information about how a loan will be repaid. As a small business, you will almost certainly not propose selling stock to

the public at large. Therefore, you will need to propose that investors will receive a significant share of ownership of the business and perhaps some monthly or annual cash payment as well. (For more details on equity investments, see Chapter 4.)

> **EXAMPLE:** An investment of $20,000 in John's Roof Repair business will result in the investor receiving a 33% interest in the business. Present plans are to distribute one-half of the annual profit of the company to the owners each year. Based on projections contained in this proposal, this means a person who invests $20,000 will receive $5,000 the first year, $17,500 the second year, and $25,000 each year thereafter. In addition, investors will be entitled to have any necessary roof repairs done to their homes or business buildings and those of immediate family members at 50% off the regular rate.

Some people worry about their ability to write in a businesslike style. If that applies to you, you'll probably want to follow the same three-step process as Antoinette:

1. List the positive facts you want to cover; you'll probably need to review the work you've done to get that information.
2. Rearrange the facts in a logical sequence that presents the most positive facts in a coherent pattern.
3. Write the facts in simple prose.

Here is Antoinette's preliminary outline of the most positive facts of her business plan. Remember, at this stage she is only doing this exercise for herself, so she has no need to be fancy.

Antoinette's Dress Shop Business Plan
Summary: Outline of Most Positive Facts

- Dress shop will cater to working women.
- 20,000 potential customers are in the city and it's a growing market.
- No competitor exploits market systematically.
- Risks such as newness of my concept to our community appear moderate and I have a plan to overcome all identified risks.
- I have a good friend with solid qualifications to be assistant manager.
- My background includes responsibility and knowledge in all critical areas.
- My personal goals coincide with the financial success of the business.
- Detailed financial projections show that I can start the business and reach my goals with $162,500.
- Creative marketing ideas include free alterations, clothing tips for working women, occasional fashion shows.

Next, Antoinette rearranges these highlights in a logical order. Here is how her second version looks.

Antoinette's Dress Shop Business Plan Summary:
Outline of Most Positive Facts (2nd draft)

1. Open a dress shop catering to professional working women/need $162,500 to do it.
2. My market analysis demonstrates the concept is sound and that I have more than enough potential customers (20,000) to make it work.
3. I have several unique marketing ideas that should attract customers.
4. No competitor targets our customers systematically.
5. Both my qualifications and Sally's prove that I can do it.
6. Financial projections show the loan can be paid back with ease.
7. The money will be well used for opening inventory, equipment, working capital, and the other things necessary for starting the business.
8. Conclusion: This business represents my long-held dream and I am eager to begin.

Antoinette's Dress Shop Business Plan Summary

[In her summary, Antoinette puts her best foot forward and tries to answer any questions the lender may ask.]

This business plan requests a loan of $110,000 to open a dress shop catering to working and professional women in New City.

Today, many women identify themselves as "professionals." This is part of an evolution in workforce patterns and no local store caters to this group's needs for moderately priced, stylish work clothing—including carrying the three most popular labels: Narak, YYY, and Pag. Antoinette's will fill this gap. We will sell stylish, good quality, and moderately priced clothing to upwardly mobile women, provide free alterations, and help our customers dress well at a reasonable cost.

Financial projections show first year revenues of $450,000, with a profit of $35,000 before loan payments and a nominal personal draw. Second year revenues rise to $540,000 and profits increase to $46,000. Profits are adequate in both years to service the loan and provide me with a draw. To secure the loan, I will consider a second trust deed on my home, which has equity of about $200,000.

I will combine loan proceeds with $50,000 in savings to provide a $160,000 cash fund. The fund will be allocated as follows: furniture, fixtures, and leasehold improvements $110,000, rent deposit $7,500, opening inventory $30,000, and contingency $15,000. Cash flow forecasts show a positive cash flow from opening, so no allocation is made for working capital.

My qualifications include three years of experience as a clothing buyer and assistant merchandise manager for the local Rack-a-Frax department store. I was able to show a 35% sales increase in my principal area of responsibility, the Designer Dress Department. During that time, I developed many industry contacts which will be invaluable at Antoinette's.

Sally Walters will be my assistant manager. She has five years' experience in the field, the last three as assistant manager of the dress department at Glendale's. We plan to open Antoinette's by Labor Day in the downtown shopping mall and have an informal commitment from the shopping center manager to lease space to us. We will both continue our activities in New City service clubs, especially those that feature women members.

_____	_____
Date	Antoinette Gorzak

Finally, Antoinette writes a narrative summary, which is shown above.

Section Introductions

When you look over your plan, you may notice that some of the sections seem incomplete or that one section doesn't flow into the next. If so, you have these options:

- Write short introductions to those sections that need more explanation.
- Rewrite the entire plan into a single comprehensive narrative, taking care to cover every important point.
- Leave the plan as is—it's possible that your circumstances make it appropriate to use rough drafts and financial documents and nothing more.

Many of you will take a middle course of rewriting some of your earlier work, presenting some of it intact, and providing written introductions and summaries for others. If you write a narrative or an introduction, keep your writing as short as possible while presenting all your conclusions and assumptions.

Sections that typically benefit by short narrative introductions include:

- **Profit and Loss Forecast.** You don't need a lengthy treatise, but you should describe the assumptions you made about the significant numbers. Explain how you derived the sales volume forecast you used to create the Profit and Loss Forecast; your backers will be extremely interested in those assumptions. Also list your major assumptions about cost of sales and fixed expenses that you used in creating the Profit and Loss Forecast. You may choose to make lists instead of writing a prose narrative. Finally, summarize the annual sales and profit figures you forecast.
- **Capital Spending Plan and Cash Flow Forecast.** This narrative should list the major assumptions you made in adjusting your monthly profits to derive the monthly cash flow. Also summarize the preopening costs you'll incur. Mention whether or not you will sell on credit or seek extended terms from your suppliers and how long

208 | HOW TO WRITE A BUSINESS PLAN

it will be before your customers pay you and before you pay your suppliers. (See Chapter 7 for more details.)

Personal Goal Statement

You may include a statement of your personal goals. It is a tricky part of your plan, even though it's a big help to potential backers who don't know you personally. Your lenders and backers want you to be happy in your new venture, since you'll be likely to work hard at it. However, people who back you will also want to be sure that you're truly committed to the financial success of your project. For instance, they won't back a beekeeper who loves bees so much she can't stand to disturb them by removing honey from the hive.

Ideally, your personal goals and commitments will tie into the business goals exactly. In reality, you probably have at least some personal goals that don't have much to do with business profitability.

> EXAMPLE 1: "My reasons for starting this business are to make a good living, prove I can be successful, enjoy the freedom of independence, and have lots of free time to work on my car collection. In addition, I would like to create a business that I can bequeath to my children."

Most people starting small businesses are tied to them full-time (if not more), and it's unrealistic to think that there will be a lot of time left to tinker with a car collection. Assuming our budding entrepreneur is willing to postpone most of his tinkering until his business is established, here's how this statement could be rewritten to sound a little better to a potential backer.

> EXAMPLE 2: "My personal and business goals largely coincide. Successful implementation of this business plan will enable me to meet the following personal goals: provide a good living for my family; work in a field I know and like; achieve the personal satisfaction of seeing my plan come true; enjoy the prestige and

independence accruing to a successful business owner; provide a legacy for my children; and provide the means to a richer and more fulfilling life for both myself and my family."

Notice that in Example 2, "time to work on cars" was translated to "provide the means to a richer life." Perhaps your statement will neither be this lyrical nor obfuscatory, but hopefully you get the picture.

Antoinette Gorzak's Personal Goal Statement

I want to accomplish a number of goals by starting Antoinette's Dress Shop.

I want to prove that I can create a successful and worthwhile business by drawing on my educational background and work experience. I feel that choosing and selling good clothes at a fair price will be an honest service to my customers and the community generally. I want to spend my time working with customers and people in the clothing business who share my values.

I want the chance to make a better living than I can make by working for others, along with the responsibility and freedom to be my own boss.

Create the Appendix

This book covers the primary business building blocks all businesses share. Of necessity, it leaves out any mention of items that are specific to any one business. Yet, in many cases, specific items are critically important to the success or failure of your business. Your job is to decide which items to include in your business plan.

For example, suppose that you are establishing a franchise business. You want to include all the information about the franchise you can, including copies of the agreements and any information the franchisor provides you about the operation. Or let's say you have invented a revolutionary new gadget. You'll want to include a copy of the patent, patent search, or patent application to support your claims.

The key to deciding what to include is whether the information helps the reader understand your proposal. Include proof of statements a lender or investor would be likely to question—for instance, horseshoeing is a growth industry. Do not include support for obvious statements—for example, people like ice cream. Don't be afraid to edit by cutting and pasting, as long as you don't unfairly change the meaning.

Here are several things that you should commonly include in your appendix:

- prior years' financial statements if you are expanding an existing business (profit and loss statements and balance sheets from at least two prior years)
- copies of proposed lease agreements
- copies of bids for any needed construction work
- plans for construction work
- drawings of business signs or logos
- a list of what will be purchased for your opening inventory
- key employees' resumes, if available, and
- copies of any newspaper stories or other publicity you have received that relates to your business. This is particularly important for people who are entering service businesses, where they are their own main product.

Finally, organize your material in a logical order and include a table of contents for the appendix.

Antoinette's Dress Shop: Table of Contents for Appendix

1. Annual Survey of Business Conditions, New City Chamber of Commerce, January 19, 20xx
2. Bank of New City Economic Forecast for 20xx
3. Article from September 27, 20xx issue of *Woman's Monthly* concerning the need for specialized clothes for the working woman
4. Newspaper articles and picture of Antoinette when she put on a large and successful fashion show for working women at the Rack-a-Frax Department Store
5. Copy of proposed store lease (critical pages only, others available on request)
6. Planned fixture layout for Antoinette's Dress Shop
7. Antoinette's Dress Shop sign drawing and bid, Smith Sign Co.
8. Leasehold improvements bid for shop, Jones Construction Co.
9. Quote from Meyer Supply on dress racks and cash register

Create Title Page and Table of Contents

Every business plan should have these two pages:

- **Title page.** This is a separate page with the title of your business plan, the date, and your name and address.
- **Table of Contents.** This appears after the Plan Summary and before the body of the plan. List the headings for the major sections of your plan as well as important subsections. After you assemble your plan and number the pages, come back and put the appropriate page number next to each heading.

Complete Your Final Edit

By now, your material should be assembled and ready for a final edit. It's wise to make a working copy of the entire plan that incorporates all the changes you've made so far, either from a computer printout or by photocopying your earlier work. Read through everything you've written to spot any inconsistencies or obvious goofs. Make any necessary corrections.

> ⚠ CAUTION
>
> **First impressions count.** You won't have time to show your potential backers a rough draft, followed by a final edit and more revisions. Somebody said that you only get one chance to make a first impression; make your first impression your best.

Let Your Plan Rest

Put your completed and organized business plan aside for a day or two. You want to come back to it as fresh as possible.

Assess the overall business message of your proposal. Does it make sense? Would you lend money on the strength of it? Can you make it more convincing by strengthening some of its sections? Can you document all your claims? If someone asks you to elaborate on your plan, are you ready with facts and figures?

Check for consistency one more time. Your plan should say the same things in the financial section that it says in the business description, and so on. For example, if Antoinette says she will do free alterations, she must budget enough money for a sewing machine.

Final Details

Your plan needs a neat and businesslike appearance to give the best impression. If you are using a word processor, make sure it has a laser or letter-quality printer. The plan should be placed in a three-hole binder or folio.

What about visuals, charts, colors, and so forth? Simply watch the sophistication level of your business plan. If you're going to market a new laser printer, your plan will include elaborate visuals that demonstrate your product's abilities as well as your ability to compete in a sophisticated market. On the other hand, if you're planning to establish a bait and tackle shop on Pier 37, your plan won't need fancy graphs and charts.

As one of the last steps, number the pages of the plan and place the numbers in the Table of Contents. If your report is thick, use divider pages with colored tabs to mark each major section, so readers can find what they want quickly.

It may seem obvious, but good writing, good organization, and good spelling can make all the difference. If you're uncertain about your plan, have it reviewed by a professional writer. If you don't know a reasonably priced experienced writer, check the local newspaper, an ad agency, or the English department at the local high school or college. For a modest fee, you may well be able to improve your work substantially. But don't go overboard—just make sure that your writing is clear and to the point.

You may want to check out a word processing service in your area if you haven't already done so. Some of these services can offer effective and inexpensive ways to improve the visual appeal of your plan at a reasonable price. Also, they may be able to offer suggestions about binding your final plan. But above all, remember that your plan's content will speak the loudest. Don't make your document so fancy that it detracts from the message or suggests that you like to spend too much in inappropriate places.

When your plan is complete, make a point to hang onto the original; don't give it away. Also, make sure you keep a list of the people who get copies and the dates they received them.

Finally, take yourself out for a terrific dinner with someone whose company you enjoy. You deserve it.

Consider Using a Business Consultant

It is often wise to have your plan reviewed after you think it is in good shape. For a modest fee, a good small business consultant or CPA who specializes in businesses similar to yours may be able to save you from a costly mistake or point out additional profit opportunities. At the very least, he should be able to suggest how to improve the way your information is presented. If he gives you minor suggestions for improvement, you can incorporate them easily. If the suggestions are more major, give some thought before making changes. Remember, this is your business and your proposal and it's up to you to make the final decisions. (See Chapter 12 for a discussion of consultants.)

Antoinette's Discouraging Moment

Antoinette was pleased with her plan after putting it together, reviewing it, and polishing it. She was convinced she had a winner. Almost as an afterthought, she decided to have a business consultant review her business plan before taking it to the bank. She was glad she did. In brief, here is what the consultant told her. "Antoinette, you have written a fine business plan and have a good idea for a business, but your financial projections contain one serious error. I believe that you have underestimated the amount of inventory you will have to carry by $45,000 to $50,000. Unfortunately, changing this number will influence all your other financial projections and will mean you have to rethink your entire plan."

The consultant then discussed the same inventory turnover problem we discovered in Chapter 7. The consultant suggested that Antoinette take a few days to decide if she wished to try and raise more money and rework her entire plan or drop the idea.

Antoinette was stunned. She expected to discover some minor flaws, not a possibly fatal one. Nevertheless, after much soul-searching, she was relieved to have uncovered the problem before, not after, she began her business. She decided that raising the extra money for inventory wasn't an insurmountable problem. The question was whether she could reasonably increase her sales projections enough to justify the increased inventory. To make this decision, she decided to again talk to a number of women in the target audience to get a better idea of how often they might patronize her store.

I shall leave the decision to you as to whether Antoinette decides to proceed with her plans or decides to go back to work for a salary. After all, it's much the same sort of difficult choice you may have to make about your own business.

Selling Your Business Plan

How to Ask for the Money You Need 216

   Write a Telephone Pitch 216

   Telephone for Appointments 216

   Meet Your Backers 217

   Ask for the Money 218

   Leave Your Plan With Your Backer 219

   Follow Up 219

How to Approach Different Backers 219

   Friends and Relatives 220

   Business Acquaintances 220

   Supporters 221

   Banks 221

   Equity Investors (Venture Capitalists) 223

   Government Agencies 224

What to Do When Someone Says "Yes" 224

Plan in Advance for Legal Details 225

   Loans 225

   Equity Investments 227

How to Ask for the Money You Need

Once your business plan has been polished to perfection, you're ready to use it as part of your campaign to get financing. If you haven't done so already, you must decide where you'd ideally like to get the money you need. You should know whether you prefer to get financing from a lender or an investor. (This is discussed in Chapter 4.)

Before you call people and make appointments, give some thought to a few preliminaries. Like it or not, you're now a salesperson. Your task is to sell your plan. Don't let this discourage you, even if your experience with selling has been negative. There are all sorts of good ways to sell things, most of which depend on a good product and an honest, straightforward presentation. I can't tell you exactly how to sell yourself and your plan, but I can make a number of suggestions.

Write a Telephone Pitch

Since some of your preliminary selling will be done over the telephone, you'll want to be prepared. Write a short statement of what you're doing and why. Simply list your two or three major reasons for entering or expanding this particular business. Then write down how much money you need and how much you'll pay the lenders or investors for using their money.

Telephone for Appointments

Avoid lengthy telephone discussions when making the call; you simply want to set up a personal appointment to discuss all the details and ask for the money. If you're not sure what to say, read the sample telephone script below. You can adapt it to suit your style and needs.

"Hello, Jack? This is Antoinette. How are you today? How's the family? Say, Jack, the reason I'm calling is that I have a great idea for a new business and I'd like to meet with you and show you my business plan to see what you think of it.

"Can we get together next Thursday morning in your office? Oh, you'd like to hear a little more about my ideas before we meet." (Antoinette briefly explains why she wants to open her business—she can read her list of reasons if she's nervous.) "Well Jack, I'm glad to hear that you like my ideas."

(Before she discusses the loan she wants, she asks Jack for an appointment. If she can personally meet with him, she will wait until then to discuss money.)

"What about next Thursday? Oh, how much money do I need? I need a good-sized loan that I can pay back in three years. So we can get together next Thursday morning in your office? Good. I'll see you at 10:00 in the morning. Bye, Jack."

Meet Your Backers

Show up on time, well-prepared to answer any questions that may arise. Then let your natural enthusiasm help you explain your business idea fully. Your basic objective in the meeting is to answer all the questions you are asked. If you can't handle a question on the spot, do not make up an answer—promise to find the information. Then promptly write, phone, or visit with the information later.

Talk about what the investment will do for your prospect. For example, bankers want to hear that their loan will be soundly secured and paid back with no problem. Your relatives, on the other hand, may be interested in family solidarity and the prestige of a family-owned business as well as making a good investment.

Offer investors/lenders a fair return, as much security as you're comfortable with, and a little romance. By romance, I mean to emphasize the fact that investing and lending money are very personal activities. Your backer wants to feel good about you and your project. Your backer also wants to share in your enthusiasm. So, in addition to presenting a potential lender or investor with a sound financial plan, make sure he knows what makes the project exciting for you.

How to Handle Past Financial Problems

What if you've previously declared bankruptcy or have had other credit problems, such as a lawsuit for a delinquent student loan? Don't try to camouflage it. The banker or investor will probably find out this sort of information from a credit reporting agency anyway, so it will help you to be up front. However, you need to come up with a plausible—and true—explanation for your past credit problems. It should also reflect your determination to meet your obligations in the future.

Here's the wrong sort of explanation for a student loan lawsuit:

"Yes, I acknowledge that I took a student loan and didn't pay it back. I didn't pay it back because the militaristic system we live under is shameful. It's my firmly held conviction that students have an obligation to take what they can to partially balance the scales."

Here's a better way to handle the same situation:

"Yes, I did have a student loan and wasn't able to pay it back. I had a rough time adjusting to the working world for several years after I graduated and couldn't come up with the money in time. Since then, I have discovered work I like to do and am good at, as evidenced by my recent work history. I have arranged a sensible monthly payment schedule, which I have been honoring."

The second explanation shows that you will play by conventional credit rules. It also tugs at the heartstrings a little, something that never hurts a good cause.

Ask for the Money

Here's one bit of essential advice about meeting with your backers: You must ask for the money. Don't make the common mistake of discussing your plan in generalities and then saying "Thank you" as you walk out the door.

As part of every presentation, you must ask the potential source of funds if he will invest in your venture or lend you the money. Repeat the following:

"Thank you for listening to my business plan. Will you invest/lend me the money I need to get started?"

If you are turned down, don't hang your tail between your legs and slink away in a puddle of embarrassed perspiration. Ask why. Sometimes the reasons why a person won't help finance your business will be more valuable to you than the money.

Leave Your Plan With Your Backer

Give your potential backer a copy of the business plan after you've met with her. If at all possible, don't mail copies of your business plan, or summaries of your plan, to people before you meet. Your presentation loses a great deal without your personality and enthusiasm. It's also a good idea to number each copy of your plan and keep track of who gets which plan. That way you can remember to follow up with everybody. Also, if you're selling stock in a private offering you need to keep track of who gets the plans.

Follow Up

After a week or ten days, telephone all of your potential backers and ask if they have any questions. If they do, you can provide answers on the telephone or make an appointment to meet. Remember to ask for the money you need.

How to Approach Different Backers

Chances are you have long since decided whom to approach first for a loan or investment. For example, you might decide to first approach your father, then the Bank of Newcastle, then the Small Business Administration. If you haven't decided yet, review Chapter 4 and develop a list of priorities now. Below are some ways you might approach specific types of backers.

Friends and Relatives

The first rule of borrowing money from people close to you is that you want to be very sure they can afford to lend it to you and that you will be able to pay it back. Everyone who works with small business financing can tell horror stories about business owners who had to deal with both the failure of their enterprise and a bunch of angry relatives. Put simply, it's no fun.

If you want to ask a relative or friend for a loan, much of your approach depends on the people involved and your relationship to them. We can't tell you much about either of these areas, but here are some general suggestions:

- Approach your friends in a respectful and organized way. Don't spring your request on anyone in a social context.
- Don't assume your relatives and friends know all your plans and accomplishments, even though they know you well. Make your presentation just as professional as for your banker, even if it's less formal.
- Tailor your presentation to your audience. For example, if you stop by your brother's place early Saturday morning wearing your banker-meeting best, he will probably laugh you out of the kitchen. But bear in mind that your brother will be as interested as a banker in seeing your well-thought-out business plan.
- Above all, give the person you're talking to a graceful way not to lend or invest. Remember, this is a business proposition, not proof of someone's feelings for you. Once everyone is assured an easy exit if they don't have the money or desire to invest, you may find they will be relaxed enough to give you a fair hearing.

Business Acquaintances

One good way to approach business acquaintances is by networking. For example, you might call your attorney or accountant or someone you know who owns a small business and say, "I've got a great business proposal in the retail clothing business. I need about $40,000 and the investor will get a 25% annual return on the money they invest, paid monthly. Do you know anybody who might be interested?"

She might reply, "Well, I'm not interested myself, but why don't you try Joe Spats? He just retired from the menswear business and has been a little restless lately." Obviously, the next step is to call Joe, mention your mutual friend's name, and set up a meeting. If he's not interested, ask if he knows anyone who might be. If you strike out with your accountant, attorney, or business friend, try your uncle, the owner of the local hardware store with whom you trade jokes, or the investor who put money into the bakery where you buy coffee.

Supporters

Supporters are people who care—often deeply—about the subject area of your business. Your best approach is to try to enlist this enthusiasm and to honestly involve these people in your dream. Often it's best to involve supporters at an early stage so that you get the full benefit of their good ideas.

If your business will have enthusiastic supporters, whether it's a music store or a dentist's office in a rural area where there is no dentist now, these people may offer financial help. Figure out ways to get the word out in the correct circles. If people care, they may respond favorably.

Banks

The main point to remember about banks is that they lend money, they don't invest it. A banker will want to know all about you and your business, but when it comes to saying "Yes" or "No," the security of the loan will be paramount.

When approaching a bank for the first time, it is important to understand that within all banks, responsibility for different tasks is divided. You want to talk to the loan officer in charge of small business loans, not the trust officer or the person in charge of getting the automatic teller machine to work right.

Bankers, like almost everyone else, prefer dealing with people they know. The ideal way to meet a bank lending officer is to know a bank vice president socially and have her refer you to the loan officer. However, if you are like most mere mortals and don't have any old school ties or country club connections, you will have to be creative. Almost anyone who owns a successful small business will have friendly contacts at a local bank, as will accountants or business consultants. See if you can arrange an introduction or at least get permission to use your contact's name. If all else fails, call the receptionist and ask the name of the small business loan officer.

Once you have a name, telephone for an appointment and briefly describe the subject matter you'll want to discuss. Show up on time with your business plan and loan package. Open the discussion by talking about your personal business and employment history. Highlight your community involvement while trying to discover common interests and acquaintances. Maybe you both have children in Little League or maybe you both belong to the Rotary Club, the Symphony Association, or the Volunteer Fire Department. Who you are in the community and what you have accomplished in other jobs or businesses is an important part of the loan application process.

While it's important to be businesslike, it's also important to take your time. After all, you want to avoid giving the banker the impression that you're in a hurry or are desperate—he is not going to approve your plan immediately under any circumstances. Expect lots of checking and probably a series of meetings. But never forget that to get a loan, you have to ask for it. As part of each meeting with the bank, ask politely but specifically about the status of your loan.

Here are a few things to emphasize when talking to bankers:

- **Your other bank business.** If you don't already patronize the bank in question, make sure the lending officer knows you plan to do so if you get the loan.
- **Security.** Remember that the banker wants to lend money, not invest it. Tell the banker how sure he is to get his money back with interest. If you can offer collateral for the loan, emphasize it. (See the discussion of bank loans in Chapter 4.)
- **Be realistic.** Your banker wants to be assured about your knowledge and enthusiasm about your business. But he also needs to know

that you have your feet on the ground. If you puff too hard, the banker is almost sure to be turned off.

- **Be persistent.** There are lots of banks. People who work with small businesses in your area can probably suggest the banks that are most likely to lend to your type of business. If you are turned down by one bank, make sure you understand why you were rejected. If it's realistic, change the items in your proposal that caused this rejection. Pay extra attention to aspects of your plan that continue to receive negative comments.

Equity Investors (Venture Capitalists)

I use the term "venture capitalist" a bit loosely to include people who invest relatively small amounts of equity financing. These may be relatives, acquaintances, or anyone else with money to invest in what looks to be a profitable business.

As you should know from reading the discussion in Chapter 4, the primary distinction between a venture capitalist and a lender involves risk, security, and amount of return. The venture capitalist is traditionally willing to take more risk in exchange for a chance to make a large profit. Here are some suggestions:

- **Prepare a summary of what you are offering.** In addition to the business plan you have already designed, you need to tell the equity investor both what you are offering (partnership, limited partnership, shares in a corporation, and so on) and what the projected return is.

- **Do not promise a certain return.** Especially if your potential investor is unsophisticated, emphasize in writing that there is always some risk associated with a high potential return. Make certain the investor knows your projections are just that—projections. In short, never guarantee a return that you may not be able to deliver. The person putting up the money should even understand there is a possibility she may lose the entire investment if things go very badly.

- **Ask for names of others who might invest.** If a potential investor turns you down for any reason, ask if he knows anyone else who might be interested in investing. Don't be surprised if someone suggests putting a deal together for you for a fee. This means he acts as a finder or broker as discussed in Chapter 4.

Government Agencies

The hardest thing about getting money from the government is finding out which program can help you. The second-hardest thing is finding out who in that agency can make a decision for or against your proposal. Compared to these two, filling out the forms is easy.

Ask your bankers if they know any of the programs. Most will have some experience with at least one of the agencies, such as the Small Business Administration (www.sba.gov), and can steer you in the right direction. If you run into a wall, try your local elected representatives. They have aides whose job it is to help people like you. If you find a program that looks good, be sure your elected representative knows about your application. (See the discussion of the SBA in Chapter 4.)

What to Do When Someone Says "Yes"

Your first job when someone indicates his interest in lending you money or investing in your plan is simple—don't faint. It's fine to prepare for a negative result so you are not too disappointed if you are rejected, but remember also to be prepared for a positive reception. If your proposal is good, it will be funded sooner or later.

One good approach is to have a number of answers ready, depending on what the lender or investor offers. It's a little like being a major league baseball outfielder in a close game, with several men on base. Depending on where the ball is hit, you need several alternative plans. You can see some pretty funny plays when a fielder fails to think ahead and throws to the wrong base.

If you're asking for a loan for a set amount of money at a certain interest rate and the lender says "Yes," presumably you will, too. But, what if the lender offers you less than you want, asks for a higher interest rate, wants collateral, or proposes a different financial formula entirely? Make sure you understand exactly what the proposal is. Think through your risks, especially if the lender wants collateral. Compare the terms—for instance, a small increase in interest rate could mean that you will end up paying more money for a longer period of time.

Don't answer on the spot. Take the proposal home and see if you can live with it. If you can't, meet with the person again and explain exactly what you can't accept and why. Then propose changes. If this doesn't result in agreement, start looking for other funding sources. It's far better to say "No" than to accept a bad deal. Anyone who has been in business for a while will tell you the times he turned down poor business proposals were at least as important to his ultimate success as the ones to which he said "Yes."

> EXAMPLE: Charlie wanted a loan of $20,000 to start a limousine service. The bank offered him $20,000, but wanted equal monthly payments of $1,018 over two years. Charlie had expected to make payments of $530 per month over five years. After he ran the different loan payments through his cash flow schedule, he discovered that he couldn't pay his own rent and grocery bill if he had to pay $1,018 per month on the loan in the first two years. After he explained his problem to the loan officer, the bank offered Charlie interest-only payments for the first two years. That was a much better deal and Charlie took it.

Plan in Advance for Legal Details

Taking money into your business requires lots of legal documentation. You will present a more professional image if you understand some of the basics.

Loans

Whatever loan you arrange will have to be reduced to writing. If you deal with a bank or another institutional lender, it will have the necessary forms. However, if your arrangement is with a friend, family member, or private investor, these details will probably be up to you.

If your loan is simple—a specific amount of money, at so much interest, to be paid at regular intervals—you can safely design it yourself. While a course in contract law is beyond the scope of this book, the sample promissory notes provided below may help you focus on this task.

However, if the loan involves complicated default provisions, security, and balloon payments, you and the person you are dealing with would be wise to have it checked by an attorney. If you have done most of the work, this shouldn't be expensive; negotiate the fee in advance.

EXAMPLE 1:

Promissory Note

Robert Lee of 1411 South St., Homer, Alaska, and Gertrude Fox of 123 Main St., Fairfax, Alaska, agree that Gertrude Fox hereby lends Robert Lee the sum of Fifty-Six Thousand Dollars ($56,000) to be repaid on the following terms:

1. Principal and interest of 10% per year will be paid in equal monthly installments on the first day of each month beginning the first day of September 20xx and continuing through the first day of August, 20xx.

2. On September 1, 20xx the entire unpaid balance of principal and interest shall be due and payable in full.

3. Should Robert Lee fail to pay an installment on the date due, as set out in Paragraph 1 of this agreement, the whole sum of the principal and interest then outstanding shall, at the option of Gertrude Fox or any subsequent holder of this note, immediately become due and payable.

4. Should Robert Lee fail to meet any condition of this agreement, and should Gertrude Fox or any subsequent holder of this note take legal action to collect it, Robert Lee shall be responsible for all attorneys' fees and costs.

_____ _____
Date   Robert Lee

_____ _____
Date   Gertrude Fox

EXAMPLE 2:

Promissory Note

$8,639.00   July 30, 20xx

For value received, the undersigned promises to repay to Sebastian Grazowtski, of New City, Oregon, the sum of EIGHT-THOUSAND SIX-HUNDRED AND THIRTY-NINE DOLLARS ($8,639.00) including interest at 12% per year. This money is to be paid in equal monthly payments of $315.00 (principal only) commencing on September 1, 20xx and continuing until November 1, 20xx, at which time the monthly payments will increase to $440.61 per month until the entire balance of principal and interest is paid.

Should default be made in the payment of any installment when due, then, at the option of the holder of the note, the entire amount of the principal and interest shall become immediately due and payable. In the event of any default on this note, the holder shall be entitled to recover all costs of collection of same, including reasonable attorneys' fees and costs.

_____   _____
Date   Sebastian Grazowtski

_____   _____
Date   Virginia Woo

Equity Investments

If you plan to arrange for an equity investment, you have considerable work to do beyond the scope of this book. In short, you need to have a detailed plan for the legal form of organization you prefer—a general partnership, limited partnership, or small corporation.

Most entrepreneurs form corporations and sell shares to raise money. They are regulated by both the federal Securities and Exchange Commission and by their state's corporation department. All require conformity to numerous regulations designed to protect investors from dishonest promoters.

While the regulations are extensive, they are designed to help the process. For example, some stock offerings can be exempt from expensive filings if they involve a small number of shareholders and a small amount of money. (Chapter 4 discusses corporations and partnerships in more detail.)

> **EXAMPLE:** Wilhelmina Whalen needed $35,000 to start a coffee shop. She decided to form a small corporation and sell an investor 25% of the company for $35,000. If the coffee shop succeeded, as she expected, the 25% investment would be worth $100,000 in three years. Harrison Flyright liked Wilhelmina and her business idea. He offered $25,000 but wanted 50% of the company. Wilhelmina thought that was too high a price and said "No." Sometime later, Harrison increased the amount to $32,000, and Wilhelmina agreed to give him 49% of the stock, thereby retaining control of her business. As a California resident, Wilhelmina incorporated her business using *How to Form Your Own California Corporation,* by Anthony Mancuso (Nolo). She issued 49% of the stock to Harrison in exchange for his cash, and was off and running.

After You Open—Keeping on the Path to Success

Introduction 230

Watch Out for Problem Areas 230

    It's Lonely at the Top 231

    Anticipate Problems Before They Arise 231

    You May Be the Problem and Not the Solution 233

    Plan Beyond Opening Day 233

    Know When You've Succeeded—Or Failed 234

    Prepare for Success 236

Getting Out of Business 237

    Lock the Doors and Leave 237

    Sell the Business 237

    Close the Business and Negotiate With Your Creditors 238

    Hold a Going Out of Business Sale 238

    Declare Bankruptcy 239

Introduction

If you have followed all the steps in this book, you have completed a thorough plan for your business. You should feel good about completing a hard, demanding task. It's also important to remember that completing your plan, finding the money you need, and opening or expanding your business are just the first three steps in your journey.

Many small business books take fairly extreme approaches. Two common ones can be summarized as follows:

- Here comes another lamb to the slaughter—hopefully this book can frighten him out of his dumb idea.
- Anybody can find fame and fortune in a small business; just read this book and get a big strongbox in which to store your surplus gold.

I hope to steer a middle course by offering you both encouragement and caution. In my view, small business is one of the last great frontiers of both individualism and opportunity, but like the prairies of yesteryear, there are more than a few rattlesnakes among the poppies. This chapter contains some highly personal recollections and observations on pitfalls and diversions you may encounter on your way to business success.

Watch Out for Problem Areas

As a small business owner, you'll have to work hard to meet your goals. It takes a lot of determination and drive to make things happen. As a result, you may focus so completely on the immediate goals at hand that you lose sight of the larger picture.

Recognizing that you don't know everything is a good first step toward business success. If you're unsure of yourself in any particular area, please take advantage of the advice and help that is there for the asking. That way, you're less likely to be sabotaged by something you didn't know—and didn't know you didn't know.

It's Lonely at the Top

As a business owner, you often make decisions in a vacuum. Most of the time you won't have immediate peers who understand your business and can also offer you good, dispassionate advice. Probably you have to go it alone, and that can be pretty tough.

You and your business become targets for an army of job seekers, government regulators, charities, competitors, consultants, salespeople, insurance brokers, and so forth. All these people have their own goals and objectives, which may or may not coincide with yours. As a matter of survival, you must become skeptical about what people claim they can do for you or your business. This isn't necessarily either bad or good, it's just the way things are. You are the only one who can decide what is good for your business.

You also have to manage relations with your three primary sources of business success: customers, suppliers, and employees. Again, each person in these groups has her own set of goals and objectives. Your job is to reconcile all those competing interests so that your business prospers.

Incidentally, I hope this doesn't read like a nightmare to you, because it isn't a nightmare. In fact, I think it's one of the best parts about being in business for yourself. As a business owner, you decide the goals and the steps to reach them. The comparison is similar to the difference between riding in the back seat of a car and driving the car. If you're like me, you're a lot more comfortable when you're driving the car.

Axiom: *If you need approval from others to function at your best, you will be uncomfortable as a business owner.*

Advice: *Get tough. Learn how to set goals and reach them. Learn when to take others' views into consideration and when to ignore them.*

Anticipate Problems Before They Arise

Your business plan describes the risks your business faces. Periodically reread that risk discussion to see if you'd like to add anything to the list.

If you're like most people, you'll admit that there may be something you missed and that you don't know what it is.

Things always go wrong in business. Your job is to notice troubles and problems before they become major hurdles. If you don't notice the mistake until others tell you about the unfortunate results, it may be too late for an easy, inexpensive cure.

If your business is like most, you'll spend some time every day creating solutions to problems. But, if you don't like playing detective and prefer sailing along on smooth waters so much that you don't see the first signs of storms, you may have a problem surviving for long.

Here's one way to keep a handle on problems. Every month, make a line-by-line comparison of your monthly actual profit and loss statement to the monthly Profit and Loss Forecast you made for your business plan. That way, you'll see problems as they develop and before they become serious. For example, if your profits are down by $1,400 and your advertising expenses are up by $2,000, you'll want to spend some time analyzing why that happened and what you should do about it.

Another way to spot problems before they become too large is to listen to what your customers, suppliers, and employees say about your business. While some of their comments may be self-serving, you can't afford to ignore all their complaints and suggestions. Experience shows that most customers will tell their friends about a problem they had with your business long before they tell you. So, you may have to develop creative ways to encourage your customers to communicate with you.

Axiom: *The business owner constantly makes small corrections to keep the business on course. The business may fail if the owner falls asleep at the wheel. Complacency kills.*

Advice: *Establish an information system that lets you know when the business goes off course. You may also choose to have an experienced business consultant review your business periodically.*

You May Be the Problem and Not the Solution

"To live is to change, and to be perfect is to have changed often." (John Henry Newman, as quoted in First Data Resources ad in *Credit Card Management*, January 1992, Volume 4, Number 10.) Unfortunately, most people aren't very good at analyzing their own strengths and weaknesses objectively and then changing their behavior to compensate. They just go ahead doing what they've always done, regardless of the outcome.

Many businesses are started by people who are very good at a skill that people demand. But many of these people know little about the complexities of starting and growing a business and can be hurt badly by their lack of knowledge about basic management skills.

Axiom: *Everybody has blind spots. Your blind spots can determine whether your business will succeed or fail.*

Advice: *Ask a friend who knows you well where your blind spots are. You can't afford not to get help if they are critical.*

Plan Beyond Opening Day

To illustrate the importance of planning for the operation of your business after it opens, I'd like to share the experiences of Molly, a friend and former student, who wanted to open a bath supply shop. Molly encountered a long series of depressing obstacles on the way to getting the money to open her business. But since she was both stubborn and a fighter, each setback made her even more determined. In truth, before long, getting the necessary money had become an obsession. Finally Molly succeeded. Unfortunately, at this point she became strangely lethargic. Molly had put an enormous push into opening her business, but she hadn't prepared herself for the gritty day-to-day realities of owning a business. Now Molly lacked energy, innovative ideas, and the knowledge of how to compete in a changing marketplace. Her business closed in 12 months, which was just about how long it took to start it. She lost a lot of money and a lot of pride.

Axiom: *You need a flexible continuing operating plan for your business.*

Advice: *Make sure you can adapt your business plan to changing circumstances.*

Know When You've Succeeded—Or Failed

Success in a small business involves meeting your objectives, especially the one that says you have a positive cash flow by a specific date. Normally it shouldn't take long to know whether your business will meet your objectives.

Many people wait a year or two to see whether the business will succeed. I think that's a mistake. Instead, figure out how long it should take for your potential customers to hear about your opening and then add a month or two. In a retail business, that's usually no more than three to six months, depending on the type of business and how good a promoter you are. Put another way, your sales will probably level out three or four months after you open. People in service, wholesale, and small manufacturing businesses may expect a longer start-up cycle. For example, a real estate agency normally allows six to 12 months for money to begin coming in. That's how long it takes to find clients, negotiate deals, and generally get known in the community.

What if your sales are less than you expected after you have been operating four months? Do you triple the advertising budget and hope that sales will pick up? I hope not. A more sensible approach is to make another business plan, adjusted to the sales you are actually getting. This is psychologically difficult for many people to do. It's all too easy to get hung up on proving that your original plans were right, rather than accepting what the numbers tell you.

EXAMPLE: Pierre, who had never run a business, bought a failed cafe. He was confident in his abilities to turn the cafe around, since he had a degree in hotel management and was an accomplished chef. Pierre projected $30,000 a month in sales and budgeted accordingly. Actual sales in that first three months were $12,000, $18,000, and $16,000. Sales leveled off at the $14,000-per-month level for the next several months, resulting in a first quarter loss of $60,000.

Pierre cut back to where he was only losing $2,000 or $3,000 per month for the next three months, but stuck to the idea that he could generate monthly sales of $30,000. In the meantime, he sold his house and his wife's jewelry to keep up with the bills. Many people suggested that he make cutbacks so that he could make a profit on $14,000 per month or, as an alternative, sell the restaurant. So far, he has refused. If he doesn't take in $30,000 a month soon, he'll go broke.

Pierre's approach is not one I would recommend. Here is how I would tackle this sort of problem. I would take the first four months' total sales and divide by four to get a monthly average. Then I would design a Profit and Loss Forecast to make a profit at that level of sales. To do this, I would have to cut back. I would also pay a lot of attention to both the quality of my food and techniques to get the word out in the community. For example, if Monday and Tuesday evenings were slow, I might close the restaurant and start a cooking class those nights. If my efforts to generate more business failed, I would think about closing.

Axiom: *You can fool yourself into waiting too long for success.*

Advice: *Before you open your doors, establish a time when you will review your business performance to see if you are meeting your goals. This forces you to compare your results to your plan. If your business is not doing as well as it should be early, you still have a chance to make changes before your money and energy run out. If you must close, it's far better to close with a small loss than to hang on and end up in bankruptcy.*

Prepare for Success

Now let's assume your business succeeds. Why shouldn't it? After all, you've planned carefully and worked hard. When it happens, be sure you relax and enjoy your success for a while before you think about your next step. Everyone needs to know how to take a vacation, especially small business owners.

If you're considering expanding, first take a long look at your business and your personal goals. Many wise people would rather make a decent profit with a small business than deal with the headaches of a much bigger business.

Let me illustrate this point with the story of Fred and Fritz, who opened a breakfast restaurant several years ago. After they learned the ropes, they made a good profit. Best of all, they went home every day at 3 p.m. Then they opened a second breakfast restaurant and things were twice as good. Next, they made plans to open two more, on the theory that if two are good, four will be better. This meant they had to run the two existing restaurants while building the new ones. Inevitably, hired employees ended up managing the existing restaurants. About then, interest rates went up and there was a recession. Finally, they got all four restaurants open. The only problem was that without their personal attention, business had dropped 40% at the original locations and was less than half of what was expected at the two new ones. Within two years, they both lost their homes as well as their businesses and were back to working for someone else. Not surprisingly, their new bosses thought it unreasonable for employees to go home at 3 p.m.

Axiom: *Bigger is not necessarily better.*

Advice: *To make your business bigger, plan as carefully as you did when you began. Resist the urge to overexpand. You will very likely continue to do well if you expand slowly and sensibly.*

Getting Out of Business

What if your business is losing money and you've already scaled down your expenses, tried innovative marketing techniques, and made sure you have a high-quality product or service? You'll need to either fundamentally change your business or get out of it. You'll be wise to make these tough decisions promptly if you keep losing money. If you decide to get out of business, you have the following basic options.

Lock the Doors and Leave

Disappearing is almost always a bad idea unless you plan never to come back. Walking out creates more problems than it solves, not to mention the hassles you will cause your landlord, your lender, your other creditors, and your friends.

Sell the Business

This may be a realistic option if your business makes a small profit, or sometimes even if it doesn't. Someone else may be satisfied with less than you are or may have visions of how to make a better profit.

If you can't raise enough cash to pay your creditors and they aren't willing to take less than the face amount of what you owe them, you may have to declare bankruptcy just to get rid of the business. Or, if you're lucky, you may find someone willing to buy your business and try to turn it around.

Make a balance sheet for your business similar to the Personal Financial Statement you created in Chapter 5. A simplified version might look like the following example, although you will want much more detail.

> EXAMPLE: Sally's bookstore has been limping along, almost breaking even for nearly two years, and Sally can't afford to keep the store open any longer. After preparing a balance sheet, Sally sees that if she can sell her business for at least $16,000 cash, she can pay her creditors and come out clean.

Sally's Bookshop: Balance Sheet

Assets

Cash	$ 200
Inventory at cost	32,000
Fixtures and equipment at estimated sales price	5,000
Total Assets	$ 37,200

Liabilities

Accounts payable	$ 15,000
Income taxes and withholding payable	1,000
Total Liabilities	$ 16,000

Close the Business and Negotiate With Your Creditors

If you're losing money every month and don't think your cash flow will improve soon, you can close your doors and make deals with your suppliers and other creditors. You can often negotiate to pay much less than what you owe. You can offer them a small lump sum payment or you can offer to make monthly payments. Either choice can be a good option if you have the money or income to make payments.

Hold a Going Out of Business Sale

This usually involves selling all your merchandise at or below cost. It frequently makes sense for retailers, because inventory of goods for resale is usually the retailer's largest asset. There are firms that make a business of liquidating businesses, or you can do it yourself. A liquidation sale can sometimes be a better idea than selling a business. Take Sally's bookshop, for example. If she could sell her assets at cost, she could pay all her creditors and end up with $21,000 in cash. Even if she only got 45¢ on the dollar, she would come out clean. Auctioneers and liquidators have lots of tricks to get the best prices for everything. It's worth investigating if you're thinking about a sale, especially if you have a lot of inventory.

Declare Bankruptcy

Federal bankruptcy laws are designed to help debt-burdened individuals and businesses get a fresh start. You declare bankruptcy by filing papers in a bankruptcy court. Your creditors are immediately barred from trying to collect what you owe them. So, at least temporarily, creditors, even the IRS, cannot legally empty your bank account, repossess your property, or cut off your utility services. However, with court approval, certain creditors may be entitled to repossess your property or resume their collection efforts.

If you own your business as a sole proprietor, you'll need to declare personal bankruptcy. Your personal debts as well as your business debts can be discharged—that is, wiped out—through the bankruptcy process.

If your business is a partnership or corporation, the business itself can go bankrupt. You won't need to declare personal bankruptcy, however, unless you have business-related debts for which you're personally responsible.

Depending on your particular circumstances, you may have a number of different bankruptcy options available. Most small business owners opt to either:

- lose some of their personal or business assets and cancel their debts, or
- arrange to make payments on past bills from future income while keeping current on new bills and retaining their property. In many cases, past bills may be paid off at a fraction of their face value.

If you are thinking about filing for bankruptcy, you'll need to research your options. Your options will be affected by issues such as:

- the dollar amount of your debt
- whether you want to keep operating the business
- your personal liability—for example, you may have pledged your home or cash for a loan, and

- the type of property you own; some of your personal property is yours to keep, regardless of your bankruptcy.

RESOURCE

For more about bankruptcy options for individuals, see *Solve Your Money Troubles: Debt, Credit & Bankruptcy,* by Robin Leonard and Margaret Reiter (Nolo). For more about bankruptcy options for businesses, see *How to File for Chapter 7 Bankruptcy,* by Stephen Elias and Albin Renauer (Nolo).

12

Good Resources for Small Businesses

Introduction	243
Business Consultants	243
SBA/SCORE	245
State and Local Agencies	246
Private Consultants	246
Books	246
Background Books	247
Choosing a Business	248
Finding Money	249
Marketing/Advertising	250
Personnel	251
Business Location	251
Corporations, Partnerships, and Legal Matters	252
Women in Business	253
General Business	254
Pamphlets	255
Magazines—Continuing Small Business Help	255
Computers and Business	256
How Will You Use a Computer?	256
What Software Do You Need?	257
How Much Computer Do You Need—And How Much Can You Afford?	258
PC or Mac?	259
Where Should You Buy a Computer and Software?	259
Online Business Resources	260
Should You Go Broadband?	260

Using Search Engines.. 261

Business-Oriented Websites... 261

Conferences and Newsgroups.. 262

Formal Education.. 263

Introduction

The key to getting the help you need is knowing in which knowledge or business practice areas you are weak. Once you've pinpointed areas where you need help, think about how you like to learn. Some people prefer classes and study groups, while others do better reading a book or a magazine. Some people benefit most by seeking out a trusted adviser who'll take the time to analyze their situation and make specific suggestions.

As much as possible, the resources below are presented in time-sensitive order. You will receive faster help from the first source listed, business consultants, than you will from the last source, formal education.

Regardless of how you choose to receive information and help, there are many excellent resources available. As a wise consumer, take care to get your money's and time's worth. Just because some person or publication promises to help you doesn't necessarily mean you'll get good results.

Check Out Nolo's Small Business Resources

Nolo (www.nolo.com), the publisher of this book, provides many ways to assist you when it comes to small business information—whether it's researching which is the best business entity, forming a corporation, partnership, or LLC, downloading agreements, or providing lots of free information. Visit the site and click "Business Formation" under "Get Informed."

Business Consultants

Business consultants are people who offer advice about how to run other people's businesses. Most have extensive business experience and want to help people like you succeed. Be careful though—there are some inexperienced and unscrupulous people who call themselves business consultants.

You'll want to select a business consultant based on your needs. The two basic categories consist of:

- **General business consultants.** They look at a business from the owner's perspective and try to solve any and all problems the business has. One of the best ways to use a general business consultant is to meet for an hour or two each month and talk about your plans and upcoming projects. Most good consultants can suggest different ways to reach your goals that will save you time and money.
- **Specialists.** These people are experts in specific fields like advertising, marketing, sales, or employee benefits. Specialists try to solve limited problems as directed by the owner. For example, you may hire an advertising agency to help you introduce a new product.

Use a consultant if you're convinced that the advice will bring in more money than it will cost or you require expertise you don't possess. Bear in mind that a consultant can only give you advice. If you don't follow that advice, then you've wasted your money and everyone's time.

Make sure that you like the consultant as a person; you probably won't listen to advice from someone with whom you're uncomfortable. Ask the consultant to outline how he proposes to approach your problem and about how much his approach will cost you. Your consultant should be open to your feedback on his proposals. If you dislike most of what he proposes, you'll be better off finding another consultant more in line with your thinking.

CAUTION

Consultant or future employee? Sometimes people use consulting as a way to find permanent employment. There's nothing wrong with that. Just make sure that you and your consultant communicate completely if you think that's an issue. You may or may not have any openings or interest in hiring the consultant. You'll want to be clear about the situation before you begin your work together.

Consulting Help

Several small business consultants whom I know and trust helped me with this book. They are available to review business plans for reasonable fees and for general guidance. Roger Pritchard (roger.pritchard @mindspring. com) advises individual small businesses and partnerships in Berkeley, California. His business is called Financial Alternatives and he can be reached at 510-527-5604. Additionally, most CPAs and tax advisers can help you with your plan. If you're not happy with the professionals in your area, I may be able to help. Call me at 415-816-2982 or email me at mckeever.mp@ gmail.com. (Be sure to mention Nolo Business Plan Book in the subject line of the email so I don't trash it as spam.)

SBA/SCORE

This agency of the federal government is organized specifically to help people like you. The primary purpose of the Small Business Administration (SBA) is to help small entrepreneurs find financial assistance. (This is covered in Chapter 4.) The SBA also runs a consulting service called the Service Corps of Retired Executives, or SCORE. This is an organized group of retired business executives who offer free consulting to any business owner.

Most SCORE consultants are genuinely interested in helping you prosper, and they have some valuable experience to share. The only cautionary note I offer is to make sure that you like the consultant and that he has some experience that will be helpful to you. For instance, some SCORE consultants with long, illustrious careers in big business may have little understanding of, or patience with, the problems of small business. If you don't feel the consultant assigned to your case is a good match, don't hesitate to ask for another.

For business owners on a tight budget, the help from SCORE can be invaluable. Make the nearest SCORE office your first stop in looking for help. Or, get more information or make use of their email counseling service at www.score.org.

State and Local Agencies

Many state and local agencies offer advice and assistance in addition to their help with securing financing. In fact, counseling and consulting may be part of the package. Refer to Chapter 4, for resources on how to locate them.

Private Consultants

To begin looking for a private general business consultant or a specialist, start with the local Chamber of Commerce, bankers, and the service clubs like Rotary or Kiwanis to find people with long community ties and stability. Many class instructors and college professors supplement their income by doing private consulting; if you take a class from a person you like and want some personal help, ask.

Books

The books covered in this section offer good information, take a helpful stance, and are easily read by most people. This is my list, not a comprehensive study of the subject. If your local library and bookstores don't have a particular book listed here, try checking with your favorite bookstore's copy of *Books in Print* to see if the book is still available. If so, you can have your bookstore order it for you, or write directly to the publisher. Or, if you're online, check with Amazon (www.amazon.com) or Barnes and Noble (www.barnesandnoble.com).

Oh, and one more thing. Several of the books I list are also published by Nolo. That's because Nolo concentrates on how-to-do-it books and avoids the double-talk that makes many business books virtually unreadable. I recommend their approach highly, especially if you don't have a graduate degree in business administration. After all, a wise man once said that if you can't explain something to a 12-year-old child, you probably don't know your subject thoroughly.

Background Books

Here are some general business books that are particularly helpful for small business owners. As you may already know, when you search for one of these books at Amazon.com or at other online retailers, the product page often contains helpful suggestions for similar books on the same subject.

- *Honest Business*, by Michael Phillips, Salli Rasberry, and Peter Turner (Shambhala Publications). This book might as well be entitled "Zen and the Art of Small Business Success." It is a remarkable book focusing on the personal and psychological qualities it takes to succeed in a small business. Much of this book's advice stands conventional small-business wisdom on its head. A must-read.
- *Small Time Operator*, by Bernard Kamoroff (Taylor Trade Publishing). Gives you the basics of keeping books, paying taxes, renting a building, becoming an employer, and other important business details more thoroughly and better than any other book. If you never buy another business book, buy this one.
- *The E-Myth Revisited*, by Michael E. Gerber (HarperCollins). Contains practical advice about small business management. Also, the author manages a telephone consulting business that specializes in small businesses and employs 30 people; call 800-221-0266 for information about management consulting by telephone.
- *E-Myth Mastery: The Seven Essential Disciplines for Building a World Class Company*, by Michael E. Gerber (HarperBusiness), which is another equally well-recommended title from the E-Myth team.
- *The Small Business Reference Guide: The Complete Guide to Small Business Taxes and Business Start-Up*, by Minute Help Press (www.minutehelpguides.com). The guide to navigating all the forms and tax requirements when you're first starting a business. When you don't have time to get an answer from a CPA, use this.

- *Growing a Business*, by Paul Hawken (Simon & Schuster). This is a well-reviewed classic on moving beyond the start-up phase.
- *The Boss's Book List*, by John M. Fischette (author and publisher). A definitive list of idea sources from business leaders.
- *Free Help from Uncle Sam to Start or Expand Your Business*, by Fred Hess (e-book). Guide to getting help from many government agencies. Includes a listing of programs and which agency to contact.

Choosing a Business

If you're having trouble selecting a business idea, you'll be interested in these books:

- *101 Best Businesses to Start*, by Russell Roberts (Crown Business). A comprehensive guide that includes cost and competitive factors on 101 businesses.
- *101 Businesses That You Can Start!* by Karen Powers (e-book). Lists numerous ideas for low-cost businesses you can operate either offline or online.
- *Ultimate Homebased Business Handbook*, by James Stephenson and Rich Mintzer (Entrepreneur Press). Run your business from home—some of the most successful companies were started from a kitchen, a spare room, even a garage.
- *The Franchise Ratings Guide: 3,000 Franchisees Expose the Best & Worst Franchise Opportunities,* by Gary M. Kowalski (iUniverse, Inc.). More helpful advice on franchising.
- *Adams Businesses You Can Start Almanac,* by Editors of Adams Media (Adams Media). Ideas and choices for starting a business.
- *To Build the Life You Want, Create the Work You Love: The Spiritual Dimension of Entrepreneuring,* by Marsha Sinetar (St. Martin's). A spiritual approach to finding satisfaction in your business.
- *Do What You Love, the Money Will Follow: Discovering Your Right Livelihood*, by Marsha Sinetar (Dell). I recommend this book, which has become a cult classic on the relationship between motivation and reward.

Finding Money

If you need more help getting your business idea funded, these books may provide some good ideas:

- *The Directory of Venture Capital & Private Equity Firms, 2014 Edition* (Grey House Publishing). A definitive list.
- *Get Financing Now: How to Navigate Through Bankers, Investors, and Alternative Sources for the Capital Your Business Needs,* by Charles H. Green (McGraw-Hill). Up to date and well-reviewed; includes lists of sources and negotiating tips.
- *Attracting Capital from Angels,* by Brian Hill and Dee Power (John Wiley & Sons). Angels can be the best money source—read this book if you're looking for an angel.
- *Business Loans From Family & Friends,* by Asheesh Advani (Nolo). This excellent book goes beyond most investment or small business guides to tell how to tap into resources of those you know.
- *Financing Your Small Business: From SBA Loans and Credit Cards to Common Stock and Partnership Interests.* by James E. Burk and Richard P. Lehmann (Sourcebooks). Get a handle on the territory before starting.
- *How to Get the Financing for Your New Small Business: Innovative Solutions from the Experts Who Do It Every Day,* by Sharon Fullen (Atlantic Publishing). Here's some practical help.
- *How to Raise Capital: Techniques and Strategies for Financing and Valuing your Small Business,* by Jeffrey Timmons, Stephen Spinelli, and Andrew Zacharakis (McGraw-Hill). Here's more down-to-earth help.
- *Going Public: The Theory and Evidence on How Companies Raise Equity Finance,* by Tim Jenkinson, Alexander Ljungqvist, and Jay Ritter (Oxford University Press). Get the overview of public stock offerings, which can be an expensive journey.

Marketing/Advertising

- *Marketing Without Advertising*, by Michael Phillips and Salli Rasberry (Nolo). An essential book about advertising and marketing. An indispensable source to help you understand your business from the customer's perspective.
- *Marketing High Technology*, by William H. Davidow (The Free Press). Although the book discusses a few specific high-tech products, it is about the principles that define a product, as opposed to a device, from the customer's perspective rather than from an inventor's point of view. Absolutely necessary for anyone considering a new product.
- *Positioning: The Battle for Your Mind*, by Al Ries and Jack Trout (McGraw-Hill). This book invents the concept of distinguishing you from your competition in the customer's mind. It explains how that process works and how positioning has become one of the most important factors in business success.
- *Repositioning: Marketing in an Era of Competition, Change and Crisis* by Jack Trout (McGraw-Hill). An update by the man who created the positioning concept.
- *Exceptional Service, Exceptional Profit: The Secrets of Building a Five-Star Customer Service Organization*, by Leonardo Inghilleri, and Micah Solomon (AMACOM). Primer on service; necessary for businesses where service counts.
- *Guerrilla Marketing: Easy and Inexpensive Strategies for Making Big Profits from Your Small Business*, by Jay Conrad Levinson (Houghton Mifflin). A classic updated; essential reading.
- *The Elements of Copywriting: The Essential Guide to Creating Copy That Gets the Results You Want*, by Gary Blake and Robert W. Bly (Longman). This text can help you create effective ad copy.
- *Web Copy That Sells: The Revolutionary Formula for Creating Killer Copy That Grabs Their Attention and Compels Them to Buy*, by Maria Veloso (AMACOM). Writing ads that sell for any medium.

Personnel

If you need to hire anyone, you may want to glance through:

- *Smart Hiring (Quick Start Your Business),* by Robert W. Wendover (Sourcebooks). Essential reading if you can't afford an HR consultant.
- *Smart Staffing: How to Hire, Reward and Keep Top Employees for Your Growing Company,* by Wayne Outlaw (Kaplan Business). Essential reading if you can't afford an HR consultant.
- *The Employer's Legal Handbook,* by Fred S. Steingold (Nolo). Steingold shows you how to comply with the most recent workplace laws and regulations, run a safe and fair workplace, and avoid lawsuits.
- *Love 'Em or Lose 'Em: Getting Good People to Stay,* 4th edition, by Beverly Kaye and Sharon Jordan-Evans (Berrett-Koehler Publishers). The inside information on keeping good people.

Business Location

Running a business out of a home has its own special issues. You'll be interested in:

- *Work at Home Now: The No-Nonsense Guide to Finding Your Perfect Home-Based Job, Avoiding Scams, and Making a Great Living,* by Christine Durst and Michael Haaren (Career Press). Step-by-step guide to a good home-based work life.

If you'll be looking for business space outside your home, see:

- *Negotiate the Best Lease for Your Business,* by Fred S. Steingold and Janet Portman (Nolo). This practical handbook explains how to analyze your space needs, find the ideal location at the right price, and negotiate a lease that will protect your short- and long-term business interests.

Corporations, Partnerships, and Legal Matters

As I discussed in Chapter 4, you may want to organize your business as a partnership, limited partnership, or closely held corporation. The following materials will prove helpful.

Corporations

- *Incorporate Your Business: A Legal Guide to Forming a Corporation in Your State*, by Anthony Mancuso (Nolo). Includes easy-to-read instructions on forming a corporation in any state, with tips on unique tax benefits, investment attraction, and more.
- *How to Form Your Own California Corporation,* by Anthony Mancuso (Nolo). Includes step-by-step instructions on how to incorporate a new or already existing business in California. The book comes complete with all tear-out forms necessary, including articles, bylaws, and stock certificates.
- *Inc. Yourself,* by Judith H. McQuown (Career Press). A popular guide to the "maze of legal and financial vagaries" of incorporating.
- *How to Form a Nonprofit Corporation*, by Anthony Mancuso (Nolo). Applies to all states. Explains all the legal formalities involved in forming and operating a tax-exempt nonprofit corporation.
- *Form Your Own Limited Liability Company*, by Anthony Mancuso (Nolo). Provides the step-by-step instructions and forms business-people need to form an LLC. Includes how to handle ongoing legal issues and tax paperwork.

Partnerships

- *Form a Partnership: The Complete Legal Guide,* by Denis Clifford and Ralph Warner (Nolo). The book includes just about everything a small business owner needs to know to establish his or her own partnership. The book also discusses limited partnerships, but in less detail.
- *Compatibility Breeds Success: How to Manage Your Relationship with Your Business Partner*, by Marvin Snider (Praeger Publishers). Deals

with the real issues of how to make a successful business with a real person.

Legal Matters

- *Legal Guide for Starting & Running a Small Business*, by Fred S. Steingold (Nolo). A comprehensive guide to making decisions about legal matters in business. Includes tax-saving methods, buying a franchise or an existing business, hiring and firing employees, and resolving business disputes.

- *J.K. Lasser's Legal and Corporation Forms for the Smaller Business*, by Arnold Goldstein (Macmillan). This book comes with a disk that includes many forms.

- *Legal Research: How to Find & Understand the Law*, by Stephen Elias and the Editors of Nolo (Nolo). A good book on doing your own legal research.

- *Everybody's Guide to Small Claims Court*, by Ralph Warner (Nolo). Can help you if you ever find yourself holding a handful of bad checks. It's a guide on how to properly prepare a small claims court case—which is far more than half the battle. It also contains good advice on who, where, and how to sue.

- *The Encyclopedia of Business Letters, Faxes, and Emails*, by Robert W. Bly and Regina Anne Kelly (Career Press). This is an indispensable guide for writers of correspondence.

- *The Complete Book of Business Legal Forms (Legal Survival Guides)*, by James Ray (Sphinx Publishing). A complete set of "ready-to-go" forms and instructions.

- *Ultimate Book of Business Forms (Ultimate Series)*, by Entrepreneur Press and Karen Thomas (Entrepreneur Press). More than 250 customizable forms covering all aspects of business.

Women in Business

These books are specifically geared to women who are starting or running their own businesses:

- *The Women's Small Business Start-Up Kit: A Step-by-Step Legal Guide,* by Peri Pakroo (Nolo).
- *A Woman's Guide to Successful Negotiating,* by Lee E. Miller and Jessica Miller (McGraw-Hill Trade).
- *Play Like a Man, Win Like a Woman: What Men Know About Success That Women Need to Learn,* by Gail Evans (Broadway Books).
- *Her Place at the Table: A Woman's Guide to Negotiating Five Key Challenges to Leadership Success,* by Deborah M. Kolb, Ph.D., Judith Williams, Ph.D., and Carol Frohlinger, J.D., (Jossey-Bass). How to get there from women who have done it.
- *Money, A Memoir: Women, Emotions, and Cash,* by Liz Perle (Henry Holt and Co.). Some women have issues about money that interfere with their success—here's how to deal with them.

General Business

Here are some good general business books:
- *Entrepreneur and Small Business Problem Solver*, by William A. Cohen (Wiley). You need this book unless you never have any business problems. It tells you how to do almost anything you want, from hiring a sales rep to negotiating a lease. Expensive, but highly recommended.
- *Industry Norms and Key Business Ratios 2014*, by Mergent (Dun & Bradstreet). Annual listing of financial results of 800 business lines; helps plan your projections. Expensive, but worth it if you're unsure about financial norms for your business. Try your library first.
- *RMA Annual Statement Studies* (Risk Management Association, www.rmahq.org). Used by banks for analyzing business loan requests. Compiles current and historical financial data for nearly 350 industries by company asset and sales size. Expensive, so try your library first.
- *Sourcebook of Zip Code Demographics* (CACI, 800-292-CACI). Provides population and income data by zip code.

Pamphlets

Well-written pamphlets may give you the information or background you need on a specific topic:

- *Small Business Administration.* The SBA has gone digital, and all SBA educational materials are now available online at: http://www.sba.gov/tools/sba-learning-center/search/everything. Some of the older print materials may be available in the library, but you'll need Internet access to take full advantage of the latest information from the SBA.
- *IRS publications.* Especially helpful publications include *Tax Guide for Small Business* and *Employer's Tax Guide.* People planning partnerships will also want to read an IRS pamphlet, *Partnerships,* IRS Publication 541. Call a local IRS number or 800-829-1040, or check its website at www.irs.gov.

Magazines—Continuing Small Business Help

Most big business publications, such as *The Wall Street Journal, Business Week,* and *Forbes,* are not directly helpful to the little guy. In addition, every industry has a trade magazine that offers practical advice specific to that industry (and you can find these magazines using any Internet search engine). For general business questions, here are several publications I find of more value to start-ups:

- *Inc.* (www.inc.com). This is primarily oriented toward big small businesses (or small big ones), but nevertheless is well put together and helpful.
- *Entrepreneur* (http://entrepreneur.com). This magazine is normally available from your local newsstand. It covers a great many business opportunities in depth and purports to give all the secrets needed to be successful in the hottest new fields.

Computers and Business

A computer can be a wonderful time-saver that enables you to accomplish more than you could imagine. Or a computer can be a frustrating time sink that interferes with your ability to make your business work. It takes time to learn how to use a computer and to correct the inevitable mistakes you'll make along the way. This section should help you assess your particular situation and figure out what kind of computer system best fits the needs of your business.

How Will You Use a Computer?

Any of the following business activities will undoubtedly be easier when done by computer:
- maintaining a large customer base
- carrying accounts receivable or accounts payable
- stocking many inventory items
- ordering products frequently
- advertising through the mail
- tracking customers' buying habits
- frequently writing letters, reports, articles, or other literature
- making catalogues, brochures, or other marketing materials
- writing a large number of payroll checks (unless you plan to use an outside payroll service), and
- engaging in extensive financial analyses that would require the use of spreadsheets.

It's important to keep in mind that using a computer won't improve your efficiency one bit if what you really need is a change of management philosophy. For example, if you're having problems keeping financial records, a new or upgraded computer or cutting-edge software won't automatically solve your problem. You'll still need to get organized and make sure the data is entered correctly.

What Software Do You Need?

Since a key reason to have a computer is to use various software programs, a good way to start figuring out which computer to buy is by defining which programs you'll use.

Computer stores and online sellers can boggle you with the vast array of available programs. Do yourself a favor and start by answering this simple question: What tasks do I want a computer to handle? Once you've made a list of tasks you want your computer to perform, you can go online or visit a computer store to see which programs have the features you want.

Before buying software:

- Consider user reviews posted online, for example, customer reviews at www.cnet.com or www.amazon.com, or read professional reviews at *PC World* (www.pcworld.com), CNET (www.cnet.com), or ZD Net (www.zdnet.com).

- Talk to a business that's already doing the same computerized tasks that you want to do. They'll probably be happy to show you how well—or poorly—their system works.

- Look at computer magazines (for example, *PC World* or *PC Magazine*), that generally devote a large portion of every issue to a side-by-side comparison of specific programs, such as accounting or payroll tools.

- Comparison shop for the best prices using a "shopping bot" such as Yahoo Shopping (http://shopping.yahoo.com/search) or Google Shopping (from the Google home page, click on the "Apps" icon in the upper right corner, then click on "More," and choose "Shopping").

Find out everything you can about the different programs and what computer systems they run on.

How Much Computer Do You Need— And How Much Can You Afford?

The software programs and tools you purchase affect how much computer you need and vice versa. Check out the system requirements for the software, including the amount of hard disk space required, whether you need a CD-ROM drive, how much memory is required, what operating systems can be used, and what type of processor is needed. Keep in mind that many programs set two standards: minimum requirements and recommended requirements. As a general rule, you should attempt to meet the recommended, not the minimum, requirements.

Also keep in mind that under Moore's Law, computer processing speed doubles every 18 months. For that reason, you should purchase a computer with the fastest processor and the most memory that fits into your budget. It's an unfortunate reality that computers are increasing their speed and storage capabilities (hard disk space) at almost alarming rates, with software manufacturers creating software that utilizes most of what the newest systems offer. The good news is that processor speed, memory, and storage continue to drop in price as they increase in efficiency.

Perhaps luckily, more and more software companies offer "cloud" computing systems; a "cloud" system means your data is stored on a remote website that you can access through an Internet connection. Frequently, these services are available on a monthly subscription basis. The advantages are that your up-front cash need is reduced, since you don't have to buy the software and your in-house computer system may not need to be as advanced. The disadvantages are that you need a very fast and very reliable Internet connection and that your data is stored elsewhere and may be more vulnerable to data theft. Think about your growth projections carefully before you choose which type to use—once installed, it is a bear to change a system.

If possible, make sure the computer system can be expanded at a reasonable cost. Potential upgrades may include a new video card, additional RAM, extra hard drives, and a DVD-RW drive. If you don't understand the upgrade potential or limitations of a computer system, you're wise to educate yourself before plunking down thousands of your hard-earned dollars. Again, websites such as CNET (www.cnet.com) and ZD Net (www.zdnet.com) can help.

PC or Mac?

When purchasing one or more computers for your small business, a basic choice you'll have to make is between IBM PC compatibles (PCs) and Apple Macintoshes (Macs). Historically, it's been less expensive to buy, repair, and upgrade PCs than Macs. And for most businesses—with the exception of companies that create music, art, and video—PCs are the preferred platform for the extensive business software that's available.

The main selling point of the Mac (or other Apple computers) has been the ease of setting up and using the hardware and software, as well as the innovative features (which are often later adopted in PCs).

In summary, for general business tasks, you're better off with a PC. If your business is involved in graphic, music, video, or creative productions, consider a Mac. Also, keep in mind that some businesses have broken away from both the Windows and Mac worlds by moving to Linux, a UNIX-based free operating system. For more information on the Linux revolution, consult Linux Online (www.linux.com).

Where Should You Buy a Computer and Software?

If you're a novice, you need to know about your three main sources for buying a computer system:

- **Purchase from a local store.** One option is to buy your computer at a nearby store, which can hopefully help you through your learning curve. Many local computer stores can assemble a computer to your specifications or business needs—check your local yellow pages. Large chains such as Best Buy and Wal-Mart often have good prices on computers and software, but may not offer the same customer service as smaller stores.
- **Mail order from a reseller.** The second option is to buy your computer from a mail-order house, for example, PC/Mac Connection or CDW, which resells computers manufactured by companies such as Apple, Hewlett-Packard, or Acer, to name just a few.

- **Order from manufacturer.** Another option is to buy your computer directly from the manufacturer, such as Apple, Hewlett-Packard, Dell, or Gateway. Most manufacturers have very good support and repair policies, but you may have to ship your system back if you have a problem.

Some computer stores, and most system manufacturers (especially through mail-order), include preinstalled software with the purchase price or give you a discount when you buy your computer system.

Useful magazines for selecting computer systems and software include *PC Magazine*, *PC World*, *MacWorld*, and *MacUser*. You may also want to go to your local bookstore or library to browse through books written for people who are buying or using computers.

Online Business Resources

Once you sign up with an Internet Service Provider (ISP) and have access to the Web, you'll be able to find information on virtually any aspect of running a small business—from raising start-up money to minimizing the tax bill for a profitable business, and everything in between. There are many sites dedicated to small business issues, often with a particular focus such as marketing or management. It's safe to say that no matter what your area of interest, you'll be able to find information to suit your needs.

Should You Go Broadband?

Your choice of ISP is affected by the speed by which you want to connect to the Internet. You can connect via dial-up modems (regular phone lines) or over high-speed broadband systems, such as DSL phone lines or coaxial cable (the same system that carries cable TV signals). Broadband costs twice as much as dial-up service and the rates are on the way up (the average monthly broadband bill is approximately $25–$30). Broadband is especially recommended if you plan on developing and regularly maintaining a website or if you will be relying on Internet downloads (or uploads) to transact business or manage sales.

Using Search Engines

Much of the navigating process online consists of searching the Web for certain words or phrases related to business issues. Search engines (websites that look for information) come and go, but none performs as consistently and efficiently as Google.com. In addition to providing links to relevant websites, Google provides thumbnail illustrations culled from the search terms as well as newsgroup commentary on the search terms. For more advanced searches using multiple fields and connectors, try Google's Advanced Search Features. If you are a heavy Google user, you can download the Google Toolbar (found at Google.com) and you won't have to keep returning to the Google home page to perform each search.

In addition to Google, there are master search engines like Copernic (www.copernic.com) or Dogpile (www.dogpile.com) that search using several individual search engines simultaneously.

Business-Oriented Websites

There are many websites providing information about business management and business plans. Particularly with the explosion of e-commerce, business has become one of the most popular online subjects. To find these sites, a good bet is to use a search engine. When you enter the terms you're interested in, such as "business plan," "contracts," or "incorporating," the search engine will retrieve the websites that contain those keywords, and hopefully the information you want.

Once you've found a site, be sure to check whether it has a collection of helpful links. Websites often provide a list of links to sites that they assume readers may want to visit. In effect, your homework has already been done for you—the creators of the site have found other worthwhile sites and are sharing their knowledge with you. This is one of the best ways to find other related sites.

Although you'll want to do your own searching for the most up-to-date and interesting sites, below are two good sites that will help in the preparation of a business plan:

- U.S. Small Business Administration (www.sba.gov). There's lots and lots of helpful information at the SBA site.
- Center for Business Planning (www.businessplans.org) provides links to relevant articles and sample business plans.

Conferences and Newsgroups

In addition to the information presented in various websites, there are lots of opportunities for businesspeople to interact on the Web, and many won't cost you a cent. Some websites offer chat rooms where you can communicate "real time" with others who are present, basically by typing in a question or comment that will appear to everyone else in the chat room instantaneously. Any replies will also appear to all participants as soon as they are submitted. Other sites maintain bulletin boards, sometimes called conferences, where users submit questions or comments which appear on the board for others to see. If another user wants to reply to a given post, she submits a response, which also gets posted. In this way, some topics generate long "conversations" among users, which are often called "threads." By reading and joining in these threads, you can learn from other people who have similar interests and perhaps more experience than you in a particular area. Of course, it's up to you to decide if other posters really know what they're talking about.

To find sites that offer chat rooms or conferences, the easiest method is to start by using a search engine such as Google. Go to https://groups. google.com and type in the subject that you're interested in, for example "business plans." That will lead you to chat rooms and message boards where the topic of business plans is discussed. Another method of locating chat rooms and message boards is to simply look around. Visit business-related sites such as Entrepreneur.com (www.entrepreneur.com) and look for chat room or message board options. The Well (www.well. com) has ongoing conferences on hundreds of topics, including small business. While many conferences are free, there is a small monthly fee to join The Well.

Another interactive area of the Internet is called the Usenet. The Usenet offers thousands of topic-related conferences called newsgroups. The scope of the Usenet's subject areas is truly staggering. Like conferences described above, a newsgroup consists of an ongoing discussion among users who post messages to the group. Unlike conferences, however, the Usenet isn't accessed from a website; it occupies its own realm of the Internet. For information about how to utilize Usenet, check Google's Usenet references (www.faqs.org/usenet), Usenet.org (www.usenet.org), or the Usenet Launch Pad (www.ibiblio.org/usenet-i/home-old.html). There are no fees to use the Usenet.

Formal Education

If you're a little weak in some important business areas, such as basic marketing, you may want to investigate some classes. But that doesn't mean that you have to enroll in a two-year MBA program with a major in marketing just to learn a little about how to sell your products.

The best way to spend your time and money wisely is to know specifically what you want to learn. If you have a certain direction in mind, you will be less likely to take a class that doesn't help you or to be taken in by a slick promoter. Study the class outline carefully to make sure you need the material covered in the class. Also make sure that the instructor is well qualified. Avoid classes that offer to solve all your problems or make you rich in one day; they are probably trying to sell you something. Here are your basic choices:

- **High school business classes.** Many high schools offer continuing education programs in evening classes. These classes provide basic, fundamental information and skills and generally don't offer the sophistication or broad coverage that you'll require. They can be an excellent choice if you lack a basic skill you'll need in your business. For example, high school bookkeeping classes and accounting classes can give you a basic foundation of knowledge and practical skills.
- **Junior or community college business programs.** Business education is a vital part of many two-year colleges. Classes often are taught by professionals from the community and offer specific, real-world

information. The more popular classes are commonly taught in both day and evening sessions. You usually can take just the classes that interest you, unless you wish to enroll in a structured degree or certificate program.

- **Short classes and extension programs.** Some colleges and universities offer a variety of classes that are not part of a degree program. Some of these classes take place in one or two days, while others take longer.
- **Universities and colleges.** Most universities and colleges offer classes only to students enrolled in a four-year program. Courses tend to be academically rigorous, but provide limited practical business information.
- **Graduate business schools.** Many universities have specialized business schools and offer graduate degrees called a Master's Degree in Business Administration (MBA) for students who have received a four-year college degree. I don't think an MBA degree is necessary to succeed in small business. I'm aware of no relationship between academic achievement and small business success. In fact, an MBA hinders some people.
- **Entrepreneurial, profit-making programs.** Private promoters organize many classes and private seminars. Some classes can be very valuable, but many are a complete waste of time and money. Fees can range anywhere from free to hundreds of dollars. And supposedly free or inexpensive seminars can be ploys to induce you to buy something later.

Business Plan for a Small Service Business

Service businesses have simple financial projections. Usually, fixed expenses are equal to total costs and the owner's objective is to make sure that sales revenue exceeds fixed expenses. Investors and lenders look for proof of the plan's revenue forecasts, since the plan succeeds or fails on that forecast. The following plan contains a thorough projection of sales revenue and a discussion of why the owner thinks the revenue forecasts are achievable.

This plan contains a different way of looking at a Cash Flow Forecast. I think this different presentation is easy to follow. You can use this new format or the format in Chapter 7.

I lost track of the owner and don't know whether she was successful. The plan is for a small personnel agency located in a city of about 70,000, which specializes in placing people in secretarial, clerical, and word processing positions. Basically, all you need to get started in this business is a state license (in many states), a desk, and a telephone. However, as in most other businesses, to do well you also need to know the business intimately, be able to manage your time effectively, have good sales ability, and be convinced that you will succeed.

This plan would benefit from a more thorough presentation of its components, and I recommend that your plan take the more thorough route.

FORM
The text of this Business Plan for a Small Service Business is included on this book's companion page on Nolo.com. See Appendix D for details.

Business Plan

CENTRAL PERSONNEL AGENCY

By: Eleanor Buss

November 3, 20xx

Table of Contents

A. Introduction and Request for Funds..3

B. My Experience and Background...3

C. Resume: Eleanor "Ellie" Buss 5

D. Business Description of Central Personnel Agency 6

E. Central Personnel Agency Marketing Plan 6

    1. How I Will Find Qualified Employees...6

    2. Competition 7

    3. Market Growth...8

F. Financial Projections 9

    1. Introduction..9

    2. Loan Security 9

    3. Profit and Loss and Cash Flow Forecasts..9

G. Personal Financial Statement: Eleanor "Ellie" Buss...................................... 10

H. Business Risk Analysis.. 11

    1. Partner Problems... 11

    2. Competition... 12

    3. Slow Times 12

    4. Owner's Ability.. 12

I. Capital Spending Plan 13

J. Personal Goals 14

A. Introduction and Request for Funds

This is a request for a loan of $6,000 to establish the Central Personnel Agency as my sole proprietorship. Central Personnel will specialize in providing South City employers with secretarial, clerical, and computer (word processing) skilled personnel. I am presently a junior partner in Mid-Mountain Personnel Services, a similar type of personnel agency with headquarters in North City. I manage the branch office in South City. Mid-Mountain provides me with an office in a good, downtown location and a moderate salary. I like what I do and feel that helping people find work is a creative and satisfying activity.

The $6,000 loan, which I am hereby requesting, will enable me to open my own employment agency, make my own business decisions, and substantially increase my income. To do this, I will be competing with my former employer, Ms. Jackie McCabe (dba Mid-Mountain Personnel Agency), to some extent, even though her headquarters is, and will remain, in North City. To minimize any hostility that could hurt business, I have kept Ms. McCabe informed of my plans. She supports them, has agreed to allow me to take over the lease on the South City Office, and is enthusiastic about working out a referral plan under which we will work cooperatively when we are dealing with employers located in each other's prime geographical area.

My best estimate of sales revenue and cash flow (both of which are spelled out in detail in this plan) shows that even using conservative estimates, I will earn a significant profit once my new business has been underway six months. My background experience in the personnel agency field, and past record of success, support my view that I will succeed. I am eager to begin.

B. My Experience and Background

As my resume sets out in detail, since 2002, I have worked for three different employment agencies in this area, successfully finding jobs for many people. This has given me the opportunity to learn the personnel agency business thoroughly, including how to find employers needing workers and how to locate and screen desirable employees.

During the years I was acquiring this valuable experience, I always planned to open my own business. In the hope of achieving this goal, I formed a partnership with Ms. Jackie McCabe, who has operated Mid-Mountain Personnel Service in North City for several years. As a junior partner, my responsibility was to open a South City branch office, which I did. My goals were to increase my income and to have more control over business decisions than I had as an employee. While the personal relationship between Ms. McCabe and myself is cordial, the partnership has not worked to our mutual satisfaction. This has been largely because Jackie's main office in North City has grown so fast it has consumed all of her energy. This has left me operating the South City branch largely by myself, at the same time that a substantial portion of the profits I have generated go to Jackie under the terms of our partnership agreement.

As part of terminating our partnership agreement, Jackie and I have agreed that I will retain the lease on the present Mid-Mountain office in South City. In addition, we have signed a written agreement (available upon request) that provides that we will share all fees and commissions when one of us places an employee with an employer in the other's primary market area. Having made this agreement, I need accomplish only two more tasks before I can open my business. The first is to take and pass the state personnel agency license examination. I expect to do this in January with little difficulty, as I have received top grades in the preparatory course given by North State Community College. My other task involves the purpose of this proposal. I need to borrow enough money to begin business.

C. Resume: Eleanor "Ellie" Buss

Address:	564 Sampson Avenue, South City, OR 96785; Telephone 567-8976
Business Address:	c/o Mid-Mountain Personnel Services, 453 Second Street, Suite 300, South City, OR 97208; Telephone 765-8970
Marital Status:	Single

Professional Experience:

May 2003 to Date **Junior Partner, Mid-Mountain Personnel Services.** As account executive, I locate employers needing assistance; meet with employers to ascertain their personnel requirements; screen, counsel, and evaluate applicants; and refer qualified applicants to employers. Also, I assist applicants in preparing resumes and in preparing for interviews. I average ten placements per month, of which one-half are positions where the applicant pays the fees; my gross average billings are $3,500 per month.

2002 to 2003 **Account Executive, Woodshaft Personnel Agency.** Responsible for all the same functions as listed above. Average gross billing was $3,500 per month, which represented an average of ten placements per month.

2002 **Trainee Account Executive, Yolo Personnel Agency.** Screened and evaluated applicants; solicited job openings with appropriate clients; completed placements; average billings $2,500 per month.

2001 **Purchasing Agent, Parsifone Electric.** Ordered material and inventory to coincide with contract process; estimated commercial and residential jobs; negotiated all materials purchased to assure cost control and maintain profit margin on bids.

2000 to 2001 **Scheduler, Graphicscan.** Production scheduling for printing and graphic studio; estimated jobs for clients.

1995 to 2000 **Production Scheduler, Acme Pre-Built Components Co.** Scheduler/coordinator for large manufacturer of structural components; coordinated finish room schedule with customer priority and transportation availability; interfaced with other departments and sales staff to ensure customer satisfaction.

D. Business Description of Central Personnel Agency

Central Personnel will specialize in secretarial, clerical, word processing, and computer operator jobs, a field in which there is constant turnover. I will also provide services for technical and midmanagement jobs, but expect it to take several years before these latter areas provide a substantial portion of my income.

My particular specialty will be women reentering the workforce after completing family-raising responsibilities. In this connection, I have developed a successful liaison with the South City Women's Resource Center. This group, which is partially funded by grants from local businesses, provides training, seminars, and counseling for reentry women and will provide me with a source of many highly motivated potential employees.

Because of my history in the personnel business in South City, I have placed many employees and expect that the already developing trend toward much of my business coming from repeats and referrals will continue. Also, in cooperation with the Women's Resource Center, I shall continue to provide detailed counseling to applicants (especially those who have been out of the labor market for several years or more) on how to compose resumes and take interviews, as well as on which jobs to seek. In addition, I plan to work closely with employers to assist them in determining what type of employee they need, how much they should pay, etc. I want employers to feel that my prescreening is honest and thorough and that by dealing with me they can save time by not having to interview clearly unsuitable candidates.

E. Central Personnel Agency Marketing Plan

1. How I Will Find Qualified Employees

The secret to success in the personnel business in South City is finding high-quality employee applicants. Because of the relatively rapid turnover among clerical employees, and because the South City economy is expanding, it is relatively easy to place highly motivated employees with good skills once they have been identified. Because of my prior experience in this business and this area, many of my initial candidates will come from repeats and referrals from people I have placed. Others will be referred as part of my work with the Women's Resource Center.

In my experience, there are several other effective marketing techniques to develop a wider community base. Classified advertising of job openings develops many prospective employees. Also, maintaining an active presence in the Chamber of Commerce and other traditional business and civic organizations enables prospective employers to recognize me as a person of integrity and stability. In addition, as discussed above, I shall continue to expand my association with the South City Women's Resource Center, a group that counsels women reentering the labor force. I also intend to provide free seminars of my own on "How to Find a Satisfying Job." Finally, I will regularly mail a brief newsletter to all major area employers listing all the job areas for which I have qualified applicants.

2. Competition

South City has three active personnel agencies in addition to the branch of Mid-Mountain, which I now run and which will close as part of the opening of my new business.

a. Bill's Personnel Services: This is the oldest and largest in the city. Recently, Bill's has suffered from their own high employee turnover, largely because it is run by an absentee owner. Bill's traditionally advertises heavily and depends on aggressive pricing policies to compete. They provide little employee counseling and, in my opinion, do not screen potential employees with sufficient thoroughness. At Mid-Mountain, I have already demonstrated that my personal approach to the needs of both employers and employees as opposed to Bill's high-volume approach is welcomed by the South City marketplace.

b. Strictly Business: This firm was recently acquired by an experienced professional counselor who heads a staff of three good counselors. Its primary emphasis is on technical management people and it handles clerical and computer operator jobs only as a sideline. Eventually, Strictly Business will be a competitor as I develop more midlevel management clients, but initially, they will not be a problem as our markets are so different.

c. The Woodshaft Organization: This agency has a staff of three and is directly competitive. Woodshaft spends about $1,000 per month on advertising, but does little work with community organizations such as the South City Women's Resource Center. The owner's husband died recently and as an understandable result, the business seems to lack energy. I believe that the Woodshaft Organization will offer the most competition over the next several years. However, because of the expanded South City job market, my own proven track record at Mid-Mountain, and my commitment to hard, creative work, I feel there is plenty of room for my new enterprise to prosper.

3. Market Growth

South City has a large number of the type of jobs I specialize in, with plenty of growth potential. Most of the other agencies are more interested in technical job categories. South City's growth as a regional financial and market center will ensure commensurate growth in job openings and should encourage the trend for women to reenter the job market. My approach to counseling both employers and employees is unique locally and I expect a continuing growth from my commitment to individual service, because this approach saves everyone time and expense in the long run.

My new downtown location (the office I will take over from Mid-Mountain) is already established, convenient, and close to the Women's Resource Center, with which I work closely.

TIP
Note: If you plan a large service business and need to borrow more money, it would be wise to back up this section with growth projection statistics. These are probably available from local banks, the Chamber of Commerce, and so on.

F. Financial Projections

1. Introduction

The key to the prosperity of Central Personnel Agency lies in quickly getting the business into the black and then building on that initial success.

The Profit and Loss and Cash Flow Forecasts in this section show a significant profit and positive cash flow from the beginning of operations. These results depend on my ability to generate revenue at the rate of $4,000 per month for the first two months and $5,000 for each month thereafter. I have no doubt about my ability to do this based on the job orders already on the books. This is because I have most of the employee applications necessary to fill these jobs on file and know how to locate the rest. And even if my revenue forecasts for the first two months are off by as much as $1,500 per month (37.5%), I will still be able to pay business expenses, service the loan, and cover my basic living expenses.

2. Loan Security

My personal financial statement is included in Section G, below. I believe my personal signature is more than enough security for a loan of $6,000, since I have substantial assets. Nevertheless, I will consider the possibility of pledging some assets as additional security if appropriate. Incidentally, my past personal credit reports will show that several years ago I got behind on my payments on several accounts (I have never defaulted or declared bankruptcy). During the period in question, I was helping several family members who were experiencing emergencies (e.g., illness or sudden loss of work). These necessitated the diversion of the maximum amount of my financial resources to members of my family who were in greater need. All these problems have since been resolved, the money repaid me, and I am happy to say that all my accounts are current.

3. Profit and Loss and Cash Flow Forecasts

Financial forecasts for Central Personnel follow.

G. Personal Financial Statement: Eleanor "Ellie" Buss

Balance Sheet

ASSETS (at market value):

Cash in banks	$ 400
Stocks	
United Inc.	450
Universal Corp.	300
Household furnishings	6,000
China collection	2,000
2 horses	4,000
Horse trailer	1,500
Surrey and buggy	3,000
Tack	1,000
Car, Mazda RX	7,000
Residence	95,000
Total Assets	**$ 120,650**

LIABILITIES:

First on property, $771 per month	$ 76,000
Auto loan, $166 per month	6,000
Credit cards	
Visa $80 per month	1,500
Macy's $40 per month	700
Business loan, $50 per month	3,000
Total Liabilities	**$ 87,200**
NET WORTH (Total Assets – Total Liabilities)	33,450
TOTAL LIABILITIES & NET WORTH	**$ 120,650**

Income & Expenses

ANNUAL INCOME:

Professional fees	$28,000
Dividends	600
Total Income	**$28,600**

ANNUAL EXPENSES:

Loan payments	
1st	$ 9,252
Car	2,000
Visa	960
Macy's	500
House-related expenses	4,000
Property taxes	950
Insurance	300
Living expenses	10,000
Total Expenses	**$ 27,962**

H. Business Risk Analysis

Every business faces risks. Central Personnel Agency is not an exception. However, I believe that the risks facing my business are manageable. I see nothing that will seriously threaten the business.

Here are the major risks I anticipate and how I plan to deal with them.

1. Partner Problems

When faced with the prospect of my leaving and taking an income source away from her, my current partner, Jackie McCabe, the owner of Mid-Mountain Personnel Services, was initially somewhat angry. However, when we discussed the fact that she had more work on her hands in North City than she could cope with and that we could cooperate on future job placements, she became supportive of my starting my own business. Nevertheless, Jackie could still open a competitive agency at any time—which might threaten my new accounts. Therefore, I am volunteering to pay her a one-third share of all future job orders developed from connections I made while the partnership was active. My budget will support this concept as long as my payments to Jackie do not exceed one-third of revenues. I do not expect this to happen, but should it, Jackie had indicated she will accept a deferred payment plan. Within six months to a year, I expect the great majority of my business will stem from new contacts and I will no longer need to pay Jackie.

2. Competition

There are several competing employment agencies in South City, as discussed in Section E, above. As I am aiming for a slightly different market from the other agencies and have a track record of success in my target area, I do not feel that the competition will hurt me. Even if the other agencies expanded their clerical placements, I think my personal rapport with my clients and the Women's Resource Center should prevent me from suffering any real problem.

3. Slow Times

People are hiring now and times are good. When the economy slows down, as it inevitably will, so too will new hires, although because of the high turnover, there is always some demand for clerical help. However, I plan to put aside money when times are good to cushion against future bad times. Also, I plan to reduce the effect of slow times by keeping my overhead low.

4. Owner's Ability

I have never operated an independent business before. However, I have been paid on a straight commission basis for some time and am used to the need to perform in order to be paid. I can see no insurmountable problems resulting from being on my own and have already determined the licenses, tax permits, and so on, I will need to begin. I plan to use the same bookkeeper and accountant who do the books for Mid-Mountain Personnel to help with paperwork. In addition, I have a friend who is a small business consultant, and I can rely on her advice should I need it.

In short, I believe that I have addressed the major risks facing my business and have demonstrated that those risks are manageable.

I. Capital Spending Plan

Most items of equipment will be leased or rented, so there will be little need for capital beyond working capital and some fees and printing costs:

Printing/stationery	$ 500
Initial advertising	1,000
License application fee	250
Employment agency license fees	250
Business license	50
Insurance deposit	50
First & last month's rent & deposit	1,030
Phone installation	200
New furniture	500
Working capital	2,000
Total Capital	**$ 5,830**

Other capital items and most of the furniture have already been paid for. The office building provides a receptionist and copy service as part of the rent.

J. Personal Goals

After trying various careers, I discovered a career I am very good at and that provides me great personal satisfaction. I feel a deep sense of personal accomplishment when a client pays a fee for completing a job hire. That validates my ability. My goal in opening the Central Personnel Agency is to make some money while doing work I basically love.

Business Plan for a Manufacturing Business

The business plan for Day International, Inc., that follows is roughly based on a real plan, although I have changed some details, including the financial projections. And because of space limitations, I have omitted a number of charts and exhibits contained in the appendix to the original plan.

Founders of the company asked for $75,000 to bring their product to market. They expected sales of nearly a million dollars by the end of the second year of operations. Here are some of the strengths and weaknesses of their business plan.

Sales Projections

The best part of the plan is the discussion of sales projections, because it gives you a sense of the support you'll have to provide if you plan to introduce a new product. Note the effort they put into developing a logical sales revenue forecast. Since most new products introduced into the marketplace do not sell well enough to produce a profit, investors and lenders want to see solid data to support a claim that your product will be different.

Also, they plan for two different products using the same technology. The first is aimed at the commercial market and is reasonably costly; the second targets the consumer market and carries a somewhat lower price.

The founders of Day International, Inc., believe that a successful business needs more than one product to survive. While there are some exceptions to that rule, diversification can achieve powerful benefits if one product meets resistance in the marketplace.

Items Excluded

This plan does not cover several important items I think should be included:

- **Marketing and advertising.** Day International, Inc., plans to have their distributors and sales representatives handle a great deal of these activities. Were this my business, I would pay a little more attention to marketing. I've learned that a new small business that leaves marketing to someone else often courts disaster. The reason for this is simple: When a product is new, no sales representatives or wholesale or retail outlets have much of a stake in its success. Until they do, they are unlikely to do much to push it.

- **Business accomplishments.** While Eleanor in Appendix A sells herself first and her business second, Frederick Jones and Phillip Court, the principals in Day International, Inc., concentrate on selling their new technology and the manufacturing specifics that will bring it to market, and keep themselves in the background. Either approach can be effective, although in the case of Day International, Inc., I wouldn't mind knowing a little bit more about why the founders think they will be good businesspeople.

- **Cash flow and capital spending plan.** This plan does not include a cash flow forecast or a capital spending plan. I think any plan needs these two items.

FORM

The text of this Business Plan for a Manufacturing Business is included on this book's companion page at Nolo.com. See Appendix D for details on accessing this page.

DAY INTERNATIONAL, INC.

AN INVESTMENT OPPORTUNITY

April 16, 20xx

DAY INTERNATIONAL, INC.

123 Smith Place

San Jose, CA

Telephone 408-555-1212

Table of Contents

A. Introduction 3

B. Company Description 4

C. Patent Status 4

D. Corporation Management 5

E. Product Description..6

F. Marketing Plan 9

G. Company Facilities 11

H. Product Development Status 11

I. Production Status.. 12

J. Product Selling Prices and Costs 13

K. Financial Statement and Projections 13

A. Introduction

After several years of development work, DAY INTERNATIONAL, INC., is ready to market two unique electronic devices, both of which use the same patented new technology. This technology utilizes computerized optic displays to create a programmable message. In commercial application, this is valuable in creating commercial signs and displays that use a scrolling technique to attract and inform customers. As a recreational product, computerized optical displays using this technology can be made to respond directly to music and voice patterns. In other words, full-color visual displays result from sound. This product application is particularly attractive to young people.

Extensive market research suggests a large market for both the commercial (Kinet-O-Scroll) and the recreational (Kinet-O-Scope) applications of this product. The commercial programmable sign market already exceeds one million dollars in the United States and is sure to grow quickly. Many units are purchased by retailers for what amounts to instant in-store advertising. In this application, the retailer can program a sign with information on that day's specials, and presto, he has created his own attractive electronic display. The product, which is described more fully in the accompanying Product Description (Section E, below), has several features not now commercially available, including a wide choice of type styles. It will also have a substantial price advantage over other products now on the market. The consumer recreational market for this product is not fully tested, but there are a number of exciting potential uses (see Section E, Product Description).

DAY INTERNATIONAL, INC., is incorporated under the laws of the state of California and is ready to begin operations. The founders have spent several years of hard work preparing for this time and have made substantial personal investments. They are eager to proceed. However, because their personal financial resources are not adequate to manufacture and distribute sufficient units, they are prepared to offer a one-third share of the corporation for an equity investment of $75,000. The enclosed financial projections demonstrate that if projections are met, there will be a very profitable return for the investor.

B. Company Description

DAY INTERNATIONAL, INC., was incorporated in California on June 1, 2009 as an outgrowth of Day Kinetics, a partnership formed in November of 2008. The corporation was organized to manufacture and sell several electronic display items for commercial and recreational purposes. The technology on which these products is based is covered by U.S. Patent (Smith #5676890123), for which an exclusive license has been obtained by the corporation. DAY INTERNATIONAL's offices are at 123 Smith Place, San Jose, CA, and the telephone number is 408-555-1212. All stock is held by Frederick R. Jones and Phillip Court who, along with several family members, occupy seats on the Board of Directors.

Two seats on the Board of Directors are still to be filled. A minority shareholder, or shareholders who invest $75,000, will be permitted to seat two directors by majority vote. The majority shareholders are willing to prepare a formal shareholders' agreement, with the idea of protecting the interests of the minority shareholders.

C. Patent Status

Phillip Court, one of the directors and officers of DAY INTERNATIONAL, INC., obtained an exclusive license to the U.S. patent on which the Kinet-O-Scroll and Kinet-O-Scope are based (Smith #5676890123) in 2008. This license was granted by the original inventor of the process, Elmo Smith, for 2% of any eventual sales of either product during the term of the patent, until Smith receives $200,000, 1.5% until Smith receives a total of $400,000, and 1% thereafter. This license is cancelable if Smith does not receive $20,000 per year, with the first payment due November 2008. The license excludes certain applications of the Smith patent that are not related to the corporation's products.

In 2010, Phillip Court assigned an exclusive sublicense for the remaining term of the patent (ten years) to DAY INTERNATIONAL, INC. The payment to Court for this sublicense is 2% of the sales, expiring when sales of $100 million have been attained. In addition, the corporation has assumed the obligation for the royalty payment to Smith. All patent documentation, license agreements, and contracts are available to the potential investor or his agent upon request.

D. Corporation Management

The founders of DAY INTERNATIONAL, INC., are: Phillip V. Court and Frederick R. Jones, Jr.

The directors, officers, and key employees of this corporation are as follows:

1. Frederick R. Jones, Jr., president, treasurer, and director;
2. Phillip V. Court, vice-president, secretary, and director;
3. Edmund R. Jones, project manager and accounts payable manager.

Frederick R. Jones, Jr., age 52, has over 25 years of experience as an engineer, project engineer, program manager, proposal manager, marketing specialist, department head, program director, marketing manager, and so on. His specialty has been in automatic control systems and advanced display systems for manned aerospace vehicles. Mr. Jones's prior associations have been with Butterworth Aircraft (1984–1999), Vokar Electronics (1999–2009), and National Computer (2009 to date).

Phillip V. Court, age 46, has over 19 years of experience as an analog design engineer and manager. He is presently Engineering Manager of Data Conservation Products at a major corporation headquartered in Santa Clara, California. Prior to this, he was the first vice-president of engineering of Ultradesign, a $200M sales semicustom integrated circuit house. Mr. Court has authored numerous applications and brochures and several articles for a national electronics publication, and holds three U.S. patents.

Edmund R. Jones, age 23, holds a Bachelor of Science degree in marketing from the University of California, Irvine. He has gained valuable work and customer interface experience at such companies as Reliable Insurance, VSV Associates, and West Coast Semiconductor. In addition to his varied work experience, he has demonstrated community service and leadership capabilities, most significant of which are his leadership of a troop of Explorer Scouts and his membership in several regional opera societies. Edmund R. Jones is the son of Frederick R. Jones, Jr.

E. Product Description

The corporation plans to manufacture two products, both based on the Smith patent. One of these is the Kinet-O-Scroll, which is designed for commercial applications. The other is the Kinet-O-Scope, which is designed for home recreational use. They are more fully described as follows:

The Kinet-O-Scroll: This consists of a scrolling "Times Square"-type message sign. Using its patented technology, DAY INTERNATIONAL, INC., can produce a moving sign that is more versatile, attractive, and economical than existing units. Basically, the Kinet-O-Scroll displays alphanumeric, graphic, and animated characters in full color. While the sign can be manufactured in numerous sizes, we plan to start with a unit with a screen measuring three feet vertically and four feet horizontally. All sorts of businesses, including restaurants, bars, banks, stores, real estate offices, airline terminals, bus stations, and so on, can use the Kinet-O-Scroll sign to inform customers of special events or offers at a comparatively low cost. The cost of the unit may further be reduced by users who make arrangements (tie-ins) for reimbursement by advertisers. This could be the case where companies that manufacture products or services that a retailer sells (e.g., clothing, insurance, soft drinks) pay for advertising or provide their product at a better discount in exchange for advertising. There are hundreds of thousands of potential locations for such a low-cost merchandising tool.

The Kinet-O-Scroll is completely developed and tested. The first 100 production units have been completed and a production capacity of over 200 units per month is established. It is projected that the sales rate will rapidly build to a minimum of 100 units per month. This sales estimate, as well as long-term sales projections for the Kinet-O-Scroll, is based on extensive research into the need for this type of product, as well as into the sales history of existing (but inferior) products. This research has also involved consumer studies in which potential customers were asked to rate a variety of existing products against our new product.

In outline form, here is what we believe to be an objective summary of the "strip sign" market and the sales potential of the Kinet-O-Scroll:

- The Kinet-O-Scroll is unique in its mode of operation and its technical capacities. For example, it provides at least twice the visual resolution of other scrolling signs.

- There are at least a dozen manufacturers of programmable strip signs that can perform a somewhat similar but less efficient function. The total annual sales of these products has been estimated to be $10,000,000. This represents a 27% increase from the year before.[1] The existent products are all very similar. No one manufacturer commands a dominant share of the market.
- The published prices of the strip signs that come the closest to having features similar to the Kinet-O-Scroll are in the $1,500 to $2,000 range. As a result of efficiencies of design inherent in the patented technique used in the Kinet-O-Scroll, DAY's published list price is under $1,000.
- DAY's service contract (available on request) is above average for the industry.
- DAY's warranty policy (available on request) is above average for the industry.

The accompanying chart shows the sales volume of programmable signs in the United States in millions of dollars. One year from now, the total market for programmable signs is estimated to be $12,000,000. The corporation forecasts sales of 1,200 Kinet-O-Scroll units by the second year of production at a wholesale price of $550. These sales forecasts are considered conservative in that they are based on a market penetration of only 5%.

Programmable Sign Annual Sales

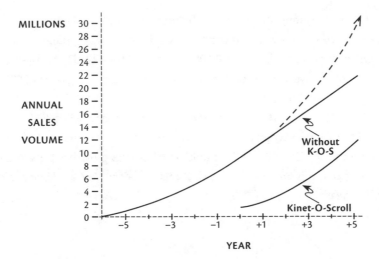

The Kinet-O-Scope: The Kinet-O-Scope features a small-sized screen that produces optic displays in response to the human voice, music, and other sounds. The display is in full color and the patterns created in response to sound are stunning. It is particularly attractive to young children experimenting with the sound of their own voice, although this is by no means the only market. People who love music, for example, are commonly fascinated by the Kinet-O-Scope. To accurately estimate the sales potential of the Kinet-O-Scope in the consumer market is difficult, as no directly comparable products exist.

In an effort to arrive at as accurate an estimate as possible, extensive consumer interviews were conducted. The Kinet-O-Scope Market Research Chart that follows summarizes the results of these interviews. When compared directly with the most similar products available (these are not nearly as good, but there is nothing else), 56% of the people asked preferred the Kinet-O-Scope. Even more persuasive, 49% of those tested would buy it for themselves, while 62% of those tested would buy it for a gift.

While there are no specific competitive products to the Kinet-O-Scope, it is clear that there is a distinct market for products of this type. This conclusion is arrived at by looking at good sales figures for Light Organs, Infinity Lights, Wave Devices, Volcano Lights, Rain Lamps, and other products that use light in innovative and creative ways.

Perhaps the best example of the size of the market is the Lava Light, a less technically advanced, but lower-cost product. According to its manufacturer, Volcano Simplex International, over 6,000,000 units have been sold in four years, with 3,000,000 sold last year. If we consider a wholesale average selling price of $90, this represents over $270,000,000.

DAY INTERNATIONAL, INC., conservatively estimates that it will sell about 2,800 units of the Kinet-O-Scope in the second year of operations, for a wholesale dollar sales volume of $420,000 ($150 per unit). Further sales growth is expected in later years. Note that this unit volume is a tiny fraction of the Volcano Light's sales volume for last year.

Market Research

	Wave	Kinet-O-Scope	Rain Lamp	Light Organ	Lava Light	Infny Light
Preferred product	9%	56%	9%	1%	10%	13%
Already own it	2%	0%	2%	3%	4%	0%
Would buy it for self	32%	49%	18%	9%	16%	24%
Would buy it as gift	43%	52%	18%	11%	5%	31%
Estimated retail price	**	$104.52	**	**	**	**

Age: Under 16: 3%   16–20: 11%   21–34: 41%   35+: 45%

**Average Total Estimate: $168.69; Actual: $160.00

F. Marketing Plan

The channels of distribution for the Kinet-O-Scroll and Kinet-O-Scope will include direct sales by corporate personnel to selected major accounts, and the use of manufacturer's representatives (sales reps), distributor's dealers (wholesalers), and international trading companies to reach the rest of the market. We do not anticipate establishing our own factory sales force. With regard to international sales, except for "opportunity sales," we will not launch our formal effort until we have adequately penetrated the domestic market. However, we will explore licensing our technology abroad.

In the beginning, DAY will team with a limited number of sales reps and wholesalers who have proven abilities in successfully introducing new electronic products. At first, the emphasis will be on developing market penetration in a few carefully chosen regions near our manufacturing facility. The reason for this approach is to properly identify effective pricing techniques and marketing strategies. Information gathered will be used to fine-tune stocking requirements, manufacturing rate requirements, and so on, for general North American distribution. In short, we want to be sure we are walking with a firm and steady tread before we begin to run.

It is particularly important that we work with good sales reps. To this end, we have contacted a number of people knowledgeable in the field (retailers, several small manufacturers of retail products, and two major wholesalers) for recommendations. We have received a number and plan to hold interviews soon. We also plan an aggressive campaign of marketing at consumer electronics and related trade shows. We have designed and built an attractive display booth that will effectively demonstrate both products in operation. We plan to attend up to ten trade shows in the next six months and will use them as a showcase around which to meet potential sales reps, wholesalers, and customers. In addition, this will be our opportunity to introduce our products to the consumer electronics industry press. As such, we have hired an experienced media consultant to work with us in developing a press package. She has already arranged for several articles about the Kinet-O-Scroll to appear in several popular electronics magazines.

DAY INTERNATIONAL, INC., anticipates expanding the principal sales areas toward the end of the first year of operation. As part of doing this, we hope our higher manufacturing volume will allow us to lower prices as well as to improve our products based on feedback from buyers. In subsequent years, DAY will continue to use sales reps and wholesalers as our main sales force, since they provide many advantages over employee salespeople. The principal advantage, of course, is that these people are paid a commission (sales reps) or fixed percentage (wholesalers) of each sale, but receive no salary.

Wholesalers have been included in the overall merchandising effort because they offer an established way to get our product onto the retailers' shelves. Many have been in business for years and offer retailers local delivery, computerized ordering, and other valuable services. They are expected to play a supportive role to our sales reps, who will have the primary responsibility to call on retailers, write orders, and so on. Many of these orders will be forwarded to the wholesaler to be filled (depending on the territory and our contractual relationship with the wholesaler), while others will be processed directly by DAY. It is important that the sales reps and the distributors work as a team. The representatives will be brought on early enough to have a strong voice in distributor selection.

G. Company Facilities

DAY INTERNATIONAL, INC., presently occupies a leased facility of slightly over 1,800 square feet at a very reasonable rental. We use this for both manufacturing and offices. We rent an additional 150 square feet of storage space nearby. There is no concern for the continuation of the lease on our principal location, as it contains three yearly options to renew at the same rate, plus a percentage increase equal to the yearly increase in the consumer price index. The existing space is adequate to support production of at least 400 Kinet-O-Scrolls per month. Nearby space is available for expansion at reasonable rates when we need it. An adequate workforce of assembly workers and shipping room personnel is available.

Several additions to the corporation's existing manufacturing equipment are required. Assuming, however, that the Kinet-O-Scroll production rate does not exceed 400 units per month, these expenditures will not exceed $30,000. When production increases above 400 units per month, we expect to show enough profit that a bank loan to finance more equipment will be easy to obtain. We can supply a potential investor with more details about these estimates upon request.

H. Product Development Status

Phillip Court began development work based on the Smith patent in 2007. The idea was to develop operational prototypes of both the Kinet-O-Scroll and Kinet-O-Scope to prove manufacturing feasibility. After design and operation of several early prototypes of each product, a full set of engineering drawing and parts specifications was prepared for each in 2008. Parts were procured from suppliers and a number of units assembled. Next, units manufactured and assembled were subjected to life testing. With some minor modifications, an operational life of up to 4,488 hours without failure was achieved for the Kinet-O-Scope. This compares to an expected typical homeowner's usage of 1,000 to 2,000 hours. We are confident from these results that with some minor material changes, which are now in the works, and the introduction of improved mechanical alignment techniques, which we plan to do soon, a 10,000-hour design goal is achievable. This is our goal.

The Kinet-O-Scroll must, of course, be designed to meet far more stringent requirements. We aim to market a product that will last at least four years, even if used 24 hours a day. Tests based on time simulations indicate that we have achieved this goal.[2]

The Kinet-O-Scroll is already in production (units are available for testing), as described in Section I of this proposal, just below. The Kinet-O-Scope can be in production within 120 days after additional financing is obtained.

I. Production Status

The Kinet-O-Scroll is the first and only DAY product currently in production. Here is a summary of both how things are going on the shop floor and how our marketing efforts are developing, as of April 16 of this year.

Material: There is no difficulty obtaining parts for the Kinet-O-Scroll. The two parts with the longest order lead time are the motor and keyboard, which at present take about eight weeks to get. There has been some recent indication of possible stretch-outs on certain semiconductor products we have been getting on a next-day basis, but this is not expected to be a significant problem. Just in case, however, we have identified several alternative suppliers.

Inventories: The first 100 Kinet-O-Scroll units have been committed to production. At the time of this writing, 35 are complete and the remainder are 90% finished, requiring only cabinets and final assembly. All materials, with the exception of the cabinets, which should arrive in ten days, are in stock to complete these units, as well as an additional 100 units. The first 100 units are primarily for demonstration purposes. We will use several at trade shows, give others to the electronics press for evaluation, and use still others as samples for our sales reps and wholesalers.

Credit Terms: Although DAY has established 30-day terms with over half of its suppliers, we are presently on cash terms with the rest, due to our low cash position and because we are a new corporation with no proven credit history. We expect to arrange 30- to 60-day terms with all our suppliers within six months. New financing will help us accomplish this.

J. Product Selling Prices and Costs

The projections included in this business plan are based on several assumptions about product selling prices and costs.

Wholesale Selling Price		
Kinet-O-Scroll	(Commercial Unit)	$550.00
Kinet-O-Scope	(Recreational Unit)	$150.00

Direct (Variable) Cost of Each Unit				
	Packaging	Direct Labor	Direct Material	Total Cost
Kinet-O-Scroll	$11.00	$24.00	$100.00	$135.00
Kinet-O-Scope	$2.00	$12.00	$ 30.00	$44.00

These figures do not allow for any corporation overhead, such as rent, management costs, and so on. They are based solely on the cost of producing each unit. All costs and selling prices have been developed through extensive market research and profitability analysis. They reflect the realities of the marketplace, as well as the price objectives of management.

K. Financial Statement and Projections

As DAY INTERNATIONAL, INC., is still in the start-up phase, we have yet to develop positive cash flow.[3] As the attached profit and loss projection and cash flow forecast indicate, however, we expect the corporation to begin to generate a positive cash flow and profit before the end of the first year of operations. To accomplish this, however, the corporation needs a total infusion of $150,000 equity capital. The founders have contributed half of that amount and are seeking additional investors for the balance. In exchange for a $75,000 investment, the investor would receive a one-third interest in the company. This would take the form of one-third of the stock in DAY INTERNATIONAL, INC., and one-third representation on the Board of Directors. As noted in Section B above, the existing shareholders are willing to design a shareholders' agreement to protect the interests and representation of the minority shareholders.

Profit projections show that if all goes according to plan, the investor can expect no return of his investment in the first year of operation and substantial profit in the second. (The accompanying profit and loss forecast shows a $338,255 profit for DAY INTERNATIONAL, INC., by the second year.) While the dividend policy of the corporation will be to pay modest dividends to investors in order to generate capital for growth, it can be expected that some of the available profits will be distributed to the shareholders. In addition, the investor can expect significant capital gains should the corporation make a public stock offering. The founders plan to do this after several years of profitable operations.

Warning to investors! Heretofore you have read an optimistic review of DAY INTERNATIONAL, INC., and its chances for future success. However, you should realize that the electronics business is a risky one. Many new products fail, while others succeed for a brief time, only to be supplanted by new technology, changing public taste, or foreign competition. While we believe we have planned carefully and well for each of these eventualities, we want to emphasize one thing loud and clear: Anyone who invests in DAY INTERNATIONAL, INC., is taking a substantial risk. While we believe chances of success are excellent, this is by no means guaranteed. In short, please do not invest money that you can't afford to lose.

Endnotes

[1] Many small manufacturing operations will have a local marketing strategy, at least to start. Don't let the sort of marketing survey presented here intimidate you. The same sort of approach can be used for any manufacturing business. For example, if you plan to make a better raisin-chocolate-chip cookie, or a crisper lemon tortilla chip for local distribution, think about ways you can convincingly tell a potential lender or investor that it will sell.

[2] Test results are based on the brush/slip ring life-methods at three times normal speed, which have been independently monitored and are available upon request.

[3] Since DAY is already in operation, it would be normal practice to include a balance sheet of operations to date. I do not do this here both because of space limitations and because we have not discussed balance sheets in the text. If your business is in operation, ask your bookkeeper or accountant to help you prepare a balance sheet and include it.

Business Plan for Project Development

P roject developments differ from normal businesses in several ways. Most importantly, the development business ends when the project is sold. That means that the developer normally knows the selling price of the project before beginning development, and it means that his profit depends almost solely on his ability to control costs. Sometimes the project is sold before it is finished, making cost control even more critical.

The cash flow projection in this example is a model for project development forecasting, and I recommend that you use it for your project.

John Reynolds plans to fix up a house that has inadequate plumbing and electrical work. In addition, the house has been unoccupied for several years and most of the windows are broken and the floors are in sad shape.

He plans to invest $5,000, paying himself a salary of $1,500 per month for three months while the house is being refurbished. When complete, he'll sell it for an immediate cash profit of $12,445 plus a note from the buyer for an additional $12,000.

Extensive documentation is required because John will need to borrow money from a bank to complete the work. With private financing it's possible to complete a development project with less data.

Obviously, a developer working on more than one project may have an ongoing business independent of any particular development.

Regardless of project specifics, the developer must establish his ownership of the property or concept, back up his assumption about its projected selling price and the terms of sale, and verify his estimates of the costs necessary to complete the project.

Copies of many of the documents referred to in this example have not been included because they are all imaginary. Of course, for a real project, all relevant documents should be included. In this instance, John Reynolds would surely include copies of the preliminary title report, showing him as property owner; copies of a title insurance policy, showing that the title is good; a copy of the note in favor of the Joneses, showing that the balance due them is really $55,000; and copies of all bids from the subcontractors who will do the work. In addition, the bank will surely require that a written appraisal of the property be included. If the bank has experience with John Reynolds on other house rebuilding projects in the particular area, it may accept his judgment as to the amount of work needed to put the house in a condition to justify the projected selling price. If not, he may have to provide a written report from the city inspector's office, stating what work must be done to get an occupancy permit.

 FORM

The text of this Business Plan for a Project Development is included on this book's companion page on Nolo.com. Please see Appendix D for details on accessing the page and all forms in this book.

Loan Request for Single-Family Residential Reconstruction

November 18, 20xx

Jonathan Reynolds
847 Market Street
Chicago, Illinois
Telephone 312-555-7896

Table of Contents

Introduction...3

Market Value of the House on Completion 3

Terms of the Expected Sale..3

Title to the Property...4

Costs to Remodel the Property...4

Sales Price 7

Cash Flow...7

Introduction

This is a request for a loan of $30,000 for the purpose of improving a single-family residence at 2246½ Hamilton Street, Chicago, Illinois. This house has been condemned by the city because of faulty plumbing and wiring, and because it has been unoccupied for about three years. As a result, there is substantial work to be completed before the house can be legally and profitably sold. According to city inspectors and a private structural engineer, the house is basically sound, except for the items referred to. Specifically, the city has stated it will issue an occupancy certificate once the tagged items are completed to its satisfaction.

Upon completion, the house will have a market value of $120,000, based on comparable sales in the area. Since I have acquired the house for $60,000, the proceeds from the sale of the house will be more than enough to pay the existing note on the house and to pay back the new loan.

Market Value of the House on Completion

Comparable Values

Address	Sold For	Sq. Ft.	Features	Age	$/Sq. Ft.
2357 7th St.	$119,000	1,385	3 br, 1 ba	50+	85.92
406 Bean Ave.	$125,000	1,500	3 br, 2 ba	45+	83.33
2765 9th St. (This house was condemned also)	$75,000	1,200	2 br, 1 ba	50+	62.50
567 Bacon Ave. (This house was condemned; the developer thinks he will sell it for $130,000 upon completion of work)	$50,000	1,400	3 br, 2 ba	60+	35.71
1988 7th St. (This house just sold after being fixed up)	$135,000	1,450	3 br, 2 ba	40+	93.10

Although I have not yet acquired a formal appraisal of the value of the house, a study of recent sales of comparable property in the area supports the value of $120,000. This area of Chicago is undergoing the "Gentrification" process whereby younger, upwardly mobile families are buying older houses and fixing them up to live in or resell. People in the market appear to be willing to pay a premium for a rebuilt house, both in terms of selling price overall and on a square-foot basis. An appraisal can be obtained from any number of qualified appraisers at the lender's request.

Terms of the Expected Sale

Lenders in this neighborhood have been lending 80% of the appraised value of a first mortgage. Buyers normally expect to make a down payment of 10% to 15% of the selling price. Many sellers are willing to carry a second mortgage on the houses for up to 10% of the selling price. This loan request is based on that set of assumptions about the terms of the resale.

Title to the Property

As evidenced by the preliminary title reports and policy of title insurance issued to me by Chicago Title Insurance, I presently own the property. The escrow closed on October 3, 2013 at the Third National Bank. A copy of the escrow documents and title policy are available upon request. I bought the property for a total price of $60,000, by making a down payment of $5,000 in cash with the seller, Mr. and Mrs. Timothy Jones of 2336 South Whale Drive in Joliet, agreeing to carry back a $55,000 mortgage on the property. The mortgage calls for monthly payments of $800 until October 3, 2014, one year from the close of escrow, when the entire remaining amount of $52,500 becomes due and payable.

Costs to Remodel the Property

As previously discussed, the house needs new plumbing and wiring, a new roof, and other repairs, including replacing most of the windows, refinishing the floors, and making improvements to the kitchen to make it marketable for the $120,000 value. I plan to have the electrical and plumbing, floor, roof, and kitchen work done by licensed subcontractors and to do most of the additional cosmetic work myself.

-4-

Here is a summary of the low bids I have received so far to the portion of the work to be completed by outside contractors. Copies of the bids are available on request.

Plumbing: Install new water and gas pipe, install new water heater, use existing sinks and tub, but install new faucets and toilet

    Low bid from Smith Brothers, 114 Prince William St., Gary, Indiana $ 12,998

Electrical: Pull new wiring throughout, install good quality fixtures and outlets, using existing boxes and wall holes wherever possible, all to code

    Frank Rochioloi, Chicago, Illinois   4,006

Roof: Install four-ply roof over entire house with 20-year guarantee, to code

    Johnson Roofing, Chicago, Illinois   800

Flooring and Carpeting: Repair flooring and install new wall-to-wall carpeting and/or linoleum throughout

    Acme Floors, Chicago, Illinois   4,958

Kitchen Cabinets: Build and install new cabinets in kitchen

    Urizola Cabinets, Chicago, Illinois   1,995

Range and Refrigerator:

    Gordon's Appliances, Chicago, Illinois   1,398

                      Total Bid Items $ 26,155

I plan to do some of the cosmetic work myself during the three months' construction time. That work will include painting inside and out, replacing window glass, and other miscellaneous items as the need arises. Cost of materials for those items will be about $500. Building permits and fees for the electrical, plumbing, and roof work will add another $500. This will put the total costs, excluding finance costs, at $18,155. As seen on the project profit and loss projection that follows, I have estimated financing and other costs to total an additional $10,200.

In making my financial projections, I made the following assumptions:

- The house will be sold within six months of the start of construction, and the Joneses' note will then be paid off. (The interest portion of this $800 note is $550.)

- Costs of the new loan of $30,000 secured by a second mortgage are assumed to be two points, which amounts to a $600 loan origination fee.
- Interest is assumed to be at a 12% annual rate, for a six-month total interest cost of $1,800 for that loan.
- Finally, I assume that I shall pay myself a salary of $1,500 per month during the time I actually work on the house.

Profit and Loss Forecast for the Remodeling and Resale of Single-Family Residential House at 2246½ Hamilton St., Chicago

Item	Amount
Sales price	$ 120,000
Less: 6% Commission	7,200
Net Proceeds	112,800
Less: Cost to acquire house	60,000
Plumbing	12,998
Electrical	4,006
Roof	800
Flooring and carpeting	4,958
Kitchen cabinets	1,995
Range and refrigerator	1,398
Miscellaneous supplies	500
Building permit, city fees	500
Subtotal Costs	78,155
Carrying costs, 6 months—interest on mortgage	3,300
Interest and loan fees on new loan, 6 months	2,400
Developer overhead (3 months' living expense at $1,500)	4,500
Total Project Cost	88,355
Project Profit	$ 24,445

Sales Price

The sales price of the 2246½ Hamilton Street house, after remodeling, is forecast to be $120,000, with a 6% real estate commission paid in cash from the proceeds of the sale. We expect to carry back a new second mortgage in favor of the buyer of approximately $12,000, which means the seller will pay a cash down payment of $12,000 and obtain a new first mortgage of $96,000 from a bank or savings and loan. The new first mortgage will pay off the existing first and second loans on the property. Thus, at the conclusion of the transaction, I expect to receive the cash difference between the total of all outstanding loan balances, sales commissions, and other cash expenses. In addition, I shall have a second mortgage on the property in the amount of $12,000.

Cash Flow

As seen on the attached cash flow for this project, there are only three infusions of cash into the project. The first one is the money from my savings account with which I made the down payment on the property and with which I obtained the engineering studies that convinced me that the project will make money. The second infusion will be the proceeds from the loan being applied for here. The third and final infusion will be from the sale of the property, and that will be sufficient to pay off the other loans on the project and leave a cash profit of $12,445. The difference between the cash profit and the book profit shown earlier is accounted for by the $12,000 second mortgage I'll carry in favor of the buyer.

Based on demand for housing in the subject area, I believe that the house will probably sell far more quickly than I have forecast; in fact, I have already had two inquiries about selling it. Based on my experience with remodeling houses of this age and location, I am sure that the $30,000 requested will be adequate to complete the repairs necessary to increase the value of the house.

Project Development Cash Flow—Remodel House at 2246½ Hamilton

	Pre-Const							Total Cost	House Sale
		Construction Period							
		Month 1	Month 2	Month 3	Month 4	Month 5	Month 6		
Sources of Cash									
Savings	5,300								
New second		30,000							
Sales—down payment									12,000
New first									96,000
Total Sources	5,300	30,000							108,000
Uses of Cash: Preconstruction									
Down payment to buy house	5,000								
City inspection fee	100								
Engineer consultant	200								
Total Preconstruction	5,300								
Uses of Cash: Construction									
Contractors	5,718	5,718	5,719					17,155	
Supplies	167	167	166					500	
Permits/fees	250	-0-	250					500	
Interest on old first mortgage	550	550	550	550	550	550		3,300	
Principal on old first mortgage	250	250	250	250	250	250		1,500	
Loan fees on new 2nd	600							600	
Interest on new 2nd	300	300	300	300	300	300		1,800	
Developer overhead	1,500	1,500	1,500	-0-	-0-	-0-		4,500	
Total Construction	9,335	8,485	8,735	1,100	1,100	1,100		29,855	
Sales—pay off savings of J.R.									5,000
Pay off old first									53,500
Pay off new 2nd									30,000
Sales commission									7,200
Total Sale									95,700
Net Cash	-0-	20,665	(8,485)	(8,735)	(1,100)	(1,100)	(1,100)	(29,855)	12,300
Cumulative Net Cash	-0-	20,665	12,180	3,445	2,345	1,245	145	145	12,445

How to Use the Interactive Forms

Editing RTFs 310

Files on the Book's Companion Page 311

Th   his book comes with interactive files that you can access online
        at **www.nolo.com/back-of-book/SBS.html**
            To use the files, your computer must have specific software
programs installed. Here is a list of the types of files provided by this
book, as well as the software programs you'll need to access them:

- **RTF.** You can open, edit, print, and save these form files with most
  word processing programs such as Microsoft *Word*, Windows
  WordPad, and recent versions of *WordPerfect*.
- **PDF.** You can view these files with *Adobe Reader*, free software from
  www.adobe.com. Government PDFs are sometimes fillable using
  your computer, but most PDFs are designed to be printed out and
  completed by hand.
- **XLS.** You can open, edit, and save the XLS spreadsheet files with
  Microsoft *Excel* and most other spreadsheet programs that read
  XLS files. Each spreadsheet program uses different commands to
  open, format, save, and print documents, so read your spreadsheet
  program's help files for specific instructions.

> **TIP**
> **Note to Macintosh users.** These forms were designed for use with
> Windows. They should also work on Macintosh computers; however Nolo
> cannot provide technical support for non-Windows users.

Editing RTFs

Here are some general instructions about editing RTF forms in your
word processing program. Refer to the form instructions (in the book
and on the Nolo site) for help about what should go in each blank.

Underlines. Underlines indicate where to enter information. After
filling in the needed text, delete the underline. In most word processing
programs you can do this by highlighting the underlined portion and
typing CTRL + U.

Bracketed and italicized text. Bracketed and italicized text indicates instructions. Be sure to remove all instructional text before you finalize your document.

Optional text. Optional text gives you the choice to include or exclude text. Delete any optional text you don't want to use. Renumber numbered items, if necessary.

Alternative text. Alternative text gives you the choice between two or more text options. Delete those options you don't want to use. Renumber numbered items, if necessary.

Signature lines. Signature lines should appear on a page with at least some text from the document itself.

Every word processing program uses different commands to open, format, save, and print documents, so refer to your software's help documents for help using your program. Nolo cannot provide technical support for questions about how to use your computer or your software.

> **CAUTION**
> **In accordance with U.S. copyright laws, the forms provided by this book are for your personal use only.**

Files on the Book's Companion Page

The following spreadsheets are in Microsoft's *Excel* format (XLS) and are available for download at **www.nolo.com/back-of-book/SBS.html**

Form Name	File Name
Cash Flow Forecast	CashFlow.xls
Personal Financial Statement	FinancialStatement.xls
Profit and Loss Forecast	ProfitForecast.xls
Sales Revenue Forecast	SalesRevenue.xls

The following sample business plans are in rich text format (RTF) and are available for download at **www.nolo.com/back-of-book/SBS.html**

Plan Name	File Name
Business Plan for a Small Service Business	SmallService.rtf
Business Plan for a Manufacturing Business	Manufacturing.rtf
Business Plan for a Project Development	ProjectDevelopment.rtf

Index

A

Accomplishment résumé. *See*
Business accomplishment résumé
Accounting, 145–146
Accounts payable, 162
Accounts receivable, 110, 119, 162
Accounts receivable factoring
companies, 88–89
Advertising, 141–144, 186–187, 250.
See also Marketing plan
After you open, 230–240
business plan as guide, 10–11
getting out of business, 237–240
watching for problem areas,
230–236
Amortized loans, 64, 82–83
Angel investors. *See* Equity investors/
investments
Annual income calculations, 118–121
Annual living expenses, 122–125
Appendix, business plan, 209–211
Apple computers, 259
Asset depreciation, 148
Assets, 79–80, 109–114

B

Balance sheet, 237–238. *See also*
Personal financial statement
Balloon payment loans, 64–65,
82–83, 169
Banker's analysis/ideal, 22–24
Bank loans, 81–84, 87, 92, 221–223

Bankruptcy, 239–240
Benefits of a business plan, 8–12
Bonds, as assets, 109–110
Bookkeeping costs, 145–146
Books for small businesses, 246–254
business form, 252–253
business location, 251
choosing a business idea, 248
finding money, 249
general business, 247–248, 254
legal matters, 253
marketing/advertising, 250
Nolo, 246–247
personnel, 251
women in business, 253–254
Borrowing money. *See* Loans
Break-even analysis, 42–59
break-even sales revenue forecast,
54–59
fixed costs forecast, 50–51
gross profit forecast, 52–54
importance of, 42–43
overview of elements, 44
for project development, 43–44
as "quick and dirty" profit
analysis, 43
sales revenue forecast, 44–50
Break-even sales revenue forecast,
54–59
Broadband Internet service, 260
Bulletin boards, online, 262–263

Business accomplishment résumé,
   98–107
   drafting your, 98–102
   in sample business plans, 271
   samples, 102–107
Business books. *See* Books for small
   businesses
Business consultants, 213–214,
   243–246
Business description, 29–37
   identifying business type, 30–32
   influence on marketing plan, 178
   overview on, 29–30
   problem statement, 32–33
   questions for, 33–37
   in sample business plans, 272
Business form, 70–72, 243, 252–253
Business goals, 20–21
Business ownership. *See* Owning a
   business
Business personality, 193–194
Business plan benefits, 8–12
Business plan completion. *See* Editing/
   finalizing your business plan
Business plan revisions, 234
Business plan samples. *See* Sample
   business plans
Business plan summary, 202–207
BusinessUSA, 93

C

Capital expenses, 140, 156, 210
Capital investment, 155, 172–176.
   See also Financial backing
Capital requirements. *See* Cash flow
   forecast
Capital spending plan, 156–159, 172,
   207–208, 279

Cash assets, 109
Cash flow, 8–9, 154, 189–190
Cash flow forecast, 159–173
   additional cash items, 170
   collections, 164–165
   credit purchases, 165–167
   credit sales in, 162–163
   cumulative net cash, 171
   depreciation, 169
   extra purchases, 169–170
   monthly net cash, 170
   online spreadsheet program, 162
   overview on, 154–155, 159, 172–173
   principal payments, 169
   profit/loss in, 162
   and required business
      investment, 172
   sample, 160–161, 307–308
   section introduction, 207–208
   withholding taxes, 167–169
Chain stores, 45–48
Chat rooms, 262
Choosing the right business, 26–60
   about risky businesses, 28
   books on, 248
   e-business basics, 40
   fine-tuning your business
      concept, 9–10
   knowing your business, 26–28
   liking the business, 28–29
   taste/trends/technology, 37–42
   writing a business plan and, 60
   See also Break-even analysis;
      Business description
Classes on business, 263–264
Closing the business, 237–240
Clothing stores. *See* Dress shop
   example
Cloud computing systems, 258

Collateral, 65–66, 73, 79–80

Colleagues, backing from, 77–79, 220–221

Commercial bank loans, 81–84, 87, 92, 221–223

Commission costs, 134

Competition, 179–181, 188

Complete business plan, 2–3, 201–202

Computers, 256–260

Computer software, 257, 259–260

Concept for business, 9–10. *See also* Choosing the right business

Conferences, online, 262–263

Consultants, 243–246

Co-owned assets, 108

Corporate bond assets, 109–110

Corporate stock offerings, 95–96

Corporations, 71–72, 252

Cosigned loans, 65, 119

Cost cutting, 79

Cost of sales
 in business plan sample, 295
 defined, 129
 determining, 130–134
 vs. fixed costs, 51
 in gross profit forecast, 52–53
 list of, 156
 monthly calculations of, 131
 in profit and loss forecast, 135–136

Costs, discretionary, 50

Costs, fixed. *See* Fixed costs

Credit card debt, 115

Credit card financing, 75

Credit card sales, 162–163

Creditor negotiations, 238

Credit purchases, 165–167

Credit reports, 125, 218

Credit sales, customer, 119, 162–165

Crowd funding online, 80–81

Cumulative net cash, 171

Customers
 business description addressing, 33–34
 as financing source, 80, 221
 focusing on, 15
 inventory turnover and, 175–176
 marketing methods to reach, 183–185
 for problem spotting, 232
 problem statement and your, 32–33, 179
 target customer description/ marketing, 181–185
 taste/trends/technology and, 37–42
 and your competition, 179–181

Customized business plan, 3

D

Day-to-day operations, 233–234

Debt, past, 218

Depreciation, 140, 148, 169

Description of business. *See* Business description

Direct product costs. *See* Cost of sales

Discounting merchandise, 169–170

Discretionary costs, 50

Dress shop example
 appendix, 211
 break-even sales revenue forecast, 56–59
 business consultant review of plan, 214
 business description, 36
 capital spending plan, 157–158
 cash flow forecast, 160–161, 172
 competition analysis, 180, 181

cost of sales, 131–132
fixed costs forecast, 51
future trends statement, 42
gross profit, 52–53, 136
introduction to, 4
inventory turnover, 173–175, 214
marketing plan, 190–192
personal goal statement, 209
personnel plan, 194–197
plan summary, 205–206
problem statement, 33
profit and loss forecast, 138–139, 150
risk analysis, 192
sales revenue forecast, 46–47
self-evaluation exercises, 17, 19–21
target customer description, 182
Drop shipping, 40

E

E-business basics, 40
Economic Development
    Administration (EDA), 94
Editing/finalizing your business
    plan, 200–214
  appendix, 209–211
  business consultant review, 213–214
  final edit, 211–213
  length of plan, 202
  list of positive facts, 204–205
  organizing your plan, 200–202
  personal goal statement, 208–209
  plan summary, 202–207
  revisions, 234
  section introductions, 207–208
  tips on writing style, 5, 204, 213
  title page/table of contents, 211, 213
  writing final portions, 202–207

Education courses, 263–264
Employees
  books on, 251
  consultants as future, 244
  corporate management
    description, 287
  vs. independent contractors, 144
  personnel plan, 193–197
  piece-rate/commission costs, 134
  problem spotting by, 232
  resumes in the appendix, 210
  staffing schedule, 194
  wages/salaries, 119, 136–137
  withholding taxes on, 167–169
Entrepreneurial programs, 264
Equipment leasing companies,
    full-finance, 88
Equipment sharing, 79
Equity investors/investments
  and legal ownership forms,
    70–72, 227
  vs. loans, 73
  overview on, 67–68, 84–86, 89
  pitching your plan to, 221–223
  regulations on, 227–228
  returns for, 68–70, 203–204, 223
Evaluating decision to own a
    business. See Choosing the right
    business; Owning a business
Evaluations, self-. See Self-evaluation
    exercises
Expanding a business
  equity investments for, 69–70
  evaluating personal goals in, 236
  funding sources for, 74, 82, 86–90
  gross profit forecast, 54
  inclusions in the appendix, 210

Expenses
  annual living expenses, 122–125
  capital expenses, 140, 156, 210
  capital investment/initial working
    capital, 155–157
  in capital spending plan,
    156–159, 172
  marketing, 185–187
  in profit and loss forecast, 147–150
  See also Fixed costs
Expertise, 26–28, 189. *See also*
    Business accomplishment résumé

F

Factoring companies, 88–89
Failure of business, 28, 234–235
Family, backing from, 73, 76–79, 220
Federal income tax expenses, 122
Federal loan programs, 91–94
Federal securities laws, 95–96
Federal withholding tax, 167–169
Finalizing your plan. *See* Editing/
    finalizing your business plan
Financial backing
  banker's analysis, 22–24
  books on, 249
  business plan to attract, 2–3, 8–9,
    83–84
  cash flow forecast and, 155
  cost cutting as, 79
  equity investments *vs.* loans, 73
  for expanding your business,
    86–90
  legal details, 225–228
  repeated attempts at, 90–91
  See also Selling your business plan
Financial backing sources, 74–96
  asset equity, 79–80

  crowd funding online, 80–81
  customers/supporters, 80
  factoring companies/factors, 88–89
  for foreign partnerships, 94
  friends/relatives/colleagues, 73,
    77–79, 220
  full-finance leasing companies, 88
  government programs, 91–94
  insurance companies/pension
    funds, 95
  money brokers/finders, 89
  overview on, 74
  personal savings, 74–76
  public offerings, 95–96
  trade credit, 76–77, 87
  See also Equity investors/
    investments; Loans
Financial problems, prior, 218
Financial projections, 275, 295–296
Finders, 89
Fixed asset depreciation, 148
Fixed costs
  in break-even analysis, 50–51
  in break-even sales forecast, 57, 58
  expenses that are not, 51
  list of, 156
  loans and, 75
  in profit and loss forecast, 129–130,
    136, 150
Foreign business investments, 94
Form of business, 70–72, 243,
    252–253
Friends, backing from, 73, 76–79, 220
Full-finance leasing companies, 88
Funding. *See* Financial backing
Funding portals, 80–81
Future trends statement, 41–42

G

General partnerships, 70
Gifts-loan hybrids, 77
Goals, personal, 14–15, 208–209, 280
Goals, specific business, 20–21
Going out of business, 237–240
Government loan programs,
   91–94, 224
Gross profit
  in break-even sales forecast, 55–59
  forecasting, 52–54
  in profit and loss forecast,
   135–136, 150
Gross sales, 44–50, 55–58, 129–130,
   131, 135–136
Guaranteed return on investments,
   69, 223
Guerrilla marketing, 142

I

IBM PCs, 259
Improvements, 140, 156, 210
Income calculations, 118–121
Incremental cost. *See* Cost of sales
Independent contractors, 144
Indiegogo, 81
Initial working capital, 155
Innovative businesses, 188, 209
Insurance, business, 122, 144–145
Insurance company loans, 95
Intellectual property, 111, 209, 286
Interest-only loans, 64–65,
   82–83, 169
Interest payments, 73, 146–147, 169
Internet access, 260–261
Internet resources. *See* Online resources
Intrastate offering, 95

Inventory
  as collateral, 65, 75, 87, 115
  in going out of business, 238–239
  opening, 156, 157, 158, 210
  in profit and loss forecast, 148
  questions about, 35, 37
  tax on, 122
  turnover of, 173–176, 214
  valuation, 151–152
  in wholesale businesses, 31
Investor funding. *See* Equity
   investors/investments
Investor guarantees, 69, 223
IRS (Internal Revenue Service),
   77–78, 144, 167, 239, 255
ISP (Internet Service Provider), 260

J

Job descriptions, 195–196

K

Kickstarter, 81

L

Leases
  inclusion in the appendix, 210
  making leasehold improvements,
   140, 156
  personal guarantees, 72
  rent expenses, 122, 137, 140–141
  resources on, 251
Leasing companies, full-finance, 88
Legal form of business, 70–72, 243,
   252–253
Legal resources, 243, 253
Lenders. *See* Financial backing; Loans
Liability calculations, 115–118

Liability insurance, 144
Life insurance, 110, 115
Limited liability companies
 (LLCs), 70
Limited liability partnerships
 (LLPs), 70
Liquidation sales, 238–239
Living expense calculations, 122–125
Living expense deferral, 75–76
LLCs (limited liability companies), 70
LLPs (limited liability partnerships), 70
Loan-gift hybrids, 77
Loan interest calculators, 147
Loans
 bank, 81–84, 87, 92, 221–223
 cosigned, 65, 119
 vs. equity investments, 73
 family/friend, 73, 77–79
 government programs, 91–94
 insurance/pension fund, 95
 interest calculations, 146–147
 interest-only, 64–65, 82–83, 169
 legal details of, 225–227
 lender verification, 125–126
 multiple attempts at securing, 90–91
 overview on, 63–64
 in personal financial statement,
  115, 122
 personal guarantees, 72
 repayment of, 51, 64–65, 73
 secured *vs.* unsecured, 65–67
 signature loans, 115
Local government assistance, 94, 246
Local zoning ordinances, 137
Location for business, 251
Long-term assets, 140, 156
Losses, 162. *See also* Profit and
 loss forecast

M
Mac computers, 259
Magazines, small business, 255
Managing a business. *See* Owning a
 business
Manufacturing businesses
 business description, 37
 cost of sales, 51, 131–133
 gross profit margins, 52
 new technology businesses, 39, 41
 overview of, 31–32
 sales revenue forecast, 48–49
 sample business plan, 281–297
 See also Inventory
Marketing, word-of-mouth, 142, 184
Marketing books, 250
Marketing costs, 141–143, 185–187
Marketing plan, 178–192
 business differentiation, 180–181
 competition analysis, 179–180
 influences on, 178–179
 marketing budget, 185–187
 marketing methods, 183–185
 risk analysis in, 188–190, 192
 samples, 190–192, 272–274,
  291–292
 target customer description, 181–183
 writing your, 188
Master's Degree in Business
 Administration (MBA), 264
Minority Small Business Investment
 Companies (MSBICs), 93
Money brokers, 89
Money sources. *See* Financial
 backing; Loans
Monthly net cash, 170
Moore's Law, 258
Mortgage assets, 110–111

MSBICs (Minority Small Business Investment Companies), 93
Mutual fund assets, 109–110

N

Negative cash flow, 154
Network marketing, 142, 220–221
Net worth calculations, 118
New businesses. *See* Start-ups
Newsgroups, 262–263
Nolo web resources, 4, 243, 246, 310–312

O

One-day plan, 3, 200–201
Online resources
  computer systems, 259
  crowd funding, 80–81
  general small business, 260–263
  government loan assistance, 93–94, 96
  IRS, 77, 255
  loan interest calculators, 147
  Nolo, 4, 243, 246, 310–312
  SBA, 255
  search engines, 143, 261
Online retail businesses, 40
Operating expenses. *See* Fixed costs
Operating plan, 233–234
OPIC (Overseas Private Investment Corporation), 94
Organizational filing, 71
Organizing your business plan, 200–202
Overseas Private Investment Corporation (OPIC), 94

Owning a business, 14–24
  banker's analysis, 22–24
  business plan to evaluate, 9
  goals in, 14–15
  key business components, 11–12
  self-evaluation exercises, 15–22
  See also Choosing the right business

P

Partnerships, 70, 252–253
Payroll tax, 137, 167–169
PCs (personal computers), 259
Pension fund loans, 95
Percentage of sales clauses, 141
Personal credit checks, 125
Personal financial statement, 108–126
  annual income, 118–121
  annual living expenses, 122–125
  assets, 109–114
  and co-owned property, 108
  lender verification, 125–126
  liabilities, 115–118
  net worth, 118
  overview of, 108
  in sample business plans, 276–277
Personal goals evaluation, 14–15
Personal goal statement, 208–209, 280
Personal guarantees, 72
Personality assessment. *See* Self-evaluation exercises
Personality of your business, 193–194
Personal property assets, 110–111, 115
Personal savings, as funding source, 74–76
Personnel. *See* Employees
Personnel agency example, 49, 265–280
Personnel plan, 193–197

Piece-rate costs, 134, 136
Pitching your plan. *See* Selling your business plan
Plan summary, 202–207
Positive cash flow, 154
Pricing guidelines, 180–181
Principal payments, 169
Private business consultants, 246
Private business lending companies, 92–93
Private offering shares, 95–96
Problem areas, 230–236
Problem statement, 32–33
Product description, 288–291
Products businesses. *See* Manufacturing businesses; Wholesale businesses
Profit analysis. *See* Break-even analysis
Profit and loss forecast, 128–152
  after you open, 232
  average cost of sales determination, 130–134
  and cash flow forecast, 154, 159, 162
  and income tax returns, 151–152
  overview on, 128–130
  reviewing your, 150–151, 235
  sample, 138–139, 306
  section introduction, 207
Profit and loss forecast instructions, 134–152
  accounting/bookkeeping, 145–146
  cost of sales, 135–136
  depreciation, 148
  fixed expenses, 136
  gross profit, 136
  insurance, 144–145
  interest, 146–147
  marketing and advertising, 141–144
  miscellaneous expenses, 149–150
  payroll tax, 137
  rent/lease, 137, 140–141
  sales revenue, 135
  wages/salaries, 136–137
Profit and loss statement, 54, 232
Profit calculations, 55–56, 162
Project development businesses
  break-even analysis notes, 43–44
  business description, 37
  gross profit, 52
  overview of, 32
  profit and loss forecast note, 128
  sales revenue forecast, 50
  sample business plan, 299–308
Promotion, 141–144, 186–187, 210. *See also* Marketing plan
Promotional pieces, 210
Property, co-owned assets, 108
Property taxes/assessments, 122
Prosper portal, 81
Public offerings, 95–96

Q

Quick plan, 3, 200–201

R

Real estate assets, 66, 110–111
Real estate loans, 115
Relatives, funding from, 73, 76–79, 220
Rental property income, 119
Renting. *See* Leases
Resources for small businesses. *See* Small business resources
Restaurants
  business accomplishment résumé example, 107

business description, 29–30
cost of sales, 131–133
future tastes and trends, 37–38
gauging success/failure, 235
risks and competition, 188
as risky businesses, 28
Résumé. *See* Business
    accomplishment résumé
Retail businesses
    beyond opening day, 233–234
    business accomplishment résumé
        example, 101–103
    business description, 35
    cost of sales, 131–133
    gross profit margins, 52
    inventory turnover, 174–176
    online, 40
    overview of, 30–31
    product inventory, 151–152
    questions for evaluating, 30
    sales merchandise, 131
    sales revenue forecast, 45–48
    See also Dress shop example;
        Inventory
Retirement plan assets, 111
Revising your business plan, 234
Right livelihood, 14–15
Risk analysis, 188–190, 192, 277–279
Risky businesses, 28
RTF instructions, 310–311
Running your business. *See* After
    you open

S

Salaries, 119, 136–137, 167–169
Sales, going-out-of-business, 238–239
Sales merchandise, 131, 169–170
Sales on credit, 162–166

Sales revenue (sales income/sales),
    55–58, 129–130, 131, 135–136
Sales revenue forecast, 44–50, 179
Sample business plans
    manufacturing business, 281–297
    project development business,
        299–308
    service business, 265–280
SBA (Small Business
    Administration), 82, 91–93, 224,
    245, 255, 262
SBICs (Small Business Investment
    Companies), 93
SCORE (Service Corps of Retired
    Executives), 245–246
Search Engine Optimization (SEO)
    consultants, 143
Search engines, 261, 262
Secured loans, 65–66, 73
Securities and Exchange
    Commission (SEC), 80–81, 95,
    227–228
Securities assets, 109–110
Securities laws, 12
Self-evaluation exercises, 15–22
    business goals, 20–21
    general/specific skills, 18–19
    likes/dislikes, 19–20
    liking the business you choose,
        28–29
    overview on, 15–16
    running a business and, 233
    strong/weak points, 17–18, 233
    using self-evaluation lists, 21–22
Selling the business, 237–238
Selling your business plan, 216–228
    approaching different backers,
        219–224
    asking for money, 216–219

handling past financial problems, 218
legal details, 225–228
meeting preparations, 217
responding to a "yes," 224–225
setting up appointments for, 216–217
telephone pitches, 216
SEO (Search Engine Optimization) consultants, 143
Service businesses
appendix inclusions for, 210
business description, 35, 37
capital spending plan, 158–159
cash flow forecast, 163–167, 171, 172
cost cutting, 79
cost of sales in, 133–134
gross profit margins, 52
overview of, 31
sales revenue forecast, 48, 49
sample business plan, 265–280
Service Corps of Retired Executives (SCORE), 245–246
Shareholder investments, 71, 72, 95–96
Signature loans, 115
Skills evaluation, 18–19
Small Business Administration (SBA), 82, 91–93, 224, 245, 255, 262
Small Business Investment Companies (SBICs), 93
Small business resources, 243–264
business consultants, 243–246
computers and business, 256–260
formal education, 263–264
magazines, 255
Nolo, 243
online, 260–263
pamphlets, 255
See also Books for small businesses

Social media, 142
Software, computer, 257, 259–260
Software development businesses, 32
Sources of money. See Financial backing; Loans
Staffing schedule, 194
Start-ups
capital spending plan, 156–159, 172, 207–208, 279
complete business plan for, 2–3
filing organizational papers, 71
financial backing, 69, 73, 80–81, 82, 91–96
gauging success/failure, 234–235
gross profit forecast, 52–54
See also After you open
Startups.co, 81
State agency funding assistance, 94, 246
State loan repayment laws, 64
State organizational filing requirements, 71
State tax expenses, 122
Stocks, as assets, 109–110, 119
Stock share investments, 71, 95–96, 227–228
Success, 10, 234, 236
Supermarkets, 45–48
Suppliers, 76–77, 165–167, 232, 238
SWAGs ("Scientific," Wild Ass Guesses), 43

T

Table of contents, business plan, 211, 268, 284, 302
Target customer description/marketing, 181–185
Tastes and styles, 38, 178

Taxes
  as annual expense, 122
  corporate, 72
  loan-gift hybrids, 77
  payroll, 137, 167–169
  strategies for, 11–12
  verification of returns, 125
  and your profit and loss forecast,
    151–152
Technology, 39–41, 178, 188–189
Telephone pitches, 216
Threads, bulletin board, 262
Title page, business plan, 211, 213
Trade credit, 76–77
Trade magazines, 255
Trends, 27, 38, 39, 41–42, 178,
    188–189
Trust deed assets, 110–111
Types of businesses, 2–3, 4, 18–19,
    30–32. *See also* Choosing the
    right business; Manufacturing
    businesses; Project development
    businesses; Retail businesses;
    Service businesses; Wholesale
    businesses
Types of business plans, 2–3

U

Unlisted securities, 110, 111
Unsecured loans, 67, 115
U.S. Securities and Exchange
    Commission (SEC), 80–81, 95,
    227–228
USDA Rural Development, 93
Usenet, 262–263

V

Valuation of inventory, 151–152
Valuation of personal property, 111
Variable costs. *See* Cost of sales
Venture capitalists. *See* Equity
    investors/investments

W

Wages, 119, 136–137, 167–169
Website marketing, 143
Websites. *See* Online resources
Wholesale businesses
    business description, 35
    cost of sales, 131–133
    gross profit margins, 52
    new technology businesses, 39, 41
    overview of, 31
    sales revenue forecast, 48–49
    See also Inventory
Withholding taxes, 167–169
Women-owned businesses, 253–254
Word-of-mouth marketing, 142, 184
Worker classification, 144
Writing tips, 5, 204, 213

Z

Zoning ordinances, 137

⚖ **NOLO** *Online Legal Forms*

Nolo offers a large library of legal solutions and forms, created by Nolo's in-house legal staff. These reliable documents can be prepared in minutes.

Create a Document

- **Incorporation.** Incorporate your business in any state.
- **LLC Formations.** Gain asset protection and pass-through tax status in any state.
- **Wills.** Nolo has helped people make over 2 million wills. Is it time to make or revise yours?
- **Living Trust (avoid probate).** Plan now to save your family the cost, delays, and hassle of probate.
- **Trademark.** Protect the name of your business or product.
- **Provisional Patent.** Preserve your rights under patent law and claim "patent pending" status.

Download a Legal Form

Nolo.com has hundreds of top quality legal forms available for download—bills of sale, promissory notes, nondisclosure agreements, LLC operating agreements, corporate minutes, commercial lease and sublease, motor vehicle bill of sale, consignment agreements and many more.

Review Your Documents

Many lawyers in Nolo's consumer-friendly lawyer directory will review Nolo documents for a very reasonable fee. Check their detailed profiles at **Nolo.com/lawyers**.

Nolo's Bestselling Books

LLC or Corporation?
How to Choose the Right Form for Your Business
$24.99

Form Your Own Limited Liability Company
$44.99

The Small Business Start-Up Kit
A Step-by-Step Legal Guide
$29.99

Legal Guide for Starting & Running a Small Business
$39.99

The Corporate Records Handbook
Meetings, Minutes & Resolutions
$69.99

Every Nolo title is available in print and for download at Nolo.com.

On Nolo.com you'll also find:

Books & Software

Nolo publishes hundreds of great books and software programs for consumers and business owners. Order a copy, or download an ebook version instantly, at Nolo.com.

Online Legal Documents

You can quickly and easily make a will or living trust, form an LLC or corporation, apply for a trademark or provisional patent, or make hundreds of other forms—online.

Free Legal Information

Thousands of articles answer common questions about everyday legal issues including wills, bankruptcy, small business formation, divorce, patents, employment, and much more.

Plain-English Legal Dictionary

Stumped by jargon? Look it up in America's most up-to-date source for definitions of legal terms, free at nolo.com.

Lawyer Directory

Nolo's consumer-friendly lawyer directory provides in-depth profiles of lawyers all over America. You'll find all the information you need to choose the right lawyer.

SBS12